How to use management ratios

How to use MANAGEMENT RATIOS

C.A. WESTWICK

A Gower Press Workbook

Published in Great Britain by Gower Press Limited
Epping, Essex
1973

© C. A. Westwick 1973
ISBN 0 7161 0100 9

Computerised origination by Autoset, Brentwood, Essex
Printed in Great Britain by Billing and Sons Ltd, Guildford, Surrey

Contents

Illustrations

Tables

Data Assembly Sheets and Ratio Calculation Sheets

Acknowledgements

This book is based on long practical experience of selecting ratios for management, including nine years at the Centre for Interfirm Comparison. Accordingly, my first and chief expression of indebtedness is due to the Centre and in particular to Herbert Ingham and Leslie Taylor Harrington.

This book owes much, both in some general principles and in matters of detail, to the body of knowledge painstakingly developed by the Centre. Certain topics appearing in the text and illustrations of this book are based on or are similar to material which was prepared by the Centre, and in such cases I have made specific and, I hope, adequate acknowledgements in the course of the book. I should like to thank the Centre for its permission to reproduce the material in question. There are other inevitable resemblances of a more general nature between the contents of the present volume and the work done by the Centre; I trust that such general resemblances will serve as a practical tribute to the Centre's principles and achievements.

I hope, however, that the book may be seen as reasonably broadly based and drawing on a variety of sources of knowledge about ratio analysis. Accordingly, I would like to thank the many people with whom I have had fruitful discussions on the subject of ratios over the past twelve years or more, including Herbert Ingham and Leslie Taylor Harrington in the first instance, and Professor W.T. Baxter, Peter Helps, W.J. Haydn Everitt, Tom Price, Richard Williams, Richard Deeley, Errol Bishop, Walter Stewart, Guenter Steinitz, D.R.C. Halford, R.S. Cutler, C.J. Platt and many others.

I am grateful to Miss M. Brownlow and Maria Rzysko of Inbucon/AIC's Group Information Department, to Kathleen Bolton and Brenda Goddard of the Library of the Institute of Chartered Accountants in England and Wales, and to Graham Rigby for help in compiling the list of suggestions for further reading.

I should particularly like to thank John Pleming and Bob Price, both of Inbucon/AIC Management Consultants Ltd, for giving me the time and the generous encouragement that got me well on the way to writing this book, and Michael Renshall of the English Institute of Chartered Accountants for help and encouragement in completing it.

I am grateful to the following individuals and organisations for permission to reproduce the material indicated:

(a) The editor of the Accountant—Appendix 1-1 which is based on an article of mine published in the 23 December 1967 issue
(b) Extel Statistical Services Ltd.—Table 2-1
(c) Moodies Services Ltd.—Table 2-2
(d) Times Newspapers Ltd.—Table 2-3
(e) National Economic Development Office and the Controller of Her Majesty's Stationery Office—Tables 2-4, 2-9, material on pages 13, 14 and 37 which originally appeared in my book *A Study of Profitability in the hosiery and knitwear industry* and the list of ratios in chapter 11 part 4
(f) The editor, *Management Today*—Table 2-5 and Diagrams 8-1 and 8-7 which originally appeared in my article 'Analysing return on equity capital' (January, 1965)
(g) Inter Company Comparisons Ltd.—Table 2-6
(h) *The Economist*—Table 2-7
(i) *The Financial Times*—Table 2-8
(j) The Centre for Interfirm Comparison—for tables and diagrams on which acknowledgements to the Centre appear
(k) A.L. Smyth, Commercial Librarian, Manchester Public Libraries—Appendix 2-2
(l) *Times Business News*—Appendix 4-1
(m) British Standards Institution—Appendix 9-1
(n) M.H. Cabourn Smith—Diagram 11-7
(o) The Institute of Chartered Accountants in England and Wales—Diagram 11-8

Finally I should like to thank my wife Wendy for believing that I could not only start to write a book but that I could finish it as well.

Views expressed in this book are my own and are not necessarily those of The Institute of Chartered Accountants in England & Wales, Inbucon/AIC Management Consultants or The Centre for Interfirm Comparison.

Introduction

Objective of Book

The objective of this book is to help directors and managers run their companies or departments more profitably or efficiently. It describes what information executives should have, where and how to get it, and how to interpret it once it has been obtained.

This book differs from the many others on the subject of management information in that it is based on the belief that the information is more useful if it is in the form of a ratio rather than an absolute figure.

Perhaps an illustration of this point from outside the world of business may help. Next time you are sitting in your car look at the dashboard. You will probably see instruments which measure speed over the ground, engine speed, oil pressure, engine temperature, and rate of charge/discharge of battery. These instruments help you to drive quickly and safely to your destination. You will no doubt have noticed that of the five instruments mentioned four are giving readings in *ratio* form (miles per hour, revolutions per second, pounds per square inch, amperes per hour); only temperature is an absolute figure. It is perhaps not surprising therefore that this book, which is about controlling a business, should also measure events by using ratios. Your business will have cost many times more than your car. Many more people are involved. Has your business got the right instruments on its dashboards and control panels? Are your staff trained to read them and interpret their messages correctly? If you are not entirely happy with the answers to these questions then reading this book should help.

Before we leave the dashboard analogy there is another point worth making. It is a matter of judgement to interpret the readings of a car's instruments and to decide what to do. A suitable speed depends on the objective of the journey, the nature of the road and of the weather, and so on. So it is with management ratios. They tell you what is happening but you have to make up your own mind what to do about it. This is

why it is not possible to lay down hard and fast rules applicable to all firms at all times as to what value a ratio should have. But guidance is given as to how and where to get such information for your firm for the period you are dealing with.

How Ratios can help Management

Ratios are a tool that enables management to analyse business situations and to monitor the performance of their own and their competitors' firms. Armed with the information provided by ratio analysis, management can take action that is relevant to the problems revealed, and can refrain from irrelevant (and perhaps costly and damaging) action which they otherwise might have taken in the absence of this information. Ratio analysis has three main uses:

1   To help diagnose a situation
2   To monitor performance
3   To help plan forward

Diagnosis is not restricted to the manager's own firm; ratio analysis helps management to study the performance of suppliers, customers, competitors, and even prospective subsidiaries and affiliates, in a systematic way.

How to make the Best Use of this Book

How can you get the best out of this book? It is assumed that your time is limited and that there are many other things you must do. Everyone should read, or at least skim through, Chapters 1 to 3. Then, each reader should study the chapter relating to his function, such as Chapter 4 for the managing director or Chapter 9 for the production manager. You should select which ratios you are going to use. It will help to reread Chapter 1 and your own functional chapter. Then you should select your standards after consulting Chapter 2 again. After you have done this you should use the work sheets at the end of your 'own' chapter to assemble the information and calculate your own and the standard ratios. You should then compare them and ask yourself what the differences mean, what they suggest you do, what other information they indicate might be helpful. Then you should act and monitor the results of your actions by using the same ratios (see Table 1).

Firms and managers differ and the same ratios will not suit all of them. Those described may need to be modified to particular circumstances. It is probable however that most of the ratios described will be found useful, and that those who drop any of them will substitute another ratio and not an absolute figure.

While acting on your own chapter, you should study those dealing with your colleagues' functions and also persuade them to read those chapters.

As it is anticipated, however, that most people will read only the chapters most relevant to their own function, material and ratios which are relevant to more than one function are either cross referenced between chapters or repeated in both chapters. Anyone reading this book straight through is bound to notice this and may find it irritating. It is hoped that he will forgive the repetition as it is designed to make the book of more immediate use to the manager who is short of time.

Historical Note

Ratios have been used by managers for a long time. Foulke [*Practical Financial Statement Analysis*, R.A. Foulke, McGraw-Hill, 1968] mentions them being used in 'the last few years of the nineteenth century' and it would not be surprising if it could be proved that they had been used earlier.

The idea of using a simple integrated set of ratios was tried by the Du Pont company in 1919 but was not made public until 1949 (see *Du Pont Chart System for Appraising Operating Performance*, C. A. Kline, Jr. and Howard L. Hessler, N.A.C.A. Bulletin, Conference Proceedings, August 1952, pp 1595-1619). Further important developments in this sphere took place in the 1950s when H. Ingham and L. Taylor Harrington made extensive studies of the choice and use of productivity, financial and operating ratios; formulated some basic principles of ratio selection; and devised the 'QAM' or 'pyramid' method of selecting ratios (see 'Pyramid structure—a pattern for comparative performance', H. Ingham and L. Taylor Harrington, *The Manager*, September 1956, pp 657-660). On this basis, they developed detailed systems (or 'family trees') of ratios meant to give an integrated view of company performance and capable of being amended to suit the needs of different industries and levels of management. This work, allied to the results of their study of methods of interfirm comparison, formed the basis for the setting up of the Centre for Interfirm Comparison in 1959, and for the later development of integrated ratio systems for many different industries and levels of management by the Centre and others.

Some of the methods of analysis presented in this book were ones which the author was particularly concerned in developing while at the Centre for Interfirm Comparison. They include:
the set of ratios dealing with gearing (Chapter 8);
alternative ways of measuring asset utilisation (Appendix 1.1);
and ratios for Stockbrokers—possibly the first to be developed for a profession (Chapter 11).

Feedback

The author would be interested to hear from readers who have:

1   Any problems in using the ratios advocated
2   Any experiences of the use of the ratios described that they consider might usefully be included in any later edition of this book
3   Any suggestions for additions to or deletions from the sets of ratios outlined in this book together with the arguments for the course of action advocated.

It would be helpful if such readers gave an indication of their experience and background.

Stage		Chapters to read
1.	Groundwork	1, 2 and 3
2.	Select ratios	1 and your chapter*
3.	Select standard	2
4.	Calculate your ratio and standard ratios	3 and work sheets at end of your chapter*
5.	Compare your ratio with standard	Your own chapter*
6.	Consider implications	Your own chapter*
7.	Decide on action	Your own chapter* plus suggestions for reading
8.	Monitor results	Work sheets at end of your chapter*
9.	Get the broader view	4, 5 and 12 and whichever of 6, 7, 8, 9, 10 or 11 you have not yet read

*Note If you are: Your Chapter(s) is/are:

managing director	4 and 5
in marketing	6
in purchasing	7
in finance	8
in production	9
concerned with personnel	10
not in manufacturing	11
in corporate planning	4, 5 and 12
in investment analysis or stockbroking	4, 5, 8 and 12
a management consultant or a management student	All (!)
a banker or credit controller	8
an accountant	All, but 8 in particular

Table 1   How to make the best use of this book

PART ONE

Chapter 1

Principles of ratio selection

1.1 Why Ratios?

Most managers are only too familiar with being asked to study figures. But these are usually absolute figures of pounds, people, tons, hours, miles, and so on. So why ratios? The answer is that *no figure is meaningful in isolation.* To give a figure meaning, whether in private or business life, it must be compared, consciously or subconsciously, with another figure. A ratio expresses simply in one number the result of a comparison between two figures.

It is, for example, of little value to look at an item of expenditure in isolation. It is important to know why this expenditure is being incurred, what benefits it is hoped to gain from it, and whether the benefits can be measured and quantified. A measure of the effectiveness of the expenditure is then the ratio of the measured benefits to the expenditure.

Thus, a ratio can be improved by operating on either part of it, or, of course, on both parts. (Technically, if a ratio is expressed as a fraction, the item on top is the numerator and the item on the bottom is the denominator.) The operation can be aimed at increasing sales (or output or amount of benefit that is being produced) for the same cost, or at decreasing the cost (or input or effort) incurred for the same sales.

This equal emphasis on numerator and denominator is one of the advantages of the use of ratios. It helps to avoid the pitfall, inherent in the use of absolute figures, of considering, for example, costs in isolation, which rapidly leads to the feeling that all costs are bad and should therefore be cut.

Let us look at three examples which show the advantages of using ratios rather than absolute figures:

1   *Transport.* When talking about the effectiveness of transport, it can be said that it took x hours to get to a place. But this is generally subconsciously related to the distance travelled, and what in fact is used is the ratio of miles per hour.

2   *Production.* Two firms in the same period produce respectively 2000 and 3000 tractors. These absolute figures of output do not indicate which firm is the more efficient, if, however, it is known that the first firm employs fifty people and the second one hundred, it is evident that the first firm has the higher productivity: its ratio of 40 tractors per employee is higher than the second firm's 30. It may not, of course, be more profitable, but that is another story.

3   *Profit.* Two firms both make a £1000 profit, but which is the more profitable? Which needed less effort to earn that profit? If firm *A* achieved its profit with £10,000 sales and firm *B* took £100,000, *A* is the more profitable, with a profit margin on sales of ten per cent against *B*'s one per cent.

1.2 How to Select Ratios

Before any ratios can be selected for an organisation, the objective or objectives of that organisation must be defined. Only if it is known where an organisation is trying to go can one measure how far it has gone.

If an organisation has a number of objectives, they must be ranked in some order or relative importance. Then, if there is a conflict between two objectives, it is known which must yield to the other. However, it must be appreciated that this ranking is not immutable. The relative order of importance of objectives is likely to change over the course of time. As one objective is achieved, another becomes more important. Priorities will also change in response to changes in outside pressures.

It must be known, too, how the achievement of these objectives has been divided up within the organisation and what are the sub-objectives of different parts of the organisation. Each part should have a reasonably clearly defined objective to aim for and the definition should be such that the sub-objective can be achieved without prejudicing the main objective of the organisation. This leads to the ten basic principles of ratio selection:

1   If possible, a manager must be provided with a single key ratio that indicates unequivocally the degree of his success, together with subsidiary ratios explaining how this success can be improved. In choosing the subsidiary ratios, it is useful to bear in mind the next six principles.
2   Ratios should be logically interrelated. A test of this is that they are mathematically related (the converse is not, however, true—see next paragraph). The formulae linking ratios in this book are given in the diagrams. Diagram 12:9 shows how the ratios in many of the diagrams are linked to each other.
3   Pseudo ratios must be avoided. Pseudo ratios—the results of dividing items that are not logically related—may be mathematically related to real ratios but do not measure any underlying business reality. The following examples of pseudo ratios may help to clarify the point:
    (a)   Interest paid/sales (per cent). Interest paid, particularly if it is on a fixed loan such as a debenture, is not affected by the level of sales, so it should not be shown as a ratio of sales but of the amount borrowed.
    (b)   Sales per production employee (£). Many firms sell, in addition to goods of their own manufacture, goods made or largely made by other firms (factored goods). This is done to offer a wide range of products to a firm's customers. The value of the sales of these factored goods is in no way the result of the efforts of the production employees and should therefore not be included in a ratio relating to them.

4   A manager must not be given ratios which cannot lead to action by him (either as an individual or, if necessary, jointly with colleagues).
5   A ratio must measure a material factor of the business, not a trivial one.
6   The ratio of the cost of obtaining the information to the likely benefit to management of having it must always be borne in mind.
7   The number of ratios provided to any one manager must be kept to the minimum.

There is no such thing as an ideal set of ratios suitable for all firms, all industries, all managers, at all times. Hence the next three basic principles:

8   Different ratios are required for different industries and even for different firms within an industry if they are operating in different ways.
9   Within a firm, different levels of management require different ratios and so do managers with different functional responsibilities but at the same level in the hierarchy.
10   A manager's need for specific ratios changes as his problems change.

This means that selecting ratios is an exercise which must be done for each firm and manager individually. There will however be considerable similarities between the results—otherwise it would not have been possible to write this book.

It also means that from time to time (say once a year) each manager should review the ratios he receives and ruthlessly weed out those which are no longer providing information that he needs for action. There is an insidious tendency for the amount of information a manager receives to grow. The quality of the information provided is vastly improved if, as with roses, the growth is vigorously pruned.

1.3 Difficulties with Ratios and How to Overcome Them

Like all management tools, ratios can be misused. There are some situations where ratios can appear to be misleading if care is not taken. These situations, and the steps to take to avoid being misled, are described below.

If, for example, the following information about two firms in the same industry is provided:

Firm	A	B
Growth (this year's sales/last year's sales)	10%	30%

Firm *A* might be criticised for its very poor growth compared with firm *B*. But one of the things affecting a firm's growth is its share of the market. It is probably easier to expand a small share than one which is already very large. So it is necessary to interpret the above ratios in the light of each firm's share of the market, which is:

Firm	A	B
Share of the market (per cent)		
Now	55	13
a year ago	50	10

Firm *A*'s poor growth rate is put in a different perspective by its very much larger share of the market. Moreover it has increased its share by five per cent while firm *B* has only captured another three per cent. The lesson of this example is that ratios must always be interpreted *in their context*.

As a further example, if a firm's ratio of selling costs to sales is high, efforts at improvement could be directed either toward increasing sales without an increase in costs or to reducing costs without a drop in sales. The latter might be impracticable because, for example, the sales force is of the minimum size necessary to cover the country without too much time wasted on travelling. Thus, when looking at ratios it may still be necessary to consider the *magnitude of the underlying figures*. Before leaving this example it is worth adding that in such a situation a firm could consider using agents in some parts of the country instead of salesmen.

Another situation where a ratio is potentially misleading is one where there is *no cause and effect linkage* between numerator and denominator, or where the link is very indirect or tenuous. These are the pseudo ratios already mentioned in this chapter. To give another example, if a firm switches from making a part to buying it in, its ratio of output to production employees will increase because either:

1   It has reduced its production employees by those who were previously making the part, or
2   It has used them to increase its output of finished goods.

But the productivity of that firm's workers has not necessarily increased. They are doing less of the work to make the product. This is why it is often better to use value added (sales less materials and bought out parts) as a measure of output.

It is most important to see that numerator and denominator are *measured and valued* in the same terms. The ratio of sales to stock, often quoted as 'stock turnover' frequently provides examples of failure to observe this rule. If, for example the figures are taken from a firm's published accounts, sales are at selling price, while stock is at cost, and sales are for a year, while stock is a figure at the year end.

Here is an example of how misleading such a ratio can be. Firm *A* and firm *B* have the following figures in their balance sheet:

	A	B
Sales for year (£)	1200	1200
Stock at balance sheet date (£)	200	200
'Stock Turnover' therefore	six times a year for both firms	

However the following information, which is not published, shows a very different picture:

	A	B
Materials used during the year (£)	800	600

	A	B
Average value of stock during the year (£)	100	400
Real stock turnover (times per year)	8	1½

The answer here is to apply the valuation and definition principles of Chapter 3 *both* to the figures of your firm *and* to the figures of any other firm with whom you are making a comparison.

1.4 Expressing a Ratio

All ratios are the result of dividing one number (the numerator) by another (the denominator) but there are various ways of expressing the answer to this division.

If the two numbers are measured in the same units the answer can be expressed as a ratio, as a pure number, as a percentage (%) or as a per mil (‰). For example £5÷ £100 can be expressed as:

1   The ratio 1:20, or
2   The pure number 0.05, or
3   The percentage 5%, or
4   The per mil 0.5‰

Method 1 is rarely used in business; however it is useful for relating more than two variables. The choice between 2, 3 or 4 is largely a matter of convention. For example, the ratio of current assets to current liabilities is usually measured by method 2 (for example 2.0 times) while the ratio of profit to sales is usually expressed as a percentage (for example 10.0%).

Ratios are often the result of dividing items measured in different units, such as money and people. In these cases none of the above methods is suitable. Indeed, care must be taken when presenting the answer to make it clear what units both numerator and denominator were measured in, such as pounds per head per year and *not* just pounds, or gallons per hour and not just gallons, and so on.

So much for labelling the ratios. An allied matter is the number of digits in the ratio. There are two points to bear in mind here: comprehension and accuracy.

Few managers (or any one else for that matter) can take in or comprehend more than about three or four digits. For most people, £153 million, or at the most £153.2 million, is just as meaningful as £153 187 529.73. In fact the former figure is probably more useful because it saves the manager the time and effort, not to mention the risk of error, in converting £153 187 529.73 in his head to £153 million.

The second point is that a ratio cannot be more accurate than the least accurate constituent of it. If £153 187 529.73 is divided by 225 000 people the answer cannot be accurate to more than two or at the most three significant figures, and should be written as:

£680 000 per head (two significant figures) or
£681 000 per head (three significant figures) *and not*
£680 833.46 per head (eight significant figures)

It is generally safe to write the result of a division as correct to one less significant figure than the less accurate of the numerator or denominator.

Just as a reminder to those who left mathematics behind them many years ago, a nought is *not* a significant figure unless it has a number other than nought on both sides of it. For example:

£500 is 1 significant figure
£0.005 is 1 significant figure
£501 is 3 significant figures
£0.105 is 3 significant figures

A final point, which I hope will not be considered pedantic. It is useful always to put a nought before a decimal point, such as £0.34 per head and not £.34. Without the nought the point can easily be overlooked by a hasty reader or disappear during photocopying or other duplicating and what was £0.34 becomes £34.

It will be seen that both our points of comprehension and accuracy lead in the same direction: fewer, rather than more, figures.

1.5 Asset Utilisation Ratios

The question of what ratios to use to measure asset utilisation is an important one (asset utilisation ratios occur in nearly every chapter of this book) but the answer is rather technical. It has therefore been dealt with in the following manner:

1   The discussion of the subject has been included in Appendix 1.1 which need not be read by those prepared to accept the conclusions on the strength of the author's experience.
2   The conclusions of the discussion have been incorporated in the text of the relevant chapters usually with little further reference to the discussion.

1.6 Presenting the Information

The frequency with which management are provided with the ratios described in this book depends on how often it is worth their taking action. This is a matter for individual management judgement. As one progresses down any management hierarchy there is a tendency for the frequency to increase.

The ratios can be presented in tables or in graphs. The latter is more expensive but it is preferable, as it has greater impact. If cost and space permits, it is useful to have a number of graphs on view simultaneously, with the graph of the key ratio for the particular manager at the top linked by suitable lines (as in the diagrams) to the graphs of the ratios measuring the factors affecting the key ratio (see Diagram 1-1).

As well as current performance, graphs can show budgeted performance, target performance, performance for 'same time last year', and competitors' behaviour (if known). It may also be possible to add limit lines to the graphs, such as, upper and lower, warning and action lines. Variations of the ratio within the upper and lower warning lines can be ignored but if the ratio crosses the warning line, and certainly if it crosses the action line, investigation and action are called for. [See M.J. Moroney, *Facts from Figures*, Chapter 11, 'Control Charts', Penguin, 1965.]

Most, if not all ratios need upper and lower warning lines because in most cases they have an optimum level. For example, too much advertising expenditure may be as harmful as too little; too fast a stock turnover may be as dangerous as too slow.

Appendix 1.1

Asset Utilisation Ratios

There are at least three different ways of expressing the relationship between the value of assets and the value of sales. They are:

1   The number of times per year the asset is 'turned over' (sales divided by assets).
2   The number of days required to 'turn the asset over once' (assets divided by average daily sales).
3   The value of assets per £1000 of sales per year (assets divided by sales divided by 1000).

The advantages and disadvantages of each method will be considered in turn.

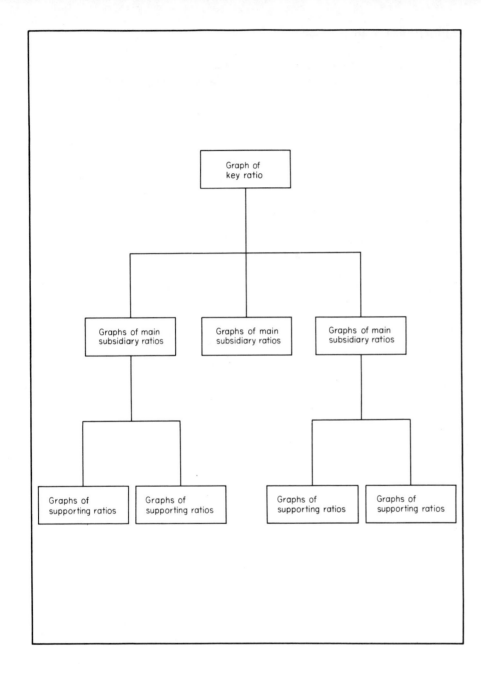

Diagram 1-1   Graphical presentation of ratios

Times per Year Method

The first method, which is the one used by Dun & Bradstreet, the leading American firm of mercantile inquiry agents, has the advantage that the number so obtained, when used to multiply the profit margin on sales, will give the profit on assets ratio. For example, if a firm's profit margin on sales is 10 per cent and it turns its assets over twice a year, then its profit on assets will be 20 per cent (10 per cent × 2).

However, when one is looking for the *causes* of a difference between a firm's turnover of assets and standard, the 'times per year' method is at a disadvantage in that the relationship between the turnover of the constituent parts of total assets and the turnover of total assets involves reciprocals, which most of us are not very happy about calculating in our heads. For example, if one divides assets between fixed and current, then, using the times a year method, the relationship is as follows:

> The reciprocal of the turnover of total assets is equal to the reciprocal of the turnover of current assets plus the reciprocal of the turnover of fixed assets.

Both the 'days' and the '£/£1000' methods avoid this disadvantage. If asset utilisation is measured in either of these ways, then the relationship mentioned in the previous paragraph would be as follows:

> The utilisation of total assets is equal to the utilisation of current assets plus the utilisation of fixed assets.

This is much simpler than the first relationship. This relative simplicity is illustrated by the figures in Table 1-1, which shows both the times per year method and the £/£1000 method applied to the same basic sterling figures. It is easy to see under the £/£1000 method that the £250 increase in total investment in relation to sales over the standard of £667 has resulted from the combination of £150 extra in current assets and £100 extra in fixed assets. Under the times per year method, little light is thrown on the total variance of 0.41 by the current and fixed variances of 1.35 and 0.50—both of which are larger than the total which they are analysing.

'Days' Method v. £/£1000 Method

On the grounds that they avoid the use of reciprocals, both the 'days' method and the '£/£1000' method are equally preferable to the 'times per year' method for use in analysing causes of differences in a total asset utilisation figure. However, the 'days' method has two disadvantages when compared with the '£/£1000' method. The first is

Method	Times per year method			£/£1 000 method		
Asset	Standard	Actual	Variance	Standard	Actual	Variance
Total	1.50	1.09	0.41	667	917	250
Current	3.75	2.40	1.35	267	417	150
Fixed	2.50	2.00	0.50	400	500	100

Table 1-1   Comparison of times per year method and £/£1 000 method

not, perhaps, a very important one; the second, however, is material. Some, with the writer, will find it bordering on the ridiculous to talk of 'turning over' such assets as land and buildings either so many times a year or in so many days. Others, perhaps with less pictorial imaginations may not, however, find this irritating.

A way of avoiding this difficulty is to use the expression 'the number of days required to turn the capital invested in an asset over once'. But this is getting very clumsy.

The second and more important disadvantage of the 'days' method arises when, and if, the analysis is continued one stage further and splits current assets into, say, raw materials stock, work in progress, finished goods and debtors. If, for its obvious analytical advantage, the arithmetical relationship is maintained whereby the figure for total current asset utilisation equals the sum of the figures for the utilisation of its constituent parts, then raw material stock turnover must be measured by dividing raw material stock (valued at cost) by average daily sales (valued at selling price). This will yield a ratio which is potentially very misleading.

Most managers, when told that their stock is turned over in so many days, will assume that on average an item stays that number of days in stock. If, however, a firm's materials-cost/sales ratio is 50 per cent (a not untypical figure for British manufacturing industry), then his assumption will be 100 per cent out. Such a situation is not likely to improve management's confidence in the reporter.

The £/£1 000 method avoids both of these disadvantages of the 'days' method. (The reason why a thousandth part of sales was chosen was because it allows the smallest asset item which it is useful to measure to be expressed as a whole number and thus simplifies presentation.)

It is therefore suggested that the £/£1 000 method be used in preference to the 'days' method in analysing the causes of a difference between a firm's sales/assets ratio and standard.

'Real' Days Method

In addition to using the £/£1 000 method, with its advantage of arithmetical inter-relationships, it may be useful to present current asset turnover in terms of 'real' days (as opposed to 'days' in the 'days required to turn over once' method) because of the easily grasped significance of this everyday unit of measurement.

This may be done by dividing raw material stocks by either the value of average daily materials issued to production (the flow of materials on to the shop floor) or the value of average daily materials purchased (the flow of materials into stock); and by dividing finished stock by either average daily sales (valued in the same way as finished stock, for example at factory cost) or by the average daily value of goods entering the finished store.

Debtors may simply be divided by average daily sales, although even here allowance may have to be made for the effect of cash discounts on the value of numerator or denominator. Work in progress is probably best divided by the average of materials issued to production and completed goods entering finished store.

Relationship Between Measurements

Diagram 1-2 illustrates the relationship between the various terms which have been used. The vertical axis measures the average value per day; the horizontal axis the average number of days. On both axes the days are 'real' days. The diagram is simplified to the extent of assuming that stock levels are not rising or falling.

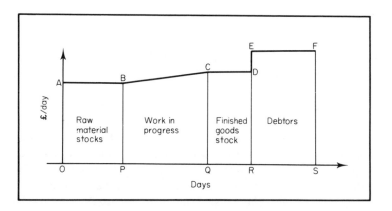

Diagram 1-2   Stock turnover ratios, flow of materials and time in stock

OA equals the average daily value of raw materials purchased, and PB equals the average daily value of raw material issued to production. OP equals the average number of days raw material stays in stock. The area OABP therefore equals the average value of raw material stock.

PQ equals the average number of days required to make a product (shop-floor time) and QC equals the average daily value of completed products. The area PBCQ represents the average value of work in progress.

QR equals the average number of days finished goods stay in stock; RD equals the average daily value of sales (at cost). The area QCDR therefore equals the average value of finished goods stock.

RS equals the average number of days' credit taken by customers, and RE equals the average daily value of sales (selling price); SF equals the average daily value of cash received from debtors. The area REFS therefore equals the average value of debtors.

The current asset utilisation ratios which are measured in terms of £s per £1000 are the areas OABP, PBCQ, QCDR and REFS divided by sales (RE × 365) divided by 1000. The ratios which are measured in terms of days are the lengths OP, PQ, QR and RS.

The fact that the vertical heights increase as one moves from left to right in the diagram emphasises that a day at a later stage in the production/sales process ties up more capital than one at an earlier stage.

The diagram illustrates incidentally the somewhat arbitrary nature of the accountant's conventional assumptions about overhead absorption and the point at which profit is made. As all the stages from O to S are necessary to earn the profit, could it not be argued that the line ABCDEF should be much smoother?

Fixed Asset Utilisation

The measurement of fixed asset utilisation, even by such a simple method as we are using, has its problems too. One of these derives from the fact that although the value of a fixed asset declines over its useful life, it is thought to be rare for the value of the sales which it helps to produce to decline at the same rate.

The result of this is a tendency for the utilisation of a fixed asset (whichever of the three methods mentioned earlier may be used to measure this) to appear to improve as the asset gets older. However, we want an improvement in utilisation to indicate an increase in the value or number of saleable objects produced and not just an increase in age. A way out of this dilemma is to measure fixed asset utilisation in two ways: by dividing the fixed asset's depreciated value by sales and then by dividing the fixed asset's original cost by sales. If one also divides the fixed asset's depreciated value by its original cost to get its percentage unexpired life, one can complete the explanation of a difference in fixed asset utilisation in the way indicated by ratios 2, 4 and 5 in Diagram 1-3.

The analysis does not have to stop at this point. The following are *some* of the ratios used to analyse causes of differences between firms' ratio of fixed assets to sales:

Ratio	*Purpose of ratio*
1 Value of land and buildings/Sales. 2 Value of plant and machinery/Sales. 3 Value of vehicles/Sales.	To narrow down in which fixed asset there is more or less invested.
4 Value of land and buildings per sq ft 5 Sales per sq ft	To indicate to what extent a high ratio 1 is due to using expensive property (ratio 4) or under-utilisation of floor space (ratio 5).
6 Plant and machinery/Direct production employees 7 Output/Direct production employees	To show how much a high ratio 2 is the result of high mechanisation (ratio 6) or low 'productivity' (ratio 7).
8 Picks woven/Maximum possible picks 9 Square yards of cloth woven per loom per year	To measure the physical (as opposed to financial) productivity of, in this case, looms. Different ratios would be used in different industries to attain the same objective.

Conclusion

To sum up: when presenting asset utilisation ratios to management, different methods of measurement should be used at different stages of the analysis of which these ratios form a part.

At the beginning when one is using the

$$\frac{\text{Profit}}{\text{Assets}} = \frac{\text{Profit}}{\text{Sales}} \times \frac{\text{Sales}}{\text{Assets}}$$

relationship the 'times per year' method should be used for its unique property of multiplying the profit margin on sales ratio to give the profit on assets ratio.

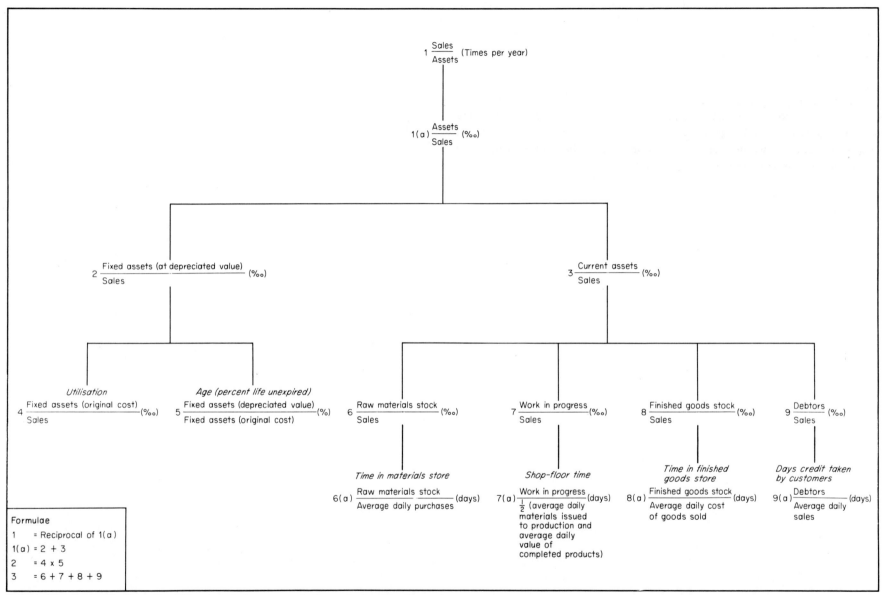

Diagram 1-3   Asset utilisation ratios. With acknowledgements to the Centre for Interfirm Comparison.

At the next two stages the '£/£1000' method should be used because by this method the relationship between the utilisation of total assets and the utilisation of its constituent parts is one of simple addition and because it avoids the potential confusion of the 'days' method. These two stages are the division of total assets between fixed and current, and the sub-division of these two groups into, for example, land and buildings, and plant and machinery on the one hand, and stocks and debtors on the other.

It is probably useful to present individual current asset utilisation ratios in terms of real days as well as so many £s per £1000 of sales; while fixed asset utilisation can be further analysed to extract the age factor.

The set of ratios shown in Diagram 1-3 was devised by the Centre for Interfirm Comparison and is used in many of its comparisons.

Chapter 2

Standards of comparison

Just as no *figure* is meaningful in isolation, so no *ratio* is meaningful in isolation. All ratios must be compared with a standard to determine whether or not they are at a satisfactory level. This chapter deals with the relative value and availability of the standards which can be used for comparison with a firm's actual results.

2.1 Internal Standards

The firm's own past

This is the most readily available and most frequently used standard. Admittedly it is not available to a new firm or to one just starting up an activity it has not previously carried on. It has the advantage of comparing 'like with like': the products and manufacturing and selling methods are the same, or similar, and the methods by which the figures have been arrived at are consistent over time.

The disadvantage of comparing performance with the same firm's past are fourfold:

1   The standards achieved in the past may have been poor and to compare with them may encourage a dangerous degree of complacency.
2   The level of activity in the economy as a whole, and in any part of it, is continually changing. This means that an apparent improvement may be the result more of a change in the economy than of an increase in the efficiency of any part of it. Here there is a danger of unwarranted self congratulation. Obviously the reverse can happen: a downturn in the economy can cause some ratios to get worse and it may be that there is little that management can or could do. Here the danger is unnecessary and unproductive self accusation.

3   The state of technology is continually, if not constantly, advancing. This means that a level of achievement which may have been perfectly satisfactory in the past is no longer acceptable now.
4   If a ratio has only the numerator or the denominator expressed in money terms (sales per employee) and if it relates to the past, its reliability is eroded by the effects of inflation. If both numerator and denominator are measured in money terms (profit/sales) it is possible that inflation has affected both equally and its effects will have cancelled out. If one of the parts of the ratio being considered is derived from information relating to the past (the cost of assets) while the other is not (sales) the effects of inflation are very unlikely to cancel out.

Budgets/targets/forecasts

These are probably better standards of comparison than a firm's own past in that they should have taken into account:

1   Changes in the level of the economy and/or the industry concerned.
2   Changes in the state of technology.
3   Changes in the value of money.

Most budgets are however heavily influenced by what has been achieved in the past and if a firm's performance in the past has been poor the budget may set a standard which is too low.

All forecasts are of course fallible; no human being is omniscient. This introduces a potential weakness in using budgets (which must be based on forecasts) as a standard of comparison that is not present in a pure comparison with the past.

Not only are forecasts fallible but, as every manager knows, each person who helps to produce a company's budget is subject to different degrees of optimism or pessimism. This is a perfectly natural, human state of affairs, but it must not be forgotten, when using a budget as a standard of comparison, that it was compiled by ordinary, warm-blooded, fallible human beings.

2.2 External Standards—Other Firms

Comparing performance with that of other firms has a number of advantages:

1   Whereas performance in the past may have been poor and therefore not a particularly good standard for comparison, if a reasonably wide and representative sample of other firms can be examined, it should be possible to perceive standards of good performance, or at least better performance than the company has so far achieved.
2   It is possible to compare results over similar periods to ensure similar economic and technological conditions.
3   Comparing performance with what other firms have achieved avoids the difficulties associated with budgets, namely their subjective elements and their (necessarily) fallible forecasts of the future.

The process of comparing the performance of a firm with that of other companies has a number of problems attached to it:

1   How similar *are* the other firms?
2   How can the information be obtained?
3   How reliable is the information?

Standards of similarity

Many managers stress the importance of comparing 'like with like', but how important is it to do this? Taken to its extreme this statement would lead to comparing a firm with one which was identical in all respects—its products, its size, its location, and so on—including its ratios! As ratios would be identical, nothing could be learned from the comparison. Obviously we must allow some difference, but how great a gap is permissible for the comparison to be useful? The answer is that the gap should not be so wide that it cannot be bridged by management action.

The size of a tolerable gap between activities varies with the ratio being compared. The more general a ratio the wider the range of firms it can be compared with. For example: all commercial organisations are out to make a profit from the use of their assets, so it is worth comparing this ratio with firms not only in the same industry but also in other, allied industries because this may indicate the desirability (or otherwise) of diversification. On the other hand it is only worth comparing the ratio of (say) 'shoes made per operative' with other shoe manufacturers.

The permissible width of the gap between firms compared depends on the time horizon of the management. The farther they are prepared to look ahead the wider the possible courses of action. For example, at one time Cunard would have compared itself with other *shipping* companies. With a wider horizon, management looked at other *travel* companies.

The firms with which it is worth while for a company to compare itself are:

1   Competitors
2   Potential competitors
3   Firms operating in fields which the company might enter (or should at least consider entering).

Obviously such comparisons must be made with thought, care and judgement but that is what management is paid for!

In comparing like with like, size need not be a major consideration. In all my work with ratios I have rarely found that the size of firms had any significant, measurable effect on the ratios. This is perhaps not so surprising as it may seem at first sight, because size will probably affect both the numerator and the denominator of most ratios and the size effect will cancel out or be diluted.

Sources of information about other companies

Broadly speaking there are two groups of sources of information about other companies:

1   Annual audited accounts of firms and data compiled from them, which will be referred to collectively as 'published sources', and
2   Comparisons specifically designed to obtain the information.

Some published sources are listed in the Appendix 1 to this chapter. Appendix 2:2 shows how to trace UK company information. The material in this appendix was originally produced by A.L. Smyth FLA, librarian of the Manchester Public Libraries

Commercial Library and Information Service, to whom I am grateful for permission to reproduce it here.

Some Trade Associations and Economic Development Councils organise exchanges of information (a list of those known is given in Appendix 2:3). The Centre for Interfirm Comparison, Lincoln's Inn Chambers, Chancery Lane, London WC2A 1JB (established by the British Institute of Management in association with the British Productivity Council) specialises in this work. A list of comparisons prepared by CIFC is given in Appendix 2.4.

A list of organisations which have conducted interfirm comparisons in Europe and North America will be found in Productivity Measurement Review No. 26 (August 1961) published by the Organisation for European Economic Co-operation.

Disadvantages of published information

Published sources of information are relatively cheap—none cost more than a few pounds—but they do have a number of disadvantages:

1   The amount of information which is published is extremely limited. It has been estimated that only 10—20 per cent of the information obtainable from an organised interfirm comparison could have been obtained from published accounts.
2   The small amount of information which is available in published accounts has often been arrived at in different ways by different firms.
3   Not all companies have to publish accounts—a division of a large organisation does not; and many small companies are exempted from some of the provisions of the Companies Act 1967. [These exemptions were increased by the Companies (Accounts) Regulations 1971. If a company is neither a holding company nor a subsidiary then it need not give particulars of its turnover if this is less than £250 000. The limit was formerly £50 000. The exemption for details of directors' emoluments was raised to £15 000.]
4   By the time some information is published—Government statistics are notorious for this—they are of more use to economic historians than to practical managers.
5   Very few firms take into account the effects of inflation on their figures, and this can have a considerably distorting effect.
6   Figures shown in the balance sheet (of stock for example) may be untypical of the level carried on average over the year. It is potentially dangerous to relate stock as shown in the balance sheet to the sales figure (if this is published) in order to arrive at stock turnover.

As management may be forced to use published information in the absence of any other it is desirable to spell out in more detail some of the limitations summarised above. These limitations are classified under the items in the accounts which are affected.

Fixed assets (land, buildings, plant, machinery, vehicles)   As a result of the combined effects of inflation and the (relatively) long life of these assets, the figure shown for them in a firm's accounts is likely to understate their current value. As the pattern of purchases of these assets over the course of time is likely to differ between firms, the effects of inflation will also differ, rendering the figures to some extent non-comparable. Some firms will have revalued their assets while most will have not. This introduces a further element of non-comparability.

Different firms adopt different rates and methods of depreciation. To some extent this will reflect differences in intensity of use, maintenance policy, and estimates of the rate of obsolescence of the assets concerned. Such differences do not make the figures non-comparable but differences due solely to different bookkeeping practices do. It is not possible to distinguish between the two causes from published information.

Only owned assets are shown in a firm's balance sheet; assets which are rented or hired are not. Such differences may not affect the ratio of profit to assets because a firm renting some of its fixed assets will have a smaller figure for the assets, but also a smaller figure for its profit (because the rent charge will have been deducted) than the firm owning all its assets. But this difference will affect such ratios as sales to assets or assets to employees and, to a lesser extent, profit to sales, because of the likelihood that the rent charge for an asset will be higher than the depreciation of the same asset.

The treatment of investment grants adopted by firms will continue to affect the figure of fixed assets shown on the balance sheet for some time. Some firms deducted the grant from the asset; other firms credited the grant to a reserve. The figure for profit may also continue to be affected by different treatments of investment grants.

Current assets (stocks, debtors, cash)   Only year-end figures for these assets are shown in a firm's balance sheet whereas the level of these assets may fluctuate considerably during the year. Different firms will probably value their stocks in different ways. These differences will affect such ratios as stocks/sales, debtors/sales, assets to sales, profits to assets, assets per employee.

The figure for debtors (and for creditors) in an associated company's balance sheet (such as that of a holding or subsidiary company) may be distorted by including the indebtedness of associated companies as a result of intra group trading in a separate item often described as holding/subsidiary company current account. The debtor turnover (sales/debtors) of such companies will tend therefore to be overstated.

Profit Because of differences in methods of depreciation and valuation of stock, and in policies of hiring or buying assets, this figure is likely to be not strictly comparable between firms. The profit of owner-manager firms may be depressed by the owners taking profits out of the firm in the form of directors' salaries (which are deductions from profit) rather than in dividends (which are not).

Transactions between associated companies (holding and/or subsidiary companies) in goods and/or services may not be at 'open market' prices (an element of levy or subsidy may be present). This will affect the profits and may affect the turnover of individual companies within a group but should not affect the consolidated results of the group.

The manner in which research and development is financed within a group and the way in which finance is raised and paid for within a group may also affect the reported profits of companies within the group but not that of the group as a whole.

Employees The figure for employees given in a firm's accounts makes no distinction between part- or full-time workers. To the extent that a firm employs people part-time its ratios of sales, assets and remuneration per employee are depressed.

No distinction is made between males, females, adults or juveniles in the figure of employees given in the accounts. This means that the ratio of average employee's remuneration may differ between firms because of a difference in the proportion of the above categories of workers employed by each firm.

If a firm uses out workers or sub-contracts some of its work its sales per employee will tend to be higher than that of a firm which does not, as out workers are not normally considered to be employees.

If a firm works more than one shift assets per employee will appear lower than for a similar firm working only one shift.

The figure of employees combines factory workers with sales and office staff. The figure of average remuneration is therefore also affected by the make-up of the total work force.

Causes of delay in publishing information

The time that elapses between the end of a firm's financial year and the publication of its results is made up of the following elements:

1   Preparation of the accounts
2   Auditing of the accounts
3   Printing of the accounts
4   Circulating the accounts to shareholders
5   Filing the accounts at Companies House
6   Searching of these files

7   Calculations (if any) on the extracted information
8   Printing and publishing the information

Directors receive information at the end of stages 1 and/or 2; shareholders at stage 4; those prepared to go to Companies House at stage 5; those who rely on sources such as *The Times 1000* at stage 8. Stage 8 may be delayed by the fact that firms' year ends differ and the need to wait for the firm with the latest year end.

The law permits up to nine months (twelve months for a company with interests abroad) to elapse between the end of a firm's financial year and the date of its AGM (s198 Companies Act 1948) and a further forty-two days to file the accounts (s126).

This means that companies have up to forty-five weeks after their year end in which to file their accounts (or fifty-eight weeks if they have interests abroad). Three recent surveys give an indication as to how long firms take in practice to present their accounts.

The Institute of Chartered Accountants *Survey of published accounts 1970–71* which relates to 300 major British companies found that the average gap between the date to which the accounts were made up and that on which they were circulated to members (stage 4) was 121 days. The median was 120 days and the upper and lower quartiles were 141 and 100 days respectively.

The Clothing EDC's *Financial League Tables for 1968/69* state that firms included in it took an average of 7½ months (228 days) from the end of their financial year to file their accounts (stage 5).

The Hosiery and Knitwear EDC's *Profitability in the Hosiery and Knitwear Industry* says that 81 per cent of the sample met the forty-five week (315 days) deadline and 90 per cent the fifty-eight week (406 days) one. The slowest firm in the sample filed their accounts eighty-six weeks (approximately one year eight months) after their year end. The most common period taken to file accounts was between twenty-five and thirty weeks. The second and third peaks in filing occurred just before the forty-five and fifty-eight week deadlines.

In addition to the slow companies in the sample there were a number of other companies which had not filed accounts for the relevant period at the time of search.

Processing methods of intermediate agencies

There are at least four methods by which the published data of firms are processed by intermediate agencies for the use of interested parties.

1   The accounts for a number of past years are summarised in one document. This is the method used to produce Extel & Moodies cards. The minimum of processing has been done but the reader is saved the laborious and time consuming search at Companies House (see Tables 2-1 and 2-2). Cards for a company may be revised several times a year as events require.

The text continues on page 36. The intervening pages display some specimens of the source material which is discussed in this chapter.

pages 16-27—Extel and Moodies Cards relating to Marks and Spencer Limited
page 28—Extract from *The Times 1000*
page 29—Extract from the *Financial League Tables for the Clothing Industry 1968/69*
page 30-31—Extract from *Management Today's* Real Growth in British Business
page 32—Extracts from publications of Inter Company Comparisons Ltd
page 33—Extract from *The Economist,* Industrial Profits and Assets
page 34-35—Extract from *The Financial Times 23 June 1971,* Trend of Industrial Profits.

MAN - R 58 MARKS AND SPENCER, LTD. MAR

ANNUAL CARD. PLEASE WITHDRAW PREVIOUS ANNUAL CARD. UP-DATED TO 17-5-71.

GENERAL STORE PROPRIETORS. Reg. 1926. Reg. Office: Michael House, Baker Street, W1A 1DN. Tel.: 01 - 935 4422.

Co. was formed to acquire business registered in 1903 and operates a chain of 249 stores throughout the U.K. Trade mark of Co. is 'St. Michael'.

ASSOCIATED COS.: (% of equity owned shown in brackets): N. Corah (St. Margaret) Ltd. (24%); John Spencer (Burnley) Ltd. (33·3%); Woolworths (Holdings) Ltd. (South Africa) (12·6%).

DIRECTORS: Lord Sieff (President); *J.E. Sieff (Chairman); *The Hon. Sir Marcus Sieff, O.B.E., B.A. (Deputy Chairman); *M.M. Sacher, M.A.; *The Hon. Michael D. Sieff; H.B. Freeman, M.C., T.D.; B.W. Goodman, F.C.A.; L.R. Goodman, Comp. T.I.; J. Levy; H.N. Lewis, B.A. (Com); D.G. Rayner; G.D. Sacher, M.A. *Joint Managing.

JOINT SECRETARIES: F.C. Hirst, F.C.A.; J.H.M. Samuel, F.C.A. **BANKERS:** Midland Bank Ltd. **AUDITORS:** Deloitte & Co.

***CAPITAL**

AUTHORISED	ISSUED
£350,000 in 10% Cumulative Preference shares of £1 ...	£350,000
£1,000,000 in 7% Cumulative Preference shares of £1 ...	£1,000,000
£81,250,000 in Ordinary shares of 25p ...	£80,788,619

*After giving effect to Scrip issue, see over.

Capitalisation issues: June each year 1949, 1950 and 1951, £49,169; 'A' Ord. capital (1949 1 'A' Ord. for 43 Ord. or 'A' Ord.; 1950 one 'A' Ord. for 44 Ord. or 'A' Ord.; 1951 one 'A' Ord. for 45 Ord. or 'A' Ord.). May 1952, £2,261,745 15s. of 'A' Ord. capital to Ord. and 'A' Ord. holders (1 for 1), June 1954, £4,523,491 10s. 'A' Ord. capital to Ord. and 'A' Ord. holders (1 for 1), Feb. 1957, £9,046,983 'A' Ord. capital to Ord. and 'A' Ord. holders (1 for 1), June 1959, £3,618,793 'A' Ordinary capital to Ord. and 'A' Ord. holders (1 for 5) (xc Aug. 5), Aug. 1961, £2,171,276 'A' Ord. capital to Ord. and 'A' Ord. holders (1 for 10) (xc Aug. 4), June 1963, £11,942,018 'A' Ord. capital to Ord. and 'A' Ord. holders (1 for 2) (xc Aug. 19), Aug. 1964, £17,913,026 'A' Ord. capital to Ord. and 'A' Ord. holders (1 for 2) (xc Aug. 17). In June 1966, 'A' Ord. shares of 5/- were converted into Ord. shares of 5/- and Capitalisation issue 480,000 Ord. shares of 5/- (1 for 5 Ord.) (xc June 3).

DIRECTORS' INTERESTS in ORD. shares of Co. at 31-3-71; Beneficial and Family: 1,953,033; As Trustees of Charitable Trusts: 3,633,383; As Trustees of other Trusts: 2,449,778. In PREF. shares: 198 10% Pref.; 2,000 7% Pref.

VOTING: One vote per Pref. share or 2 Ord. shares, but Pref. only vote in certain circumstances.

DIVIDENDS: 10% Pref. due May 1 and Nov. 1. 7% Pref. due Jan. 1 and July 1. 7% Pref. entitled to priority for capital at 112½p per share.

ORD. DIVIDEND PAYMENT DETAILS: Year end March 31. Latest accounts published 14-5-71.

	%	Per Share	Announced	Paid	Holders	Ex Date
1969	Int 11¾	7.05d.	14-10-68	10-1-69	15-11-68	28-10-68
	Fin 21 7/12	1/0.95d.	11-4-69	18-7-69	16-5-69	28-4-69
1970	Int 12½	7.5d.	9-10-69	16-1-70	4-11-69	27-10-69
	Fin 25	1/3d.	16-4-70	17-7-70	19-5-70	11-5-70
1971	Int 13¼	7.95d.	5-10-70	15-1-70	10-11-70	2-11-70
	Fin 29¼	7.3125p	20-4-71	16-7-71	17-5-71	3-5-71
	Cap.50	-	20-4-71	-	17-5-71	

DEBENTURES: 5½% Deb. stock 1985/90. Authorised, Issued and Outstanding: **£5,000,000.** Redeemable at par on 30-6-90 or earlier on Co.'s notice on or after 30-6-85. Trustees: Prudential Assurance Co. Ltd. Issued privately June 1960 at 97½%.

6½% Debentures 1989/94. Authorised. Issued and Outstanding: **£10,000,000.** Issued to Prudential Assurance Co. £5,000,000 in Oct. 1964 at 98% and £2,500,000 in June 1965 at par. Balance issued at par in June 1966.

7¼% Deb. stock, 1993/98. Authorised and Issued **£15,000,000.** Issued to Prudential Assurance Co. £7,500,000 on 16-1-67 at 97¾%, and balance on 16-1-68 also at 97¾%.

7¾% First Mort. Deb. Stock 1995/2000. Authorised £15,000,000. Issued **£15,000,000.** Issued to Prudential Assurance Co. Ltd. £7,500,000 in Jan. 1968 at par, and balance in Jan. 1970 also at par.

DIVIDENDS OF EARLIER YEARS ON ORD. AND "A" ORD. (%, less tax): 1952, 80, Cap.100 in 'A' Ord. shares; 1953, 50; 1954, 65, Cap. 100 in 'A' Ord. shares; 1955, 45; 1956, 50; 1957, Int 20, Cap.100, Fin. 20, 1958, 42½; 1959, 37½, Cap. 20; 1960, 40; 1961, 47½, Cap. 10.

YEAR ENDED MAR.31	ISSUED ORD. (& "A" ORD.) £	TURNOVER £000	DIVS.& INT.RECD. £	NET PROF. BEF.TAX £	CORPN. TAX £	PROFITS TAX £	INCOME TAX £	TOTAL TAX £	NET PROF. AFT.TAX £	10% PREF. DIVIDEND £.
1962	23,884,035	172,826	488,645	**21,334,923**	-	3,050,000	7,750,000	10,800,000	**10,534,923**	21,438
1963	23,884,035	184,878	410,046	**22,455,128**	-	3,200,000	8,150,000	11,350,000	**11,105,128**	21,438
1964	35,826,053	201,494	563,000	**25,070,000**	-	3,650,000	9,200,000	12,850,000	**12,220,000**	21,000
1965	53,739,000	219,791	817,000	**27,656,000**	-	3,950,000	10,850,000	14,800,000	**12,856,000**	21,000
1966	53,739,000	238,015	1,300,000	**29,818,000**	e 11,350,000	-	-	11,350,000	**18,468,000**	h 35,000
1967	53,859,000	j 255,770	1,004,000	**30,859,000**	11,700,000	-	-	11,700,000	**19,159,000**	i 35,000
1968	53,859,000	j 282,306	1,029,000	**33,871,000**	13,750,000	-	-	13,750,000	**20,121,000**	35,000
1969	53,859,000	j 317,336	1,667,000	**38,123,000**	a 16,350,000	-	-	16,350,000	**21,773,000**	35,000
1970	53,859,000	j 360,935	1,940,000	**43,705,000**	a 18,750,000	-	-	18,750,000	n**24,955,000**	35,000
1971	53,859,000	j 416,685	1,862,000	**50,115,000**	e 18,900,000	-	-	18,900,000	**31,215,000**	35,000

YEAR ENDED MAR.31	7% PREF. DIVIDEND £	PROF.AFT. PREF.DIVS. £	% ON ORD. & "A" ORD., LESS TAX: EARNED	PAID	COST OF ORD.DIVS. £	RETAINED PROFIT FOR YEAR £	CHARGES: DEPN. £	REPAIRS & MNTCE. £	DEB. INTEREST £	DIRS.' EMLTS. £	†EXCPL. ITEMS EXCLUDED £	AVERAGE NO. OF EMPLOYEES
1962	42,875	10,470,610	71.6	Int 15 Fin 32½	6,948,761	3,521,849	1,163,773	1,577,530	354,109	191,649	-	d
1963	42,875	11,040,815	75.5	Int 15 Fin 37½ Cap.b 50	7,680,210	3,360,605	1,412,862	1,398,235	385,968	186,209	-	d
1964	43,000	12,136,000	55.4	Int 11¼ Fin 27½ Cap.b 50	8,503,000	3,653,000	1,609,000	1,781,000	383,000	173,000	-	d
1965	43,000	12,792,000	40.1	Int 8¾ Fin 20	9,194,000	3,598,000	1,844,000	1,516,000	519,000	188,000	-	d
1965			c 32.0									
1966	h70,000	18,363,000	34.2	Int 11¾ Fin 19½ Cap. g	h16,793,000	h1,570,000	1,993,000	1,623,000	826,000	271,000	-	d
1967	i70,000	19,054,000	35.4	Int 11¾ Fin 19½	i16,831,000	i2,223,000	2,177,000	1,432,000	1,030,000	271,000	-	d
1968	70,000	20,016,000	37.2	Int 11¾ Fin 20½	17,370,000	2,646,000	2,488,000	1,638,000	1,588,000	293,000	-	k29,072
1969	70,000	21,668,000	40.2	Int 11¾ Fin 21 7/12	17,953,000	3,715,000	2,987,000	1,933,000	2,132,000	343,000	-	k31,210
1970	70,000	24,850,000	46.1	Int 12½ Fin 25	20,197,000	4,653,000	3,534,000	2,123,000	2,714,000	363,000	-	k32,992
1971	70,000	31,110,000	57.8	Int 13¼ Fin 29¼ Cap. 50	22,890,000	8,220,000	4,177,000	2,409,000	3,178,000	361,000	-	k34,372

†Exceptional items excluded from profit shown in accounts. (a) At 45%. (b) In 'A' Ord. shares. (c) Estimated earnings after allowing for Corporation Tax at 40%. (d) Not disclosed. (e) At 40%. (g) One for 5 to Ord. holders to compensate for loss of voting control. (h) Dividends deducted gross (Income Tax deducted from Pref. and Ord. dividends and retained, £2,647,000). (i) Dividends deducted gross. (j)Before deduction of refunds, £7,145,000 in 1967, £8,311,000 in 1968, £10,428,000 in 1969, £13,150,000 in 1970 and £18,987,000 in 1971, amount not disclosed in earlier years. (k) Including 11,931 part-time in 1968, 13,306 in 1969, 14,548 in 1970 and 15,753 in 1971. Remuneration all employees - £17,803,000 in 1968, £20,247,000 in 1969, £22,649,000 in 1970 and £27,176,000 in 1971. (n)Over-provision of £1,050,000 for Corporation Tax due to reduction in rate to 42½% disclosed in 1971 accounts.

Table 2-1 Example of Extel card. (a) Annual card

MARKS AND SPENCER, LTD.

PRIORITY PERCENTAGES:

	Deb. stocks (Net)	10% Pref.	7% Pref.	Ordinary	Retained	Total
1971	£1,907,000	£35,000	£70,000	£22,890,000	£8,220,000	£33,122,000
	0–5¾%	5¾–6%		6–75¼%	75¼–100%	-

ANALYSIS OF SALES

	STORE SALES IN U.K. CLOTHING £000	FOODS £000	EXPORT SALES £000	TOTAL £000
1966	178,480	55,985	3,550	238,015
1967	186,430	65,580	3,760	255,770
1968	201,133	76,400	4,773	282,306
1969	224,214	86,840	6,282	317,336
1970	255,701	97,214	8,020	360,935
1971	297,765	109,571	9,349	416,685

LONDON PRICES OF 25p ORDINARY SHARES.

Cal. Year	1962	†1963	†1964	1965	†1966	1967	1968	1969	1970	*1971
Highest	$6\frac{3}{32}$	88/-	57/4	53/9	40/7	46/3	60/9	57/3	312½p	335p
Lowest	84/3	61/10	48/-	42/-	30/4	31/1	37/4	40/3	255p	193⅛p

*To Apr. 16. †Adjusted to give effect to Capitalisation issues: 1961, Prices prior to Capitalisation to Aug. 3, 7⅜, 5¾, - Quotation Aug. 3, 140/-, 130/-; 1963, Prices to Aug. 6, $5\frac{3}{16}$, 92/6d. - Quotation Aug. 18, 105/-, 100/-; 1964, Prices to Aug.5, 86/-, 72/6d. - Quotation Aug. 14, 76/-, 72/-; 1966, Prices to May 18, 48/9d. 43/- - Quotation June 2, 47/-, 45/-.

***GROSS YIELD INDICATOR** based on Dividend 42½% (28⅓%), Earnings 57·8% (38·5%) (14.45p (9.625p) per share), Capital £53,859,079 (£80,788,619).

PRICE p	312 (208)	336 (224)	360 (240)	384 (256)	408 (272)	432 (288)	456 (304)
DIVIDEND YIELD %	3.41	3.16	2.95	2.77	2.60	2.46	2.33
EARNINGS YIELD %	4.63	4.30	4.01	3.76	3.54	3.34	3.17
P/E RATIO	21.59	23.25	24.91	26.57	28.24	29.90	31.56

*Figures in brackets adjusted for proposed 1 for 2 Scrip issue.

BALANCE SHEETS. MARCH 31.

	1969 £	1970 £	1971 £
CAPITAL	55,209,000	55,209,000	55,209,000
RESERVES			
Surp. on Valuation of Properties	22,738,000	22,738,000	22,738,000
Retained Profits	41,858,000	46,555,000	51,114,000
DEBENTURE STOCK	37,500,000	45,000,000	45,000,000
	£157,305,000	£169,502,000	£174,061,000

	1969 £	1970 £	1971 £
CURRENT ASSETS			
Stock	23,574,000	24,879,000	29,642,000
Debtors, &c.	4,908,000	5,991,000	5,843,000
Tax Resv. Certs.	-	-	7,000,000
Cash	20,298,000	20,643,000	23,916,000
	48,780,000	51,513,000	66,401,000
CURRENT LIABILITIES	45,579,000	49,910,000	*60,889,000
NET CURRENT ASSETS	3,201,000	1,603,000	5,512,000
FIXED ASSETS			
Properties	141,257,000	152,913,000	†154,617,000
Fixtures, &c.	10,254,000	12,372,000	‡13,932,000
INVESTMENTS	2,593,000	2,614,000	-
	£157,305,000	£169,502,000	£174,061,000

*Creditors, etc. £24,548,000 (1970, £17,695,000); Corporation Tax £20,587,000 (£18,750,000); Dividend £15,754,000 (£13,465,000). †At valuation £88,457,000; Additions, at cost £71,480,000, total £159,937,000, less £5,320,000 depreciation. ‡At cost less depreciation.
Note (1971): Properties: Freeholds £110,830,000; Leaseholds £43,787,000.
At 31-3-71 there were commitments in respect of Properties in course of development of approx. £22,000,000 (£15,500,000).
Capital expenditure authorised by Directors, but not yet contracted for, amounted to approx. £11,000,000 (£9,500,000).
NET ASSET VALUE (BOOK VALUE), excluding intangibles, at B/s. date per 25p Ord. share: 1971, 59.2p.

14-5-71.

REPORT for year ended 31-3-71. For figures, see tables.
INCOME AND CORPORATION TAXES ACT, 1970. Close Co. provisions of Act do not apply to Co.
SCRIP ISSUE. It is proposed that capital be increased to £82,600,000 by 108,600,000 Ord. shares of 25p and that £26,929,539.75 be capitalised and applied in paying up in full 107,718,159 Ord. shares of 25p (1 for 2 held May 17). New shares shall not rank for any dividend payable in respect of year ended 31-3-71.
Meeting, The Dorchester Hotel, Park Lane, W.1, June 7 at noon.
CHAIRMAN'S STATEMENT. Year's results, and consistent growth of business can be attributed to three main factors:- (1) massive Investment they are making year by year in store development; (2) managerial and technological effort which they and their suppliers devote to creating, producing and improving 'St.Michael' garments and foodstuffs; (3) thought and efforts they devote to maintaining confidence and goodwill of customers and staff. This has been another year of intensive growth for business with interesting new developments in merchandise and stores. Increase in selling space is largest they have ever achieved in one year. Great upsurge in sales has enabled them to absorb many increases in costs and thus to maintain profit margin. At the same time, they have improved substantially remuneration and working conditions of staff.
"ST. MICHAEL" CLOTHING. During last financial year, clothing sales, which include growing footwear and household textiles departments, have increased by £42,064,000 to £297,765,000. This has been the most unpredictable year for fashion trade he can recall and doubts about future trends of fashion still persist. However, designers, selectors and advisers visit main textile fairs and garment exhibitions in Europe and America and have produced some excellent ranges of fabrics, colours and styles. Similarly, technologists are constantly seeking, in collaboration with producers, scientific and technical developments in fibres, fibre blends and dyestuffs, so as to improve quality and performance of goods, 99% of which are British made. This has been a year of inflation, with production and transport costs rising at a faster rate than any they have experienced since 1951. Nevertheless, volume of business which stores generate, enables them, and consequently suppliers, to absorb some of extra costs and to improve productivity. Policy of upgrading quality of merchandise continues and 'St. Michael' goods are appealing to a widening section of public, at home and abroad.
"ST. MICHAEL" FOODS. Food sales have this year reached £109,571,000 compared with £97,214,000 last year. Rate of growth in the second half of year has accelerated, in spite of unavoidable price increases due to substantial rises in cost of many raw materials, transport and labour. They have extended range of prepared vegetables, bakery goods, dairy products, fresh meat and poultry. Developments take into account increasing sophistication of tastes of public.
FINANCE During course of year, they sold a small number of Store Properties, for £7,500,000, to Prudential Assurance Co. and leased them back on new terms. This transaction, although slightly increasing their annual rental charge, has provided them with further funds which, together with existing cash and with retentions they expect to accumulate in future, gives them ample finance to carry out their development programme for a number of years ahead.
EXPORTS. Export Department is making steady progress. They are concentrating efforts on developing a closer relationship with selected retailers abroad. A number of them, particularly in English-speaking countries, operate 'St. Michael' shops, most successful of which are stocked exclusively with Co.'s merchandise.
DECIMALISATION. Changeover to decimal currency was effected with great smoothness in stores. They made this opportunity for a complete re-equipment with most modern electric cash-handling machines at cost of some £3,000,000.

17-5-71.

Card revised (Chairman's Statement amended.

LATER INFORMATION WILL BE PUBLISHED ON NEWS CARD.

Table 2-1 *continued.* (a) Annual card *continued*

PLEASE WITHDRAW PREVIOUS CARD. EXTEL AUXILIARY SERVICE COPYRIGHT.

MAN - R 58 MARKS AND SPENCER, LTD. MAR

CAPITAL EMPLOYED £000

YEARS ENDED Mar.31	BANK LOANS & OVERDRAFT £	†%	LOANS £	†%	MINORITY INTEREST £	†%	PREFERENCE £	†%	ORDINARY £	†%	*NET RESERVES £	†%	NET CAP. EMPLOYED £	INTAN-GIBLES £
1961	-	-	5,460	7.5	-	-	1,350	1.9	21,713	29.9	44,181	60.8	72,704	-
1962	-	-	7,920	10.1	-	-	1,350	1.7	23,884	30.3	45,701	57.9	78,855	-
1963	-	-	7,877	9.5	-	-	1,350	1.6	23,884	29.0	49,437	59.9	82,548	-
1964	-	-	7,832	6.5	-	-	1,350	1.1	35,826	29.7	75,696	62.7	120,704	-
1965	-	-	12,784	9.8	-	-	1,350	1.0	53,739	41.2	62,729	48.0	130,602	-
1966	-	-	15,234	11.1	-	-	1,350	1.0	53,739	39.0	a67,401	48.9	137,724	-
1967	-	-	22,680	16.6	-	-	1,350	1.0	53,859	39.5	58,392	42.9	136,281	-
1968	-	-	30,000	20.5	-	-	1,350	0.9	53,859	36.9	60,929	41.7	146,138	-
1969	-	-	37,500	23.8	-	-	1,350	0.9	53,859	34.2	64,596	41.1	157,305	-
1970	-	-	45,000	26.5	-	-	1,350	0.8	53,859	31.8	69,293	40.9	169,502	-
1971	-	-	45,000	25.9	-	-	1,350	0.8	53,859	30.9	73,852	42.4	174,061	-

*Reserves less intangibles shown in end column. †Percentage of Net Capital Employed. (a)Including provision for Corporation Tax.

EMPLOYMENT OF CAPITAL £000

YEARS ENDED Mar.31	FIXED ASSETS BEF. DEPN. PROPERTY £	FIXED ASSETS BEF. DEPN. OTHER £	TOTAL AFT.DEPN. £	TRADE INVESTS. £	CASH & CASH EQUIVT. £	QUICK LIABS. £	STOCK & W/P. £	*%	DEBTORS A £	CREDS. B £	RATIO B:A	CURRENT ASSETS C £	CURRENT †LIABS. D £	RATIO C:D	‡OTHER ASSETS £
1961	52,251	a 6,055	56,340	3,543	12,257	7,327	12,541	7.5	1,983	6,633	3.3	26,780	13,960	1.9	-
1962	57,174	a 7,188	62,029	3,708	10,768	8,428	14,128	8.2	2,181	5,530	2.5	27,076	13,958	1.9	-
1963	60,488	a 7,780	65,547	2,906	14,321	9,330	14,808	8.0	1,863	7,568	4.1	30,992	16,898	1.8	-
1964	b97,505	a 6,364	103,869	2,675	15,488	10,091	15,615	7.7	1,873	8,725	4.7	32,976	18,816	1.8	-
1965	104,319	a 6,652	110,262	2,205	16,850	10,580	17,365	7.9	3,604	9,104	2.5	37,819	19,684	1.9	-
1966	113,196	a 7,021	118,766	2,147	15,098	11,197	20,286	8.5	3,396	10,772	3.2	38,780	21,969	1.8	-
1967	124,344	a 7,688	129,863	2,060	13,981	22,745	20,976	8.2	3,470	11,324	3.3	38,427	34,069	1.1	-
1968	133,506	a 8,964	139,544	2,469	16,526	24,792	20,907	7.4	3,912	12,428	3.2	41,345	37,220	1.1	-
1969	145,050	a10,254	151,511	2,593	20,298	27,975	23,574	7.4	4,908	17,604	3.6	48,780	45,579	1.1	-
1970	157,612	a12,372	165,285	2,614	20,643	32,215	24,879	6.9	5,991	17,695	3.0	51,513	49,910	1.0	-
1971	159,937	a13,932	168,549	-	30,916	36,341	29,642	7.1	5,843	24,548	4.2	66,401	60,889	1.1	-

*Percentage of Turnover. †Including Bank Loan and Overdraft. ‡Other Assets less Other Liabilities.(a)After Depn.(b)Properties revalued.

CAPITAL CHANGES

DATE			CUM. PRICE	EX DATE	EX PRICE	FACTOR APPLIED	CASH RAISED £000
Aug. 1961	Cap. Issue of 8,685,104 5/- "A" Ord. (1 for 10 Ord.or "A" Ord.)		135/-	4.8.61	132/-	.909	
Aug. 1963	Cap. Issue of 47,768,070 5/- "A" Ord. (1 for 2 Ord.or "A" Ord.)		102/6	19.8.63	72/6	.667	
Aug. 1964	Cap. Issue of 71,652,106 5/- "A" Ord. (1 for 2 Ord.or "A" Ord.)		62/6	17.8.64	41/9	.667	
Oct. 1964	£5,000,000 6½% Deb.Stock 1989/94 issued at 98%						4,900
July 1965	£2,500,000 6½% Deb.Stock 1989/94 issued at par to Prudential Assurance Co.Ltd.						2,500
June 1966	£2,500,000 6½% Deb.Stock 1989/94 issued at par						2,500
June 1966	Cap. Issue of 480,000 5/- Ord. (1 for 5 Ord.) 212,556,318 Non-voting "A" Ord. converted into Ord.	Ord. "A"Ord.	46/- 38/-	3.6.66	38/-	.998	
Jan. 1967	£7,500,000 7¼% Deb.Stock 1993/98 issued to Prudential Assurance Co.Ltd. at 97¾%						7,331
Jan. 1968	£7,500,000 7¼% Deb.Stock 1993/98 issued to Prudential Assurance Co.Ltd. at 97¾%						7,331
Jan. 1969	£7,500,000 7¾% Deb.Stock 1995/2000 issued to Prudential Assurance Co.Ltd. at par						7,500
Jan. 1970	£7,500,000 7¾% Deb.Stock 1995/2000 issued to Prudential Assurance Co.Ltd. at par						7,500
1971	Cap. Issue of 107,718,159 25p Ord. (1 for 2)					.667	

INCOME STATISTICS £000

YEARS ENDED Mar.31	A *NET CAP. EMPLOYED £	B TURNOVER £	RATIO B:A	NET PROFIT BEF. INT & TAX AMOUNT £	% ON A	% ON B	C NET PROF. BEF.TAX £	TAXATION CHARGED £	TAXATION AS % OF C	NET PROF. AFT.TAX £	COST OF DIVS.PAID £	DEPN.& RETD. PROF. £	CAPITAL COMMIT-MENTS £
1961	65,741	166,501	2.5	20,714	31.5	12.4	20,495	10,200	49.8	10,295	6,381	4,929	2,000
1962	72,704	172,826	2.4	21,689	29.8	12.5	21,335	10,800	50.6	10,535	7,013	4,686	2,500
1963	78,855	184,878	2.3	22,841	29.0	12.4	22,455	11,350	50.5	11,105	7,744	4,774	3,000
1964	82,548	201,494	2.4	25,453	30.8	12.6	25,070	12,850	51.3	12,220	8,567	5,262	3,750
1965	120,704	219,791	1.8	28,175	23.3	12.8	27,656	14,800	53.5	12,856	9,258	5,442	5,000
1966	130,602	238,015	1.8	30,644	23.5	12.9	29,818	11,350	38.1	18,468	14,251	6,210	8,000
1967	137,724	255,770	1.9	31,889	23.2	12.5	30,859	11,700	37.9	19,159	16,936	4,400	8,500
1968	136,281	282,306	2.1	35,459	26.0	12.6	33,871	13,750	40.6	20,121	17,475	5,134	9,500
1969	146,138	317,336	2.2	40,255	27.5	12.7	38,123	16,350	42.9	21,773	18,058	6,702	14,500
1970	157,305	360,935	2.3	46,419	29.5	12.9	43,705	18,750	42.9	24,955	20,302	8,187	15,500
1971	169,502	416,685	2.5	53,293	31.4	12.8	50,115	18,900	37.7	31,215	22,995	12,397	22,000

*At beginning of year.

*PRIORITY PERCENTAGES - CONSOLIDATED EARNINGS

YEARS ENDED Mar.31	FUNDED DEBT £	%	PREFERENCE £	%	ORDINARY £	%
1961	134,131	1	64,313	2	6,317,055	62
1962	216,892	2	64,313	3	6,948,761	67
1963	236,405	2	64,313	3	7,680,210	70
1964	235,000	2	64,000	3	8,503,000	71
1965	318,000	2	64,000	3	9,194,000	73
1966	496,000	2	105,000	3	16,793,000	92
1967	618,000	3	105,000	4	16,831,000	89
1968	913,000	4	105,000	5	17,370,000	87
1969	1,173,000	5	105,000	6	17,953,000	84
1970	1,493,000	6	105,000	6	20,197,000	82
1971	1,907,000	6	105,000	6	22,890,000	75

*Cumulative.

IND Copyright. EXTEL STATISTICAL SERVICES LTD., 37/45, PAUL ST., LONDON, EC2A 4PB
23.8.71 Reproduction prohibited. No responsibility is accepted for any error or omission. Tel: 01-251 0681. Extra Cards 01-251 1437 21(22)

Table 2-1 *continued.* (b) Auxiliary service

Marks & Spencer, Ltd.

ORDINARY SHARE RECORD

YEARS ENDED Mar.31	NEW PENCE PER SHARE *NET ASSET VALUE ACTUAL	ADJD.	† CASH FLOW GROSS	NET	% EARNED ON ORDINARY LESS TAX ACTUAL	ADJD.	Excl. Invest. Allces. ACTUAL	ADJD.	DIVIDENDS PAID LESS TAX		ACTUAL %	ADJD.%	TIMES COVERED	EX DIV.	PAYABLE	NET U.K. RATE
1961	75.5	20.3	3.50	1.53	76.9	20.7			Int		15	12.8	1.6	14.11.60	2.1.61	
									Fin		32½			29. 5.61	1.7.61	
									Cap	a	10					
1962	72.5	21.7	3.63	1.43	71.6	21.3			Int		15	14.1	1.5	13.11.61	1.1.62	
									Fin		32½			14. 5.62	19.7.62	
1963	76.5	22.7	3.87	1.47	75.5	22.4			Int		15	15.5	1.4	12.11.62	17.1.63	
									Fin		37½			31. 5.63	18.7.63	
									Cap	a	50					
1964	77.5	34.3	4.27	1.63	55.4	24.7			Int		11¼	17.2	1.4	11.11.63	17.1.64	
									Fin		27½			15. 5.64	17.7.64	
									Cap	a	50					
1965	54.0	36.0	4.53	1.70	40.1	26.7			Int		8¾	19.1	1.4	9.11.64	15.1.65	
									Fin		20			3. 5.65	16.7.65	
1965					b32.0	21.3										
1966	c51.0	34.0	6.33	2.53	b34.2	22.8			Int		11¾	20.8	1.1	8.11.65	14.1.66	
									Fin		19½			2. 5.66	15.7.66	
									Cap	d						
1967	52.0	34.7	6.57	1.37	b35.4	23.6			Int		11¾	20.8	1.1	31.10.66	13.1.67	
									Fin		19½			1. 5.67	14.7.67	
1968	53.0	35.3	6.97	1.60	b37.2	24.8			Int		11¾	21.5	1.2	30.10.67	12.1.68	
									Fin		20½			29. 4.68	12.7.68	
1969	55.0	36.7	7.63	2.07	b40.2	26.8			Int		11¾	22.2	1.2	28.10.68	10.1.69	
									Fin		21 7/12			28. 4.69	18.7.69	
1970	57.0	38.0	8.80	2.53	b46.1	30.7			Int		12½	25.0	1.2	27.10.69	16.1.70	
									Fin		25			11. 5.70	17.7.70	
1971	59.2	39.5	10.92	3.83	b57.8	38.5			Int		13¼	28.3	1.4	2.11.70	15.1.71	
									Fin		29½			3. 5.71	16.7.71	
									Cap		50					

*Excluding Intangibles. †Adjusted. (a)In "A" Ord. shares. (b)Based on Corporation Tax. (c)Excluding provision for Corporation Tax. (d)One for 5 to Ord. holders to compensate for loss of voting control.

YIELD COMPARISONS

YEARS ENDED Mar.31	REPORT RECEIVED	PRICE	GROSS YIELD % EARNINGS A	GROSS YIELD % DIVIDEND B	F.T. - ACTUARIES GROUP YIELD % EARNINGS C	GROUP YIELD % DIVIDEND D	"500" YIELD % EARNINGS E	"500" YIELD % DIVIDEND F	YIELD RATIOS EARNINGS A:C	EARNINGS A:E	DIVIDEND B:D	DIVIDEND B:F
1961	17.5.61	115/6	3.33	2.06								
1962	22.5.62	91/3	3.92	2.60								
1963	23.5.63	95/-	3.97	2.76	5.25	3.26	7.92	4.45	0.76	0.50	0.85	0.62
1964	21.5.64	65/6	4.23	2.96	5.80	3.56	7.98	4.61	0.73	0.53	0.83	0.64
1965	11.5.65	34/6	5.81	4.17	7.22	4.54	9.79	5.44	0.80	0.59	0.92	0.77
1966	9.5.66	38/6	a4.44	4.06	a5.80	4.48	a7.11	5.27	0.77	0.62	0.91	0.77
1967	8.5.67	38/-	a4.66	4.11	a5.97	4.42	a7.08	5.22	0.78	0.66	0.93	0.79
1968	8.5.68	48/6	a3.84	3.32	a4.87	3.86	a4.79	3.63	0.79	0.80	0.86	0.91
1969	8.5.69	48/-	a4.19	3.47	a5.62	4.32	a5.43	3.73	0.75	0.77	0.80	0.93
1970	15.5.70	57/6	a4.01	3.26	a5.80	4.40	a7.42	4.92	0.69	0.54	0.74	0.66
1971	14.5.71	395p	a3.66	2.69	a4.76	3.31	a5.94	3.86	0.77	0.62	0.81	0.70

a)Based on Corporation Tax.

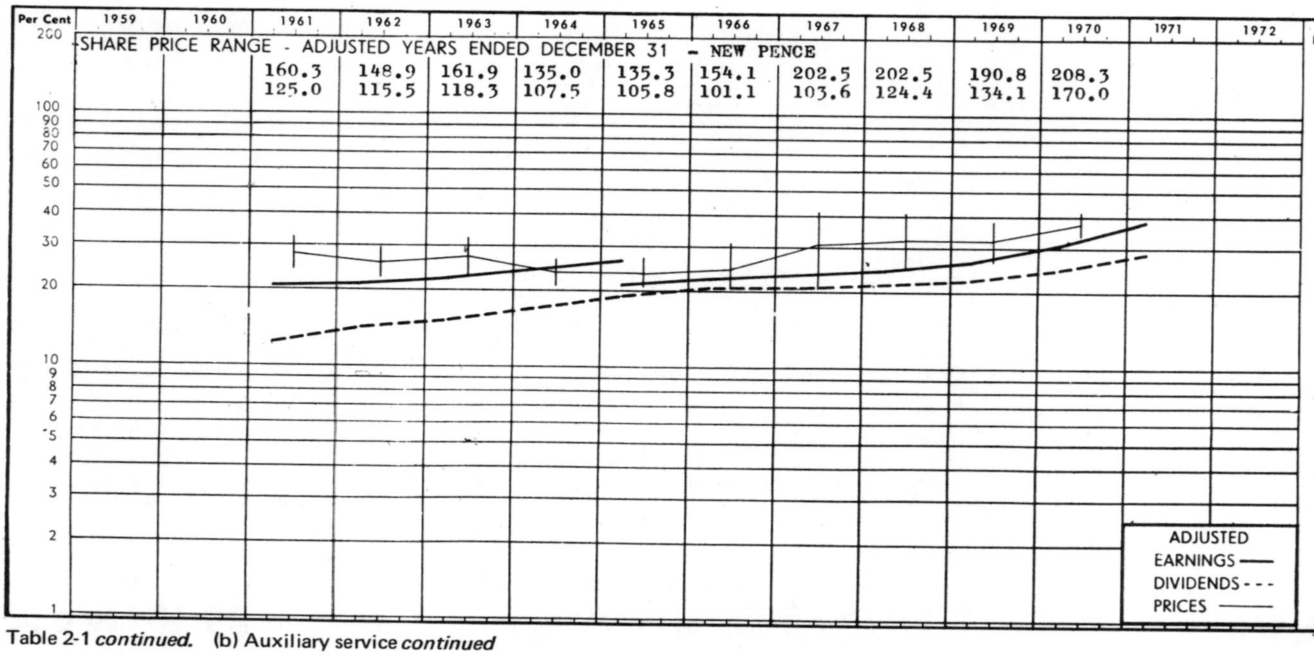

Per Cent
1959
1960
1961
1962
1963
1964
1965
1966
1967
1968
1969
1970
1971
1972
NEW PENCE
SHARE PRICE RANGE - ADJUSTED YEARS ENDED DECEMBER 31 - NEW PENCE
160.3 125.0
148.9 115.5
161.9 118.3
135.0 107.5
135.3 105.8
154.1 101.1
202.5 103.6
202.5 124.4
190.8 134.1
208.3 170.0
ADJUSTED
EARNINGS
DIVIDENDS
PRICES

Table 2-1 *continued.* (b) Auxiliary service *continued*

20

MAN - R 58
NEWS CARD

EXTEL BRITISH COMPANY SERVICE

MARKS AND SPENCER, LTD.

PLEASE WITHDRAW PREVIOUS NEWS CARD.

MAR

UP-DATED TO 12-10-71.

ISSUED EQUITY CAPITAL: £80,788,619.

GROSS YIELD INDICATOR based on Dividend *29¼%. Earnings 38·5% (9·625p per share), Capital £80,788,619.

PRICE p	240	260	280	300	320	340	360
DIVIDEND YIELD %	3.05	2.81	2.61	2.44	2.29	2.15	2.03
EARNINGS YIELD %	4.10	3.70	3.44	3.21	3.01	2.83	2.67
P/E RATIO	24.94	27.01	29.09	31.17	33.25	35.32	37.40

*Adjusted for increased interim.

SHARE PRICES. 25p ORD. (LONDON): 1971, High 312p, Low 128½p. To Sept.15. Adjusted for Scrip issue during year. (Prices prior to Scrip to July 16, 444p, 193½p. Quotation July 23, 455p, 440p).

ORD. DIVIDEND PAYMENT DETAILS. Year end March 31. Last accounts published 14-5-71.

		%	Per Share	Announced	Paid	Holders	Ex Date
1969	Int	11¾	7.05d.	14-10-68	10-1-69	15-11-68	28-10-68
	Fin	21½	1/0.95d.	11-4-69	18-7-69	16-6-69	28-4-69
1970	Int	12½	7.5d.	9-10-69	16-1-70	4-11-69	27-10-69
	Fin	25	1/3d.	16-4-70	17-7-70	19-5-70	11-5-70
1971	Int	13¾	7.95d.	5-10-70	15-1-70	10-11-70	2-11-70
	Fin	29¼	7.3125p	20-4-71	16-7-71	17-5-71	3-5-71
	Cap.50		-	20-4-71	-	17-5-71	26-7-71
1972	Int	9%	2.4375p	12-10-71	14-1-72	-	9-11-72

CONSOLIDATED INTERIM STATEMENT (UNAUDITED). For half year to approx. Sept.30.

	SALES			DIVS.&	TRADING	DEB.		PROFIT		PROFIT
	CLOTHING	FOOD	EXPORTS	TOTAL	INT.RECD.	PROFIT	INT.	DEPN.	BEF. TAX	TAX	AFT. TAX
	£000	£000	£000	£000	£000	£000	£000	£000	£000	£000	£000
1969	117,958	47,078	3,739	168,775	910	22,490	1,298	1,765	20,337	8,750	11,587
1970	135,438	50,694	4,153	190,285	959	25,743	1,590	2,047	23,065	8,700	14,365
1971	151,296	60,760	4,580	216,636	754	27,444	1,590	2,130	24,298	9,200	15,098

5-10-70.
INTERIM REPORT. For figures for half-year to 30-9-70, see table.

P.T.O.

MARKS AND SPENCER, LTD.

12-10-71.
INTERIM DIVIDEND of 9%%, less tax, on Ord. for year to 31-3-72.
INTERIM REPORT. For figures for 26 weeks to 2-10-71, see table.-
Directors state that the Profit before Tax for this half-year is arrived at after charging cost of exceptional price reductions following reduction of S.E.T. and reduction of Purchase Tax rates. In both these instances, benefits were passed on to public, in form of lower prices, at a cost to Co. of approx. £1,250,000.

Table 2-1 *continued.* (c) News card

MOODIES Services

MARKS & SPENCER (T)

MARKS AND SPENCER LIMITED

FILING	REMOVE	PREVIOUS	SECURITY	PRICE	YIELD	EARNINGS YIELD	CARD ISSUED
	FOLDER						17/1/72 Reprint

DESCRIPTION & ADDRESS   Regd. 1926 to acquire business of store proprietors (originators of "Penny Bazaar"), registered 1903.   Retailers of clothing and foods under the "St. Michael" trade mark through its chain of 246 stores in the U.K. and also for export.   This Co. is not a "Close" Company.
REGISTERED OFFICE: Michael House, 47/67, Baker Street, W1A 1DN.   TEL: 01-935 4422.

DIRECTORS, ETC.   J. E. Sieff (Chairman & Joint Managing): Hon. Sir. M. Sieff, B. A. (Deputy Chairman & Joint Managing): M. M. Sacher, M. A. (Joint Managing): H. B. Freeman: B. W. Goodman, F. C. A.: L. R. Goodman, Comp. T. I.: J. Levy: H. N. Lewis, B. A. (Com.): D. G. Rayner: G. D. Sacher, M. A. and 8 alternates.   JOINT SECRETARIES: F. C. Hirst, F. C. A.: J. H. M. Samuel, F. C. A: BANKERS: Midland Bank Ltd.   AUDITORS: Deloitte & Co.

FINANCIAL YEAR   Ends 31st March.   Annual Meeting at Dorchester Hotel, Park Lane, London W. 1 on 7th June 1971 at 12 noon.

DEBENTURES

	Issued	Outstanding	Int. Due	Redemp.	Security
$5\frac{1}{2}$% 1st. Mort.Deb.Stk.	£5,000,000	£5,000,000	--	1985/90‡‡	1st Fxd &
$6\frac{1}{4}$% 1st. Mort.Deb.Stk.	10,000,000A	10,000,000	30J. 31D.	1989/94B	Fltg. pari
$7\frac{1}{4}$% 1st. Mort.Deb.Stk.	15,000,000C	15,000,000	30J. 31D.	1993/98E	passu
$7\frac{3}{4}$% 1st. Mort.Deb.Stk.	15,000,000D	15,000,000	30J. 31D.	1995/2000F	

‡ Pari passu stock may be issued up to 60% value of freehold and leasehold properties (existing specific mortgages to be reckoned as part of the 60%) but no prior or pari passu floating charge may be created.
‡‡ Red. at par (a) 30th June, 1990 or (b) earlier, all or part after 29th June, 1985.
A. Issued to Prudential Assurance Co. Ltd.   £5,000,000 at 98% in Oct. 1964; £2,500,000 in June 1965 at par; £2,500,000 in June 1966 at par.
B. Red. at par (a) 30th June 1994 or (b) earlier, all or part after 29th June, 1989.
C. £7,500,000 Issued to Prudential Assurance Co.Ltd. in Jan. 1967 at $97\frac{3}{4}$% and £7,500,000 at $97\frac{3}{4}$% in Jan. 1968.
D. Issued to Prudential Assurance Co. Ltd. at par in Jan. 1969. A further £7,500,000 was issued in Jan.1970.
E. Red. at par (a) on 31st March 1998 or (b) earlier all or part on notice from Co. at any time after 31st March 1993.
F. Red. at par (a) on 31st Jan. 2000 or (b) earlier all or part, on 3 months' notice from Co. at any time after 31st Jan. 1995.

TRUSTEES: Prudential Assurance Co. Ltd.
Directors' borrowing powers equal to twice amount of paid-up capital of this Co.
DEBENTURE CHANGES - for details of later changes (if any) see Small Card.

CAPITAL & SUMMARY

	Authorised	Issued & Paid-Up	Div. Information Year to 31st March 1971		
				Required (Gross)	Available
10% Cum. Pref. £1 Shs.	£350,000	£350,000	1May. 1Nov.	£35,000	£31,215,000
7% Cum. Pref. £1 Shs.	1,000,000	1,000,000	1Jan. 1Jly.	70,000	31,180,000
Ord. 25p Shares	54,100,000	53,859,000	Yr's Div. *$42\frac{1}{2}$%	22,890,000	31,110,000
	£55,450,000	£55,209,000	*Int. $13\frac{1}{2}$% decl. 5 Oct. 1970 pd. 15 Jan. 1971		
CAPITAL CHANGES - for details of later changes (if any) see Small Card.			Fin. $29\frac{1}{2}$% decl. 20 Apr. pd. 16 July, 1971.		

FOR CAPITAL ISSUES SEE PAGE 2

CAPITAL RIGHTS: 10% Pref. have priority for capital without further participation.   7% Pref. rank next and in a winding up entitled to repayment at 112½p without further participation.
VOTING RIGHTS: One vote per 10% or 7% Pref. or 2 Ord. shares but Pref. only if div. is six months in arrear, on resolution for capital reduction, winding up or on matters affecting their rights.

	COVER
Required (Net)	Available
£1,907,000	£33,122,000

Business :	Chain Stores
Last Accounts Published	17th May 1971

Table 2-2   Example of a Moodies card. (a) Large card

21

CAPITAL ISSUES:

Date	Issue	Terms and Purpose	Date Ex-Bonus or Ex-Rights
June 1950	196,674 "A" Ord. 5/- shs.	2-3/11% Scrip Issue to Ord. & "A" Ord.	
June 1951	196,674 "A" Ord. 5/- shs.	2-11/50% Scrip Issue to Ord. & "A" Ord.	
June 1952	9,046,984 "A" Ord. 5/- shs.	100% Scrip Issue to Ord. & "A" Ord. (1 for 1)	
June 1954	18,093,966 "A" Ord. 5/- shs.	100% Scrip Issue to Ord. & "A" Ord. (1 for 1)	1.7.54
Feb. 1957	36,187,932 "A" Ord. 5/- shs.	100% Scrip Issue to Ord. & "A" Ord. (1 for 1)	25.2.57
Aug. 1959	14,475,172 "A" Ord. 5/- shs.	20% Scrip Issue to Ord. & "A" Ord. (1 for 5)	5.8.59
Aug. 1961	8,685,104 "A" Ord. 5/- shs.	10% Scrip Issue to Ord. & "A" Ord. (1 for 10)	4.8.61
May 1963	47,768,071 "A" Ord. 5/- shs.	50% Scrip Issue to Ord. & "A" Ord. (1 for 2)	19.8.63
Aug. 1964	71,652,106 "A" Ord. 5/- shs.	50% Scrip Issue to Ord. & "A" Ord. (1 for 2)	17.8.64
June 1966	480,000 Ord. 5/- Shs.	20% Scrip Issue to Ord. (1 for 5)	3.6.66
	--	Existing "A" Ord. shs. then conv. into Ord. Shs.	--

PRICE RANGE (LONDON)**

		1961	1962	1963	1964	PRICE 6.4.65	1965	1966	1967	1968	1969	1970
6% Deb. Stock	High	100	103¼	105	101½	98½	101¼	99½	Red.			
	Low	96	96	99	99		96	95½				
3½% Deb. Stock	High	87½	92¾	94¼	95½	94	98¼	Red.				
	Low	83	83½	90½	90½		93					
10% £1 Pref. Shares	High	33/9	33/3	35/-	33/3	30/-	31/6	30/6	29/7	29/-	26/1	22/9
	Low	30/6	30/6	30/6	30/9		29/10	26/-	27/6	26/9	20/3	20/9
7% £1 Pref. Shares	High	25/-	24/1	24/10	23/10	21/6	22/4	21/3	21/6	20/4	18/9	16/3
	Low	20/6	20/3	22/6	21/-		19/7	18/9	19/10	18/7	13/3	14/2
Ord. 25p Shares	High	133/9‡	121/10	88/-‡	57/4‡	52/6	53/9	40/7‡	46/3	60/9	57/3	62/6
	Low	104/4‡	74/3	61/10‡	48/-‡		42/-	30/4‡	31/1	37/4	40/3	51/-
"A" Ord. 25p Shs.	High	108/1‡	100/7	72/10‡	48/9‡	34/8¼	40/6	Conv.				
	Low	84/5‡	78/-	52/3‡	32/3‡		31/9					

** Ord. and 7% Pref. also at Northern , Midland, Dublin, Scottish.
‡ Prices adjusted for Scrip Issue during year.

NOTES TO PROFITS ANALYSIS (from page 5)

A. On £53,739,000 Capital after 50% Scrip Issue Aug. 1964.
B. On £23,884,035 Capital after 10% Scrip Issue Aug. 1961.
C. Incls. £347,456 Deprec. no longer required on Trade Invests.
E. £124,867 Net Surplus on Sale of Properties and Investments also transferred to General Reserve.
F. Both on £53,859,000 Capital after 20% Scrip Issue to former Ord. holders June 1966 prior to "A" Ord. conversion
G. Gross.
L. Deb. Discount & Expenses.
M. On £35,826,000 Capital after 50% scrip issue May 1963.
P. After crediting £270,000 Dividends from Subs. out of Profits of Prior Years.
R. Int. Div. (Net) Fin. Div. (Gross).
S. Incls. £173,000 Deb. Discount & Expenses less £63,000 surplus on sale of assets.
V. Moodies Estimated Corpn. Tax Equiv. at 40% rate 31.4%.

NOTE: In 1964 £33,389,000 Surplus on Revaluation of Properties transferred to Capital Reserve & £2,337,000 being book value of certain Fixtures & Fittings was transferred to Properties Account prior to Valuation Mar. 1964. In 1966 £305,000 and in 1967 £629,000 Net surplus on sale of Fixed Assets transferred to General Reserve. In 1971 £7,104,000 from Retained Profits utilised in making a special contribution to Staff Benevolent Fund and £2,393,000 net surplus on disposal of assets and £1,050,000 Corpn. Tax overprovided in previous year transferred to Retained Profits.

Table 2-2 *continued.* (a) Large card *continued*

MARKS AND SPENCER LIMITED

MISCELLANEOUS STATISTICS

	Employees			No. of Stores
Yrs.to 31Mar.	Avge. No. Full time	Part Time	Remun.	
1968	17,141	11,031	£17,803,000	1966 240
1969	17,904	13,306	£20,247,000	1967 240
1970	18,444	14,548	£22,649,000	1968 241
1971	18,619	15,753	£27,176,000	1969 243
				1970 245
				1971 246

At 31Mar.	Directors & Families Interests –Ord. Shs. Beneficial	As Trustees
1969	2,370,452	6,620,617
1970	2,183,562	6,388,479
1971	1,953,033	6,083,161

INTERIM STATEMENTS: £000's.

6 mos to	Sales	Trading Profit	Other Income	Total Profit	Deb. Interest	Deprec.	Profit before Tax	Tax	Profit after Tax
26Sept. 1969	168,775	22,490	910	23,400	1,298	1,765	20,337	8,750	11,587
1970	190,285	25,712	959	26,671	1,559	2,047	23,065	10,000	13,065

POINTS FROM DIRECTORS' REPORT   20th April, 1971

Finance for Development : In order to provide further finance for Store development, arrangements were made with Prudential Assurance Co. Ltd. during year for sale and lease-back of 13 store properties. Capital sum received amounted to £7,500,000.

Points FROM CHAIRMAN'S REVIEW *Issued* 17th May 1971
Co. announce once again, record sales and profits. Gross sales have increased by £55,750,000- largest increase in any single year - to £416,685,000 in fifty-three weeks, as against £360,935,000 last year. Of this total, store sales amounted to £407,336,000 and export sales to £9,349,000.
During course of year, Co. sold a small number of Store Properties, for £7,500,000, to Prudential Assurance Co. and leased them back on new terms. This transaction, although slightly increasing annual rental charge, has provided Co. with further funds which, together with existing cash and with retentions Board expect to accumulate in future, gives ample finance to carry out development programme for a number of years ahead.
This has been another year of intensive growth for business with interesting new developments in merchandise and stores. Increase in selling space is largest ever achieved in one year. Great upsurge in sales has enabled Co. to absorb many increases in costs and thus to maintain profit margin.

Table 2-2 *continued.*   (a) Large card *continued*

Store development is a continuous process. In year under review 32 projects were completed, representing addition of 300,000 sq.ft of new selling space. In new financial year Board expect to construct 3 new stores, 1 replacement store and 20 important extensions, with an additional footage of 200,000 sq. ft. This will bring number of stores to 249, most of them extended or built in last decade, with a total selling area of nearly 5,000,000 sq. ft.
Although Board have concentrated developments on extending stores in large areas of population, they continue to acquire prime sites where Co. is not represented, in new towns and in new shopping centres. During last financial year clothing sales, which include growing footwear and household textiles departments, have increased by £42,064,000 to £297,765,000. Food sales have this year reached £109,571,000 compared with £97,214,000 last year. Rate of growth in second half of year has accelerated, in spite of unavoidable price increases.
Export Department is making steady progress. Co. is concentrating efforts on developing a closer relationship with selected retailers abroad. A number of them, particularly in English-speaking countries, operate "St. Michael" shops, the most successful of which are stocked exclusively with Co's. merchandise.

MARKS AND SPENCER LIMITED   -31st March-

BALANCE SHEET ANALYSIS
(in thousands of £)

	1969	1970	1971
Ord. Shares	53,859	53,859	53,859
10% Pref. Shs.	350	350	350
7% Pref. Shs.	1,000	1,000	1,000
5½% Deb. Stk.	5,000	5,000	5,900
6½% Deb. Stk.	10,000	10,000	10,000
7⅛% Deb. Stk.	15,000	15,000	15,000
7¾% Deb. Stk.	7,500	15,000	15,000
Capital Reserves:-			
Surplus on valn. of props.	22,738	22,738	22,738
Retained Profits	41,858	46,555	51,114
	157,305	169,502	174,061

	1969	1970	1971
Current Assets:			
Cash & Short Term Deposits	20,298	20,643	23,916
Tax Reserve Certs.	Nil	Nil	7,000
Debtors & Prepayments	4,908	5,991	5,843
Stocks at cost or under and Stores	23,574	24,879	29,642
	48,780	51,513	66,401
Less Current Liabs. & Provisions:			
Creditors & Accruals	17,604	17,695	24,548
Taxation	16,350	18,750	20,587
Dividends	11,625	13,465	15,754
Net Current Assets:	3,201	1,603	5,512
Add Fixed Assets:			
‡Properties:			
Freeholds	100,682	107,666	110,830
Long L'holds (over 50 years)	39,655	44,416	41,931
Short Leaseholds (under 50 years)	920	831	1,856
Fixtures etc. at cost less depreciation	10,254	12,372	13,932
Trade Invests. at cost	2,593A	2,614A	Nil
Net	157,305	169,502	174,061
Profits before tax & interest	40,255	46,419	53,293
B/S Asset Value–Equity (pence)	55	57	59

Asset Cover	31st March, 1971
Net Tangible Assets	174,061
Deb. Stocks	45,000
	129,061
Pref. Capital	1,350
Available for Equity ##	127,711

##Subject to prem. on 7% Pref.

Priority Percentages	% of Capital Contributed	% of Earnings Taken
Deb. Stocks	0 - 45	0 - 5¾
10%Pref. Shs.)	45 - 46	5¾ - 6
7%Pref. Shs.)		
Ord. Shares	46 - 100	6 - 75

‡ Properties as independently valued at 31st Mar. 1964 plus subsequent additions at cost less depreciation.

Gross Book Value	1969	1970	1971
Properties	145,050	157,612	159,937

A. Incls. "2,341" in 1969 & "2,349" in 1970 Quoted Invests. with market valuation "9,184" in 1969 and "8,001" in 1970. Also Incls. "252" in 1969 and "265" in 1970, unquoted investments, with Directors valuation "458" in 1969 and "528" in 1970.

NOTES TO 1971 BALANCE SHEET:
(1) Investments   A special contribution of £7,104,000 was made to Staff Benevolent Fund during March, 1971, by transferring Co's. quoted and unquoted Investments to Fund.   At date of transfer market value of quoted Investments was £6,863,000 and unquoted Investments were valued by Directors at £241,000.   Total cost of these Investments was £2,614,000.   For Corporation Tax purposes total amount of this contribution will be allowed against profits over a period of ten years.
(2) Property Commitments   At 31st Mar. 1971 there were commitments in respect of Properties in course of development of approx. £22,000,000.   Capital expenditure authorised by Directors, but not yet contracted for, amounted to approx. £11,000,000.
(3) Subsidiary Companies   Co's. subs. none of which is trading, are not represented in Balance Sheet as their figures are insignificant.

Table 2-2 continued.   (a) Large card continued

MARKS AND SPENCER LIMITED

PROFITS ANALYSIS (£'s)

Yrs.to 31 Mar.	Turnover (£m's.)				Trading Profit	Other Income	Total	Deprec.	Repairs & Maintce.	Staff Benevolent Fund.
	Foods	Clothing	Over-seas	Total						
1961	28.5	138.0		166.5	23,084,748	436,189	23,520,937	1,014,561	1,591,140	150,000
1962	33.0	139.8		172.8	24,129,324	493,549	24,622,873	1,163,773	1,577,530	150,000
1963	39.0	145.9		184.9	25,429,356	410,046	25,839,402	1,412,862	1,398,235	150,000
1964	45.0	156.5		201.5	28,454,000	563,000	29,017,000	1,609,000	1,781,000	150,000
1965	50.0	169.8		219.8	30,906,000	817,000	31,723,000	1,844,000	1,516,000	150,000
1966	56.0	178.5	3.5	238.0	33,231,000	1,300,000	34,531,000	1,993,000	1,623,000	200,000
1967	65.6	186.4	3.8	255.8	34,765,000	1,004,000	35,769,000	2,177,000	1,432,000	200,000
1968	76.4	201.1	4.8	282.3	39,049,000	1,029,000	40,078,000	2,488,000	1,638,000	200,000
1969	86.8	224.2	6.3	317.3	44,244,000	1,667,000	45,911,000	2,987,000	1,933,000	393,000
1970	97.2	255.7	8.0	360.9	50,940,000	1,940,000	52,880,000	3,534,000	2,123,000	441,000
1971	109.6	297.8	9.3	416.7	58,908,000	1,862,000	60,770,000	4,177,000	2,409,000	530,000

Yrs.to 31 Mar.	Drcts' Emolts.	Trustees Remun.	Deb. Int. (Gross)	Income Tax	Profits Tax	Corpn Tax	Earned for Divs.
1961	200,871	688	218,990	7,700,000	2,500,000	—	10,144,687
1962	191,649	889	354,109	7,750,000	3,050,000	—	10,384,923
1963	186,209	1,000	385,968	8,150,000	3,200,000	—	10,955,128
1964	173,000	1,000	383,000	9,200,000	3,650,000	—	12,070,000
1965	188,000	—	519,000	10,850,000	3,950,000	—	12,706,000
1966	271,000	—	826,000	—	—	11,350,000(40%)	18,268,000
1967	271,000	—	1,030,000	—	—	11,700,000(40%)	18,959,000
1968	293,000	—	1,588,000	—	—	13,750,000(40/42½)	20,121,000
1969	343,000	—	2,132,000	—	—	16,350,000(45%)	21,773,000
1970	363,000	—	2,714,000	—	—	17,700,000(45/42½)	26,005,000
1971	361,000	—	3,178,000	—	—	18,900,000(42½/40)	31,215,000

Yrs.to 31 Mar.	Pref. Divs. 10%	Pref. Divs. 7%	Earned for Ord.	Ord. & "A" Ord. Divs.	Ord. & "A" Ord. Shs. % Paid Int.	Fin.	Earned	Sundry Adjusts	General Reserve
1961	21,438	42,875	10,080,374	6,317,055	15.0	32.5	75.8	Dr. 75,000	3,987,702
1962	21,438	42,875	10,320,610	6,948,761	15.0B	32.5B	70.5B	Cr. 269,956C	3,171,276
1963	21,438	42,875	10,890,815	7,680,210	15.0	37.5	74.4		3,375,133E
1964	21,000	43,000	12,006,000	8,503,000	11.25M	27.5M	54.7M	Dr. 60,000	3,500,000
1965	21,000	43,000	12,642,000	9,194,000	8.75A	20.0A	39.5AV	Dr. 202,000L	3,000,000
1966	21,000	41,000	18,206,000	14,189,000R	11.75	19.5	33.8		3,695,000
1967	70,000G		18,854,000	16,831,000R	11.75F	19.5F	35.0	Dr. 191,000L	2,371,000
1968	70,000G		20,016,000	17,370,000G	11.75	20.5	37.2	Dr. 110,000S	—
1969	70,000G		21,668,000	17,953,000G	11.75	21.583	40.2	Dr. 48,000	—
1970	70,000G		25,900,000	20,197,000G	12.5	25.0	48.1	Cr. 44,000	—
1971	70,000G		31,110,000	22,890,000G	13.25	29.25	57.8	—	—

Yrs.to 31 Mar.	Carry Forward / Retained Profit	Issued Ord. & "A" Ord. Ord.	"A" Ord.	Conv.	Audit Remun.	Staff Pensions
1961	2,107,525	600,000	21,112,759	Conv.		
1962	2,578,054	600,000	23,284,035	do.		
1963	2,413,526	600,000	23,284,035	do.		
1964	2,626,000P	600,000	35,226,000	do.		
1965	2,872,000	600,000	53,139,000	do.		
1966	3,194,000	600,000	53,139,000	Conv.		
1967	2,655,000	53,859,000		Conv.	11,000	431,000
1968	2,536,000	53,859,000		do.	11,000	442,000
1969	3,667,000	53,859,000		do.	11,000	500,000
1970	5,747,000	53,859,000		do.	14,000	507,000
1971	8,220,000	53,859,000		do.	14,000	566,000

FOR NOTES TO PROFITS SEE PAGE 2.

Table 2-2 continued.   (a) Large card continued

MARKS AND SPENCER LIMITED.

HISTORICAL RECORD

ADJUSTED - WHERE APPLICABLE - TO ALLOW FOR SHARE BONUSES AND RIGHTS ISSUES MADE DURING PERIOD COVERED

CAPITAL EMPLOYED - SOURCES AND GROWTH (£000's)

YEARS END 31 Mar.	GROUP LIABILITIES: LONG TERM DEBT: BANKERS	OTHER	TOTAL	%	OUTSIDE SHARE-HOLDERS	%	FUTURE TAX & OTHER PROVS.	%	PARENT COMPANY SHAREHOLDERS' INTEREST: ISSUED PREF. CAP.	%	ORD. HOLDERS' FUNDS: ISSUED CAP.	RESERVES: CAP.	REV.	TOTAL	%	TOTAL CAPITAL EMPLOYED
1966	Nil	15234	15234	11	Nil	Nil	11350	8	1350	1	53739	22857	33194	109790	80	137724
1967	Nil	22680	22680	17	Nil	Nil	Nil	Nil	1350	1	53859	22737	35655	112251	82	136281
1968	Nil	30000	30000	20	Nil	Nil	Nil	Nil	1350	1	53859	22738	38191	114788	79	146138
1969	Nil	37500	37500	24	Nil	Nil	Nil	Nil	1350	1	53859	22738	41858	118455	75	157305
1970	Nil	45000	45000	26	Nil	Nil	Nil	Nil	1350	1	53859	22738	46555	123152	73	169502
1971	Nil	45000	45000	26	Nil	Nil	Nil	Nil	1350	1	53859	22738	51114	127711	73	174061

CAPITAL EMPLOYED - HOW USED (£000's)

YEARS END 31 Mar.	FIXED ASSETS LESS DEPREC. & AMOUNTS W. O.: PROP-ERTY	PLANT ETC.	TRADE INV.	OTHER	TOTAL	CURRENT ASSETS: CASH & EQUIV.	STK. & W. I. P.	DEBT-ORS	TOTAL	CURRENT LIABILITIES: DUE BANK-ERS	DIVS. & TAX	CREDIT-ORS	TOTAL	NET. CURRENT ASSETS	RATIO CURRENT ASSETS / LIABS.	TOTAL ASSETS EXCL. G'WILL.	GOOD-WILL	TOTAL CAPITAL EMPLOYED
1966	111745	7021	2147	Nil	120913	15098	20286	3396	38780	Nil	11197	10772	21969	16811	1.8	137724	Nil	137724
1967	122175	7688	2060	Nil	131923	13981	20976	3470	38427	Nil	22745	11324	34069	4358	1.1	136281	Nil	136281
1968	130580	8964	2469	Nil	142013	16526	20907	3912	41345	Nil	24792	12428	37220	4125	1.1	146138	Nil	146138
1969	141257	10254	2593	Nil	154104	20298	23574	4908	48780	Nil	27975	17604	45579	3201	1.1	157305	Nil	157305
1970	152913	12372	2614	Nil	167899	20643	24879	5991	51513	Nil	32215	17695	49910	1603	1.0	169502	Nil	169502
1971	154617	13932	Nil	Nil	168549	30916	29642	5843	66401	Nil	36341	24548	60889	5512	1.1	174061	Nil	174061

PROFITABILITY TREND - CASH FLOW - CAPITAL COMMITMENTS

YEARS END 31 Mar.	CAPITAL EMPLOYED (£000s)	TURNOVER £m's	AS % CAP. EMPL. INCL. G'WILL.	AS % CAP. EMPL. EXCL. G'WILL.	PRE - TAX PROFITS BEFORE INTEREST £000s	AS % CAP. EMPL. INCL. G'WILL.	AS % CAP. EMPL. EXCL. G'WILL.	AS % OF TURN OVER	AFTER INTEREST	TAX RATIO TAX CHARGED £000s	AS % OF PROFIT AFTER INT.	CASH FLOW (£000's) RE-TAINED PROFIT	DEPREC.	TOTAL	CAPITAL COMMIT-MENTS £000's
1962	78855	172.8	219			27.3		12.4	21185	10800	51	3372	1164	4536	2500
1963	82548.	184.9	224		22691	27.5		12.3	22305	11350	51	3210	1413	4623	3000
1964	120704*	201.5	166		25303	21.0*		12.6	24920	12850	52	3503	1609	5112	3750
1965	130602	219.8	168		28025	21.4		12.8	27506	14800	54	3448	1844	5292	5000
1966	137724	238.0	172		30444	22.1		12.8	29618	11350	38	4017	1993	6010	8000
1967	136281	255.8	188		31689	23.3		12.4	30659	11700	38	2023	2177	4200	8500
1968	146138	282.3	193		35459	24.3		12.6	33871	13750	41	2646	2488	5134	9500
1969	157305	317.3	202		40255	25.6		12.7	38123	16350	43	3715	2987	6702	14500
1970	169502	360.9	213		46419	27.4		12.9	43705	17700	40	5703	3534	9237	15500
1971	174061	416.7	239		53293	30.6		12.8	50115	18900	38	8220	4177	12397	22000

DISTRIBUTION - EQUITY SHARE RECORDS ORD. 25p. SHARES *** ‡‡‡

YEARS END 31 Mar.	DISTRIBUTION PRIORITY PER CENT: FXD. CHGS.	PREF. DIV.	ORD. DIV.	EARNED %	EARNED • PER. SH. Pence	DIVIDEND PAID %	PER. SH. Pence	TIMES COVERED	ERNGS. AS % OF EQUITY ASSETS	NET‡‡ ASSETS PER SH.	SHARE PRICES CALENDAR YEAR HIGH (Pence)	LOW (Pence)	PRICE/ EARNINGS RATIO	YIELD RATIO ERNGS.	DIV.
1962	2	2½	68	20.9	5.23	14.1	3.53	1.5	27.3	19	149	116	25.3		47
1963	2	2½	71	22.0	5.50	15.6	3.90	1.4	27.3	20	162	116	25.2		52
1964	2	2½	72	24.3	6.08	17.2	4.30	1.4	19.2	31½	162	107	22.2		50
1965	2¼	2¾	74	26.3	6.58	19.2	4.80	1.4	20.1	32½	135	106	18.3		47
				20.9	5.23			1.1	16.0				23.0		
1966	2½	3	93	22.5	5.63	20.8	5.20	1.1	16.6	34	135	101	21.0		70
1967	3	3½	90	23.3	5.83	20.8	5.20	1.1	16.8	34½	154	104	21.3a		73
1968	4	5	87	24.8	6.20	21.5	5.38	1.2	17.5	35½	202	124	25.3a		80
1969	5	5½	84	26.8	6.70	22.2	5.55	1.2	18.3	36½	191	134	23.0a	68	74
1970	5	5½	79	32.1	8.03	25.0	6.25	1.3	21.0	38	208	170	22.3a	50	57
1971	5¾	6	75	38.5	9.63	28.3	7.08	1.4	24.4	39½			26.8a	49	55

A771

* "33, 389" in '64 added on Revaln. of Properties.
‡‡ Incls. Goodwill (if any).
a. Based on prices at issue of accounts (prev. yearly average).
*** "A" Ord. shares up to and incl. 1965, Ord. shs. thereafter.
‡‡‡ Takes account of 1 for 2 scrip issue July, 1971.

FOR SUBSEQUENT NEWS (IF ANY) SEE THIS COMPANY'S CARD IN SMALL SERVICE

Table 2-2 *continued.* (a) Large card *continued*

MARKS & SPENCER LTD. (T)

LAST A/CS. PUBL'D 17th May, 1971 | CARD ISSUED 17.1.72 Reprint
MEETING 7th June 1971

TRANSFERS Michael House,
67, Baker Street, London W1A 1DN.
TEL. Welbeck 4422.

BUSINESS Operates 246 retail stores in Great Britain.
This Company is not a "Close Company".

CAPITAL EMPLOYED £M's.

— SOURCES —	1970	1971	— USES — 31st Mar. —	1970	1971
EQUITY FUNDS					
CAPITAL	53.86	53.86	CASH & SECS.	20.64	30.92
RESERVES	69.29	73.85	STOCKS & W.I.P.	24.88	29.64
			OTHER CUR. ASS.	5.99	5.84
	123.15	127.71	TOTAL CUR. ASS.	51.51	66.40
PREF. CAPITAL	1.35	1.35	LESS CUR. LIABS.		
LONG TERM DEBT	45.00	45.00	DUE BANKERS	Nil	Nil
DEFERRED LIABS.	Nil	Nil	OTHER CUR. LIABS.	49.91	49.89
	169.50	174.06	NET CUR. ASS.	1.60	5.51
			FIXED ASS. (NET)	167.90	168.55
EQ. ASS. VAL.	38p	39½p	GOODWILL	Nil	Nil
CAP. COMMITS.	15.50	22.00		169.50	174.06
NET CASH FLOW	9.24	12.40			

CAPITAL

	OUTSTANDING £	DIV. DATES	REDEMPTION
1st M. Deb. Stocks	45,000,000	30J.31D.	par '85/2000
10%Cum.Pr.£1 Shs.(56544)	350,000	1M.1N.	
7%Cum.Pr.£1 Shs.(56546)†	1,000,000	1J.1J.	
Ord.25p.Shares (56540C)	53,859,000		

REVISED — Changes overleaf

	YEAR	DIV.	PER CENT	PER UNIT	DECLARED	PAYABLE
DIVI-	69/70	Int	12½	-/7½	10Oct'69	16Jan'70
	69/70	Fin	25	1/3	16Apr'70	17Jly'70
DENDS	70/71	Int	13¼	-/7.95	5Oct'70	15Jan'71
	70/71	Fin	29¼	7.3125p	20Apr'71	16Jly'71
	71/72	Int.	9¾	2.4375p	13Oct'71	14Jan'72

YIELD GUIDE

ERNGS	DIV.	PRICE	1970	1971
5.7	4.3	170	20.64	30.92
4.6	3.5	210	24.88	29.64
3.9	2.9	250	5.99	5.84
3.3	2.5	290	51.51	66.40
2.9	2.2	330		
2.6	2.0	370		

PROFIT TRENDS

TO 31 Mar.	CAP. EMP'D.	PRE TAX PFTS (1) BEF. INT.	(2) AFTER INT.	AS % OF CAP. EMP'D. OF (2)	TAX AS %	ERND. PAID ORD %	D ORD % (ADJUSTED)
'67	136.1	31.7	30.7	23.3	38	23.3	20.8
'68	146.1	35.5	33.9	24.3	41	24.8	21.5
'69	157.3	40.3	38.1	25.6	43	26.8	22.2
'70	169.5	46.4	43.7	27.4	40	32.1	25.0
'71	174.1	53.3	50.1	30.6	38	38.5	28.3

RANGE (ADJ.)

(LONDON)	1968	1969	1970	1971 (to 13Dec)
ORD H	202	191	208	330
L	124	134	170	192

COVER £000's
% OF ERNGS. TAKEN
CALC. ON
38.5 29.25 ... 541,907 33,122

EX DIV.	NET U.K. RATE
27Oct'69	--
11May'70	--
2Nov'70	--
3May'71	--

RECENT SCRIP & RIGHTS ISSUES

TERMS	EX.	RANKING FOR
1 for 2 Scrip	26.7.71	7/72 Int.

†† Includes goodwill (if any).
b. £5m. at 5½% Red. '85/90. £10m. at 6½% Red. '89/94. £15m. at 7¼% Red. '93/98. £15m. at 7¾% Red. '95/2000.
† In Liq. repayable at 112½p.
p. New Pence.
i. 70/71 earnings but see 13.10.71.
e. Takes into account increased int. div.
PTO

Particulars contained in this memorandum are not guaranteed, but are based on information believed to be reliable. 200

Made & Printed by MOODIES SERVICES LTD., Moodies House,6,7 & 8,Bonhill St.,London,E.C.2.

Making	216,636,000	190,285,000
Trading Profit	27,444,000	25,743,000
Add:Interest & Divs.	754,000	959,000
Deb.Interest	1,590,000	1,590,000
Deprec.	2,310,000	2,047,000
Profit before tax	24,298,000	23,065,000
Corpn.tax at 40%	9,200,000	8,700,000
Profit after tax	15,098,000	14,365,000

Profit before tax for this half-year is arrived at after charging cost of exceptional price reductions following announcement of halving of S.E.T. and reduction of Purchase Tax rates. In both these instances, benefits were passed on to public, without delay in form of lower prices, at a cost to company of approx. £1,250,000.

MARKS & SPENCER LIMITED.

21st April, 1971. SCRIP ISSUE: Directors propose to recommend a Scrip Issue in proportion of one for every two Ord. shares held at close of business on 17th May, 1971. Renounceable Certs. will be posted 23.7.71.
REVISED EQUITY CAPITAL (Giving effect to above)
Ord. 25p. Shares £80,788,000
(Meeting 7th June) (X.C. 26.7.71)

POINTS FROM CHAIRMAN'S REVIEW Issued 17th May, 1971. Co. announce once again, record sales and profits. Gross sales have increased by £55,750,000 - largest increase in any single year - to £416,685,000 in fifty-three weeks as against £360,935,000 last year. Of this total, store sales amounted to £407,336,000 and export sales to £9,349,000. During last financial year clothing sales which include growing footwear and household textiles departments, have increased by £42,064,000 to £297,765,000. Food sales have this year reached £109,571,000 compared with £97,214,000 last year. Rate of growth in second half of year has accelerated, in spite of unavoidable price increases.

8th June 1971 REMARKS AT MEETING Excellent progress was made in April and May, the first two months of current year.

18th Aug. 1971 ALLOTMENT LETTERS Company is prepared to accept renunciation of Allotment Letters representing new shares up to 12.00 mid-day on Friday 20th Aug. 1971.

13th Oct. 1971 INTERIM STATEMENT 26 wks. end

Sales: At Stores:	2.10.71	26.9.70
Clothing	151,296,000	135,438,000
Foods	60,760,000	50,694,000
Total	212,056,000	186,132,000
Exports	4,580,000	4,153,000

D13/10

Table 2-2 continued.   (b) Small card

Rank by turn-over	COMPANY	Headquarters	Main activity	Chairman and Managing Directors (in italics) § ǁ
1 (2)	British Petroleum	London	Oil Industry	Sir Eric Drake (J.M.D.)
2 (1)	'Shell' Transport & Trading[2]	London	Oil Industry	Sir David Barran (J.M.D.)
3 (3)	British-American Tobacco	London	Tobacco & Cosmetics	R. P. Dobson
4 (4)	Imperial Chemical Industries	London	Chemicals, Fibres, Paints, etc.	Jack Callard
5 (5)	Unilever Ltd.	London	Detergents, Margarine, Foods	E. G. Woodroofe
6 (6)	Imperial Tobacco Group	London	Tobacco and food products	Sir John Partridge
7 (7)	Shell-Mex & B.P.	London	Petroleum Distributors	
8 (8)	British Leyland Motor Corpn.	London	Motor Vehicle Manufacturers	Lord Stokes (M.D.)
9 (9)	General Electric Co.	London	Electrical Engineers	Lord Nelson of Stafford, *Sir A. Weinstock*
10 (10)	Courtaulds	London	Man-Made Fibres, Textiles, Chemicals	Lord Kearton
11 (11)	Esso Petroleum	London	Oil Industry	N.P. Biggs, *A. W. Pearce, L.R. Pincott*
12 (15)	Ford Motor Co.	London	Motor Vehicle Manufacturers	Sir Leonard Crossland, *W. B. Batty*
13 (14)	Dunlop Holdings	London	Rubber Goods & Sports Requisites	Sir Reay Geddes
14 (20)	Metal Traders	London	Dlrs. In Metals, Minerals, Chemicals	Sir John Brown. *A. F. Baer*
15 (13)	Associated British Foods	London	Wholesale & Retail Bakers, etc.	G. H. Weston

	TURNOVER		*CAPITAL EMPLOYED			NET PROFIT BEFORE INTEREST AND TAX							
	Total £000	Export £000	£000	Rank Latest year	Rank Previous year	Latest year £000	Rank	Previous year £000	% to turnover Latest year	% to capital employed Latest year	Previous year	Employees	‡Equity market cap £M
1	2,614,200	111,300	1,890,500	2	2	466,500	1	384,300	17.8	26.4	25.1	27,200[1]	2233.8
2	2,608,197[3]	—	2,043,560	1	1	347,230	2	335,435	13.3	18.2	18.9	—	2259.4
3	1,668,450[4]	32,080	795,020	4	5	167,710	4	141,560	10.1	25.1	23.3	120,000	795.9
4	1,462,400**	253,200	1,695,600	3	3	186,500	3	212,700	12.8	11.8	14.1	194,000	1359.4
5	1,292,000	87,500	570,800	8	8	74,100	7	68,600	5.7	13.5	12.6	100,553[1]	567.5
6	1,266,600	6,800	568,342	9	9	72,083	8	62,027	5.7	13.6	11.4	68,460	510.9
7	1,063,000[5]	—	364,000	13	13	—[6]	—	—[6]	—	—	—	14,997	UQ
8	1,020,964	351,000	436,550	11	11	25,616	34	55,594	2.5	6.3	16.0	199,524	215.0
9	890,669	202,000	583,599	7	6	81,819	6	71,433	9.2	13.2	11.8	206,000[1]	579.5
10	659,583	113,618	554,309	10	10	59,423	10	67,046	9.0	11.6	14.7	160,000	296.7
11	611,985	21,599	404,443	12	12	11,846	76	14,809	1.9	3.4	4.5	11,309[1]	UQ
12	589,100	232,500	264,100	23	23	27,000	32	43,100	4.6	11.3	18.0	65,000[1]	UQ
13	541,000	41,000	316,681	19	18	38,369	19	36,116	7.1	12.9	13.4	107,000	147.4
14	530,193	2,619	10,324	446	404	1,643	391	407	0.3	18.4	3.1	107[1]	5.0
15	524,355	3,710	159,403	44	44	27,284	30	24,961	5.2	18.4	19.5	82,880[1]	176.0

*Total tangible assets less current liabilities and sundry provisions (other than bank loans and overdrafts and future tax). †As percentage of capital employed at beginning of the year. ‡At July 2nd, 1971. § Officials are listed only if there is room. ǁM.D.=Managing Director; J.M.D.=Joint Managing Director. ¶As percentage of capital employed at end of the year. [1] U.K. only. [2] Based on 40% of Royal Dutch/Shell Group. [3] Before deduction of Duties, Levies, etc. [4] Including Import and Excise duties. [5] Including Customs Duty. [6] Profits included in those of Royal Dutch/Shell and B.P. Group. **Including figures for Imperial Metal Industries with sales of £207,751,000.

Table 2-3   Extracts from *The Times 1000 1971-72.*

Name	A/Cs dated	Parent company	Total assets £000	Total profits £000	% profits to assets	Sales in £000	% profits to sales	Ratio sales to assets	No of employees	Sales per employee	Total remuneration in £000	Average remuneration per employee	Exports	% exports to sales	1963/64 total assets in £000	Asset growth rate per annum %
Trutex Ltd	31.12.1968		1,176	211	18.0	2,101	10.1	1.8	860	2,443	561	652	13,800	0.7		
†F C Goode and Co Ltd	14.12.1968	Sharp, Perrin and Co Ltd	52	9	17.0	167	5.3	3.2					24,092	14.4	52	0.1
Paula Lee Ltd	19.11.1968		70	11	16.3	253	4.5	3.6					14,843	5.9		
David Towler and Co Ltd	10 months to 30.9.1968	Edgar Allen and Co Ltd	77	11	14.8	205	5.5	2.7					1,678	0.8	123	-9.0
Cumberland Fashions Ltd	31.12.1968		347	49	14.1	729	6.7	2.1	354	2,060	204	578	200,687	27.5		
Collins (Juveniles) Ltd	31.12.1968		368	34	9.2	562	6.0	1.5	257	2,186	147	572				
John Thorpe and Co (Nottingham) Ltd	30.9.1968		131	9	6.8	236	3.8	1.8	143	1,651	77	535	1,763	0.7		
Truly-Fair (Manchester) Ltd	17.5.1968		183	12	6.7	562	2.2	3.1	274	2,050	119	435				
Babychic Ltd	29.3.1969	John Heathcoat and Co Ltd	398	24	6.0	528	4.5	1.3					31,926	6.1		
A and L Lister Ltd	31.12.1968		175	9	5.2	386	2.4	2.2	187	2,067	121	646	85	—		
Sharp, Perrin and Co Ltd	31.12.1968	Courtaulds Ltd	932	46	4.9	1,970	2.3	2.1					47,163	2.4		
Chilprufe Ltd	31.12.1968	Coats Patons Ltd	796	16	2.0	1,312	1.2	1.6	540	2,429	353	654	138,898	10.6	688	2.9
Brookside Clothing Co Ltd	30.11.1968		128	0.1	0.1	239	0.1	1.9	107	2,236	55	516	16	—		
Totals and weighted averages			4,781	432	9.1	9,083	4.8	1.9	2,722	2,251	1,637	601	450,859	5.0	811	1.5

	Property	Plant
Capital expenditure	103,655	152,344
Less disposals at written-down value	6,622	19,597
New capital expenditure	97,033	132,747
Future capital commitments £40,000		

Blank spaces under number of employees indicates no figures were available

Blank space under Exports indicates no direct exports were shown by the company.

Blank space under 1963/64 total assets indicates that no comparable figures were available from public records.

†Subsidiary companies whose results have been incorporated with a holding company also appearing in this sector. Their figures are therefore omitted from the sector totals.

—Indicates figures between £100 and −£100 and percentages between 0.1 and −0.1.

Table 2-4 Extract from the *Financial League Tables for the Clothing Industry 1968/69*. Sector 8, children's wear (companies are shown in order of profitability).

	Net profit before tax[1] %growth 1960-69	Invested capital[2]	Col 1 minus Col 2	Net capital employed[3] % growth 1960-69	Depreciation + retained profit[4] % growth 1960-69	Years of profits fall, losses or stagnation
IDV	+2052	+5180	−3128	+5292	+1889	2
Blackwood Hodge	+1779	+ 205	+1574	+ 221	+ 282	1
GEC	+1556	+ 606	+ 950	+ 486	+1064	1
Ready Mixed Concrete	+1452	+1664	− 212	+1462	+3526	1
London Merchant Sec.	+1272	+ 581	+ 691	+1294	+1672	1
Rank Organisation	+1207	+ 566	+ 641	+ 212	+1108	1
Thorn Electrical	+1204	+ 750	+ 454	+ 526	+1576	0
Grand Metrop. Hotels	+1056	+3205	−2149	+4589	+1902	1
Tesco	+ 941	+ 873	+ 68	+ 826	+1172	0
Lesney Products	+ 792	+1393	− 601	+1623	+ 965	1
European Ferries	+ 775	+ 971	− 196	+1198	+1773	1
Foseco Minsep	+ 686	+1570	− 884	+1368	+ 420	1
Transport Development	+ 645	+ 624	+ 21	+ 630	+ 555	1
J.B. Eastwood	+ 625	+1601	− 976	+2351	+ 497	3
Bovis Holdings	+ 615	+ 558	+ 57	+ 720	+ 520	1
Nottingham Manufacturing	+ 537	+ 521	+ 16	+ 480	+ 491	0
Pegler-Hattersley	+ 530	+ 447	+ 83	+ 600	+ 483	2
Joseph Dawson	+ 527	+ 148	+ 379	+ 317	+1014	1
Trust Houses Forte	+ 492	+ 418	+ 74	+ 757	+3211	2
Tarmac Derby	+ 481	+ 293	+. 188	+ 581	+ 311	2
Ozalid	+ 479	+ 489	− 10	+ 543	+ 387	0
Empire Stores	+ 477	+ 202	+ 275	+ 321	+ 629	0
Inchcape	+ 473	+ 307	+ 166	+ 560	+ 516	4
Coalite & Chemical	+ 464	+ 179	+ 285	+ 215	+ 447	0
Chubb	+ 445	+ 547	− 102	+ 546	+ 332	0
Taylor Woodrow	+ 435	+ 382	+ 53	+ 284	+ 249	1

Table 2-5 Extract from *Managment Today's* Real Growth in British Business *(Management Today,* December 1970).

	Net profit before tax[1] %growth 1960-69	Invested capital[2]	Col 1 minus Col 2	Net capital employed[3] % growth 1960-69	Depreciation +retained profit[4] % growth 1960-69	Years of profits fall, losses or stagnation
Cunard	+ 415	− 20	+ 435	+ 34	+ 27	6
Cadbury Schweppes	+ 387	+ 655	− 268	+ 711	+ 359	2
Plessey	+ 386	+ 644	− 258	+ 773	+ 390	2
George Kent	+ 352	+ 429	− 77	+ 389	+ 297	1
Carreras	+ 342	+ 131	+ 211	+ 132	+ 186	2
Associated Dairies	+ 338	+ 209	+ 129	+ 219	+ 327	0
Whitbread	+ 338	+ 680	− 342	+ 760	+ 305	0
Marchweil	+ 324	+ 641	− 317	+ 231	+ 189	1
Scottish & Newcastle	+ 315	+ 352	− 37	+ 365	+ 202	1
Furness Withy	+ 312	+ 68	+ 244	+ 104	+ 102	2
Redland	+ 289	+ 327	− 38	+ 702	+ 379	3
Carrington	+ 271	+ 977	− 706	+1819	+ 811	3
English China Clays	+ 269	+ 272	− 3	+ 322	+ 206	0
BSR	+ 260	+ 295	− 35	+ 317	+ 383	3
Beecham	+ 259	+ 189	+ 70	+ 249	+ 246	2
McKechnie Bros	+ 255	+ 98	+ 157	+ 140	+ 95	3
International C. Air	+ 241	+ 250	− 9	+ 334	+ 337	2
Rugby Portland Cement	+ 240	+ 289	− 49	+ 264	+ 240	0

Table 2-5 *continued*

Notes to Table 2-5

The data for each company provide its growth profile. Bold type for the name means that growth in pre-tax profits has equalled or exceeded growth in invested capital (i.e. return on shareholders' equity has risen over the decade). The difference between the first two columns measures the extent of the improvement (or decline) in the company's profitability. The increase in net capital employed (which includes debt) should be compared with growth in invested capital: if the former is greater than the latter, then the company's profit growth may be partly accounted for by borrowing—by 'gearing up'. Depreciation and retained profit—in other words the increase in plough-back—are shown in column 5. The last column shows the number of financial periods (out of 9) in which profits either fell or failed to rise significantly. Where financial years coincide with calendar years, the comparisons run from 1960 to 1969. In other cases the base is the financial year nearest to calendar 1960, i.e. year ended 31 March 1961 compares to year ended 31 March 1970. Companies which did not trade in substantially the same form as public companies engaged in commerce or manufacturing in 1960 have been excluded.

The statistics in almost all cases have been taken from Exchange Telegraph.

1. Profit less depreciation and loan interest, etc, but before tax and minority interest.

2. Preference and ordinary capital plus net reserves and intangibles = fixed assets, less depreciation, plus net current assets, minus loans and minority interest.

3. Equals loans, minority interest, preference and ordinary capital plus net reserves.

4. Profit after minority interest, tax and dividends, plus depreciation.

(a) ICC Survey (Knitwear, Hosiery, Corsetry & Lingerie)

	Date of Accounts	Turnover		Total Assets		Current Liabilities		Profit Before Tax and Group Relief		Payments to Directors	
		This Year	Last Year	This Year	Last Year	This Year	Last Year	This Year	Last Year	This Year	Last Year
A.A. Manufacturing Knitwear Co. Ltd	17.10.71	172,481	196,727	96,077	88,939	48,323	45,948	7,903	5,951	N/F	21,332
William Ackroyd & Co. Ltd	31.5.71	596,774	615,676	213,837	176,472	90,848	50,944	5,985	29,802	17,104	18,273
Atkins Brothers (Hosiery) Ltd (Group)	31.3.71	4,072,242	4,048,453	2,700,412	2,626,358	719,014	790,235	249,249	322,770	42,186	40,704
Frymann & Fletcher Ltd (Group)	27.3.71	620,571	525,460	411,115	421,668	179,624	191,577	3,400	(68,044)	12,541	10,550
Jarol Ltd	19.6.71	491,847	430,232	266,330	218,450	115,469	93,632	17,411	20,576	13,322	11,425
Nova (Jersey) Knit Ltd (Group)	31.3.71	6,099,586	3,870,350	4,517,310	2,076,165	2,209.841	1,198,024	683,936	348,509	16,549	9,450
Youthlines Ltd	31.3.71	37,342	95,823	144,670	180,852	39,971	84,463	8,310	581	750	750

(b) Computerised Business Ratio Service (Motor component and accessory manufacturers) TABLE 1 PROFITABILITY*

	A/C Date	Profit Before Tax £000			Total Assets £000			Profit/Total Assets Percentage		
	70/71	1970	1969	1968	1970	1969	1968	1970	1969	1968
Champion Sparking Plug Company Ltd	31.12	2,033	1,906	1,607	5,189	5,035	4,273	39.2	37.9	37.6
Eaton Axles Ltd	31.12	802	716	559	2,632	2,025	1,558	30.5	35.4	35.9
Dartmouth Auto Castings Ltd	31.07	909	1,134	632	3,818	4,026	3,978	23.8	28.2	15.9
L. Gardner and Sons Ltd	31.12	1,385	1,225	1,132	6,577	6,071	5,664	21.1	20.2	20.0
Harmo Industries Ltd	31.12	1,131	972	812	5,399	4,099	3,589	20.9	23.7	22.6

*Note: Other tables cover the following ratios

PROFIT MARGIN	Profit before tax to sales
CAPITAL USAGE	Sales to total assets
RETURN ON CAPITAL	Profit before tax to capital employed
LIQUIDITY	Current assets to current liabilities
STOCK TURNOVER	Sales to stocks
CREDIT PERIOD	Debtors to sales
EXPORT RATIO	Export to sales

Table 2-6   Extracts from publications of Inter Company Comparisons Ltd

Profit and Loss Account July-September 1970

Industry	Building Materials		
	Latest (£000s)	% change	
		qtr	year
Number of Companies		(20)	(76)
Profit	32,481	− 3.9	+ 1.2
Investment and other income	1,455	+ 5.6	+ 7.7
Total Income	**33,936**	**− 3.5**	**+ 1.6**
Depreciation	10,386	+ 8.2	+ 15.0
Directors' Emoluments	958	+ 6.4	+ 5.9
Administrative Charges	2,491	+ 69.7	+ 69.8
Loan Interest	2,749	+ 47.3	+ 31.4
Profit Before Tax	**17.352**	**− 18.7**	**− 10.0**
Corporation Tax (net)	8,485	− 16.9	− 7.1
Minorities	1,008	+ 29.1	+ 7.6
Preference Dividend	169	+ 5.0	+ 5.1
Net Equity Earnings	**7,690**	**− 24.6**	**− 13.8**
Ordinary Dividends	5,965	− 15.3	− 7.1
Plus Non-Recurring Credits	305	+ 21.0	+286.6
Retained Earnings	**2.030**	**− 40.3**	**− 9.4**
Dividend Cover	1.3	− 7.1	− 6.7

Balance sheet July-September 1970

Industry	Building Materials		
	Latest (£000s)	% change	
		qtr	year
Number of Companies		(20)	(76)
Fixed Assets	193,010	+ 10.1	+ 11.9
Less Depreciation	76,723	+ 10.6	+ 4.9
Land and Property (net)	**52,902**	**+ 6.2**	**+ 11.3**
Plant and Equipment (net)	**63,385**	**+ 12.8**	**+ 19.5**
Trade Investments	15,739	− 5.7	+ 3.6
Intangible Assets	13,372	+ 41.7	+ 14.3
Stocks	37,875	+ 11.4	+ 11.4
Debtors	58,844	+ 3.8	+ 10.7
Gilt-edged	−	−	− 68.1
Cash	3,798	+ 2.3	+ 9.6
Other Marketable Investments	3,057	+258.8	+ 3.6
Creditors	35,242	+ 12.7	+ 19.0
Other Current Liabilities	15,645	− 1.0	+ 4.1
Bank Overdrafts	22,564	− 10.9	+ 0.9
Net Current Assets	**30,123**	**+ 32.0**	**+ 8.8**
Total Net Assets	**175,521**	**+ 13.3**	**+13.2**
Financed by:			
Corporation Tax	8,511	+ 4.2	+ 13.7
Capital Reserves	25,435	+ 13.1	+ 18.5
Revenue Reserves	41,186	+ 0.2	+ 12.8
Minorities	5,444	+ 28.7	+ 5.3
Loan Capital	39,656	+ 59.8	+ 40.7
Preference Capital	2,963	−	− 10.3
Ordinary Capital	52,326	+ 2.3	+ 1.9
Scrip Issues	6	+100.0	− 96.4
Capital Commitments	7,611	− 36.7	− 28.4

Table 2-7   Extract from *The Economist,* Industrial Profits and Assets

INDUSTRY	Number of Companies	Trading Profit (1)	% change	Profits before Int. & Tax (2)	Pre-Tax Profits (3)	Tax (4)	Earned for Ordinary Dividends (5)	% change	Ord. Dividends (6)	% change	Cash Flow (7)	Net Capital Employed (8)	Net Return on Capital % (9)	Net Current assets (10)
AIRCRAFT & COMPONENTS	2	3,649	−23.6	2,318	1,545	189	1,196	−30.7	1,374	+2.5	970	41,723	5.6	20,654
		(4,776)		(3,128)	(3,128)	(1,171)	(1,727)		(1,341)		(1,356)	(41,391)	(8.9)	(21,973)
BUILDING MATERIALS	58	121,128	+8.5	81,358	65,669	27,216	34,818	+10.3	26,050	+0.9	45,256	589,195	13.8	154.856
		(111,649)		(72,490)	(60,508)	(26,134)	(31,559)		(25,816)		(38,631)	(553,466)	(13.1)	(149,850)
CONTRACTING & CONSTRUCTION	52	73,790	+12.3	50,121	40,784	17,726	21,812	+13.0	9,953	+9.8	33,320	337,890	14.8	89,880
		(65,697)		(44,345)	(38,199)	(17,966)	(19,307)		(9,062)		(28,787)	(265,288)	(16.7)	(73,413)
ELECTRICAL EX ELECTRN ETC	12	61,826	+8.3	46,439	35,870	15,962	15,760	+6.7	10,810	+4.6	19,746	350,963	13.2	134,660
		(57,071)		(42,378)	(34,888)	(16,023)	(14,771)		(10,338)		(18,519)	(327,643)	(12.9)	(136,864)
ENGINEERING	13	212,320	+5.6	157,375	132,636	61,137	66,827	+4.0	40,578	−4.3	75,461	1,181,060	13.3	457,954
		(201,086)		(148,820)	(130,002)	(60,420)	(64,228)		(42,394)		(67,354)	(1,109,264)	(13.4)	(437,082)
MACHINE TOOLS	19	23,825	+33.3	17,323	12,853	5,547	6,792	+86.0	3,002	−11.3	9,139	165,938	10.4	72,757
		(17,873)		(12,091)	(8,661)	(4,591)	(3,651)		(3,384)		(5,057)	(154,707)	(7.8)	(61,714)
SHIPBUILDING	1	183	−50.5	88	84	46	7		34		29	3,242	2.7	1,000
		(370)		(288)	(274)	(62)	(180)		(168)		(66)	(3,273)	(8.8)	(950)
MISC CAPITAL GOODS	33	48,852	+10.6	37,948	31,968	13,611	16,457	+16.2	10,582	+6.3	14,764	249,745	15.2	107,048
		(44,166)		(34,023)	(29,022)	(13,154)	(14,164)		(9,957)		(12,995)	(240,095)	(14.2)	(109,268)
TOTAL CAPITAL GOODS	290	545,573	+8.5	392,970	321,409	141,434	163,669	+9.4	102,383	−0.1	198,685	2,919,756	13.5	1,038,809
		(502,688)		(358,103)	(304,682)	(139,521)	(149,587)		102,460		(172,765)	(2,695,127)	(13.3)	(991,114)
ELECTRONICS RADIO & TV	9	40,239	+19.0	22,102	16,797	6,351	10,380	+27.5	5,172	+27.9	22,918	147,249	15.0	84,556
		(33,812)		(17,355)	(13,611)	(5,469)	(8,142)		(4,045)		(20,171)	(143,624)	(12.1)	(76,771)
HOUSEHOLD GOODS	32	29,903	−0.4	22,114	20,054	8,673	11,052	+2.3	7,205	−3.6	10,653	155,739	14.2	67,057
		(30,034)		(22,482)	(20,217)	(9,081)	(10,803)		(7,473)		(9,721)	(147,391)	(15.3)	(68,175)
MOTORS & COMPONENTS	26	230,136	−14.5	127,560	81,060	42,313	31,146	−51.7	25,461	−40.9	110,913	1,377,962	9.3	347,387
		(269,115)		(166,686)	(132,660)	(61,161)	(64,518)		(43,057)		(117,997)	(1,215,134)	(13.7)	(365,354)
MOTOR DISTRIBUTORS	28	23,073	+27.2	17,559	11,875	5,025	6,478	+64.5	3,751	+14.4	6,892	138,311	12.7	31,954
		(18,137)		(13,313)	(8,185)	(3,857)	(3,939)		(3,278)		(4,236)	(126,054)	(10.6)	(25,124)
TOTAL CONSUMER DURABLE	95	323,351	−7.9	189,335	129,786	62,362	59,056	−32.4	41,589	−28.1	151,376	1,819,261	10.4	530,954
		(351,098)		(219,836)	(174,673)	(79,568)	(87,402)		(57,853)		(152,125)	(1,632,203)	(13.5)	(535,424)
BREWERIES	20	174,666	+12.8	144,187	118,501	50.051	64,258	+18.1	42,103	+8.3	50,406	1,206,638	12.0	48.511

Table 2-8   Extract from *The Financial Times 23 June 1971,* Trend of Industrial Profits. This covers the results (with the preceding year's comparison in brackets) of 1,018 companies which publicised their reports during the first five months of 1971. The cumulative record, of the 1970 series covered the results of 2,694 public companies (Figures in £000). Notes on compilation of the table are given on page 35.

The classification follows closely that of the Institute and Faculty of Actuaries, which has been adopted by the Stock Exchange Daily Official List.

Column (1) gives trading profits, plus investment and other normal income properly belonging to the financial year covered. The figure is struck before charging depreciation, loan and other interest, directors' emoluments and other items normally shown on the profit and loss account. Excluded are all exceptional or non-recurring items such as, for example, capital profits unless the latter arise in the ordinary transaction of business.

N.B.—Certain companies, including merchant banks, discount houses, insurance and shipping companies, are exempted from disclosing the full information required under the Companies Act 1948.

Column (2) gives profits before interest and taxation, that is to say profits after all charges, except loan and other interest, but before deducting taxation provisions and minority interests. In the case of banks no figure can be shown because of non-disclosure (see foregoing paragraph.)

Column (3) gives pre-tax profit, that is to say profits after all charges including debenture and loan interest but before deducting taxation provision and minority interests.

Column (4) groups all corporate taxation including foreign liability and future tax provisions but excludes adjustments relating to previous years.

Column (5) gives the net profits accruing on equity capital after meeting:

1. Minority interests,
2. All prior charges—sinking fund payments, etc, and Preference dividends; and
3. Provisions for staff and employees, pension funds where this is a standard annual charge against net revenue.

Column (6) sets out the gross cost of dividend on equity capital.

Column (7) is the capital generated internally over a year's trading. For the purposes of comparison equity earnings plus depreciation less equity dividends is the recognised method of computing this figure.

Column (8) constitutes the total net capital employed. This is the total of net fixed assets, trade investments and current assets—excluding intangibles such as goodwill—less current liabilities except bank overdrafts.

Column (9) represents the net return on capital employed. Column (2) as a percentage of Column (8) provides an indication of average profitability.

Column (10) Net current assets are arrived at by the subtraction of current liabilities and provision from current assets. It must therefore be regarded mainly as an indication of the volume and the value of industrial activity and is not necessarily a true guide to actual liquid resources.

2   Selected figures and ratios for a number of firms are tabulated in one document. This is the method of *Management Today* and the NEDO league tables and Inter Company Comparisons Limited. Firms can be tabulated in order of size (as in *The Times 1000*) or some criteria of profitability (as in the NEDO league table) or growth (*Management Today* Growth League) or separately for each ratio (as in Inter Company Comparisons) (see Tables 2-3 to 2-6).

3   The figures for a number of firms are added together to produce a 'consolidated' profit and loss account and balance sheet for an industry. This is the method which was used in the *Economist* Industrial Profits and Assets (this ceased publication at the end of 1970) and is used in the *Financial Times* Trend of Industrial Profits (see Tables 2-7 and 2-8).

4   Selected ratios for individual firms are calculated and then the median and the upper and lower quartile ratios are calculated.* This is the method which I used in my book *A study of profitability in the hosiery and knitwear industry* for the Hosiery and Knitwear Economic Development Council. Table 2-9 is an example of one of the tables from that book.

The 'League Table' approach (method 2) has two advantages over the statistical approaches of methods 3 and 4:

1   It is possible to see the combination of ratios achieved by each individual firm—to see, for example, how fast a firm with a high profitability turns its stock over.

2   Businessmen in the industry can add to the figures their own knowledge of the firm's operations and thus improve the interpretation of the ratios.

The 'consolidated' approach (method 3) has the disadvantage that all the figures will be heavily influenced by the larger firms. The 'median' approach (method 4) may overcome or circumvent some of the limitations of published data. Ratios calculated from figures in published accounts which suffer from the limitations already discussed, tend either to be too large or too small. Use of the quartiles excludes the largest and smallest quarters of the range and may therefore exclude the most distorted figures.

Searching accounts at Companies House

When using the accounts of a company filed at Companies House there are a number of practical points which are worth bearing in mind:

1   Is auditors' report qualified? If so, what is qualification?
2   Is turnover defined? If so, how?
3   Do the directors and/or their family have a controlling interest in the company?
4   Are accounts for a period other than a year?
5   Are there any anomalous items in assets, liabilities or profits?
6   Information for two years should be extracted. This will not take twice as long as searching one year—at a guess only 150 per cent of the time—and will provide information on trends, and even some sort of averaging. Furthermore, the longer the period to which profits relates the less will it be affected by differences in the accounting treatment of stock and depreciation.
7   Costs, income and assets not connected with the industry concerned should be removed if possible.

Organised interfirm comparisons

As mentioned above, comparisons of ratios which can be derived from published accounts of companies have many limitations which make them inadequate as a basis for management decisions. Only a very small fraction of the comparative ratios needed by management (and recommended in this book) is available in published accounts, and even that information is probably not sufficiently comparable to enable management to make decisions based on a study of it.

In order to enable firms to obtain reliable and adequate comparative data properly organised interfirm comparisons are needed. These involve firms in pooling their data under agreed conditions of confidentiality and comparability with some central organisation. The latter carefully checks and processes the data, then issues reports showing each participant's results anonymously under code numbers (together with medians and quartiles etc). Ideally, the comparisons should relate to a carefully chosen set of ratios and supporting data which show each participant in systematic and logical fashion how his performance compares with that of others and why it

---

*1 Median and quartiles are calculated by listing all the figures for a ratio (such as profit/total assets) from the smallest to the largest. The median is the figure in the middle of the list, the lower quartile is one quarter of the way up the list, the upper quartile is three quarters of the way up.

2 The median is used, rather than the arithmetical average, as a measure of typical performance because it is less affected by extreme values which may be untypical and/or the result of the distortions arising from the use of published data.

3 The quartiles and the median divide the sample into four equal parts and give an indication of the range of results. Half the sample lies between the upper and lower quartiles (termed the interquartile range).

4 As the process of calculating the median and quartiles is repeated for each ratio, the median for each ratio is likely to be derived from a different firm.

	Number of firms	Lower Quartile	Median	Upper Quartile
Product group				
A Multi product	48	4.2	8.0	12.5
B Stockings and tights	25	(0.6)	3.9	12.6
C Half hose	16	2.8	7.4	15.4
D Knitted outerwear	52	1.9	7.5	11.4
E Knitted innerwear	17	2.5	7.1	15.0
F Knitted fabric	37	6.1	11.0	16.0
H Dyeing	25	8.8	14.9	22.0
Asset size (£ million)				
L Under 0.25	127	1.8	6.6	12.4
M 0.25 to 0.5	30	3.6	9.2	16.1
N 0.5 to 1.0	25	8.5	11.7	17.1
O 1.0 to 3.0	19	5.5	10.8	14.8
P/Q Over 3.0	19	7.8	11.4	13.5
All firms	220	3.2	8.9	13.7

( ) indicates a loss

Table 2-9   Profit/Total assets (percentage) ratio

differs. The ratios and other yardsticks should cover every significant aspect of performance and should be supplemented by background data which enables participants to take into account the effect on comparative performance of company characteristics and practices such as size; product range; location; production, distribution and marketing methods; and other relevant factors. Ideally, too, the comparisons should provide participants not only with the tables of results, but also with a well-designed guide to their use; if desired, the organiser should provide specially-written individual reports to participants and arrange to visit them to discuss the results and their meaning. The comparisons should be organised on a regular (e.g. annual) basis.

The above principles of proper interfirm comparison were formulated during the British Institute of Management's research which preceded the setting-up of the Centre for Interfirm Comparison, and have been fundamental features of the Centre's operations since its foundation in 1959. The Centre, which is regarded both nationally and internationally as a leading organisation in the field, has now prepared interfirm comparisons in over eighty industries and trades and it is increasingly carrying out work in enabling companies to compare their performance with that of firms in other countries (especially Europe).

Participation in properly organised interfirm comparison involves firms in paying a fee which is, of course, higher than that payable for statistical surveys based on published accounts. It also involves firms in the time and trouble of providing data for the comparisons—although it must be said that a well-organised firm should have internal data of the kind in question fairly readily available. Fees currently quoted (1973) by the Centre for Interfirm Comparison for new projects range from about £150 to £600 per firm per comparison—the exact figure depends upon the degree of detail of the comparisons; the amount of individual analysis; whether or not firms are visited; and whether the scheme is on a national or international basis.

The results of full interfirm comparisons tend to cover fewer firms than is the case with published accounts surveys—but against this (and offsetting also the cost of participation) must be put the immense advantages of relevance, depth and comparability of data which means that the results can be of real value to management in raising productivity and profitability.

For obvious reasons, the full results of these properly organised interfirm comparisons are made available only to participants. Table 2-10 is an example of the method of presenting the results of the comparison used by the Centre for Interfirm Comparison. It is a much condensed example. A full report would typically cover, say, thirty/forty companies, and between 100 and 200 ratios, as well as anonymous supporting data about company characteristics and practices and interpretative guidance. The figures in Table 2-10, although based on actual results, are imaginary.

2.3 External Standards—Work Measurement

This family of techniques provides standards for the shopfloor ratios of Diagram 9-3. The principal methods are:

1. *Time study*—recording the times (measured with a stop watch) and the rate (or pace) of working for a specified job under specified conditions, and then analysing the data so as to obtain a standard time for carrying out the job at a defined level of performance.
2. *Activity sampling*—making a large number of observations over a period of time. Each observation records what is happening at that instant and the percentage of observations recorded for a particular activity or cause of delay is a measure of the percentage of time during which that activity or cause of delay occurs.
3. *Synthesis from standard data*—building up a time for a job by, first of all, breaking the job down into elements for each of which a standard time is already available from time studies of other jobs containing these elements, and then adding up these standard times for each element of the new job.
4. *Predetermined motion time systems* (PMTS)—Building up the standard time for a job from a series of times which have been established for basic human motions (grasp, crank, side step, and so on). Method-Time

A brief example of interfirm comparison – using the pyramid of ratios for general management

This example is intended to show the way in which the pyramid ratios for a comparison are presented, and how conclusions may be drawn from them. The actual figures used are hypothetical, but are typical of the results found by the Centre for Interfirm Comparison in its work in many industries. In practice a comparison normally covers more firms, and also includes more detailed data, such as those referred to in 'What the Comparison Shows Firm 6'.

RATIOS	FIRMS									MEDIAN*
	1	2	3	4	5	6	7	8	9	
1. Operating profit/Operating assets	20.2	17.9	14.3	13.3	11.3	7.9	7.4	3.9	3.1	11.3
2. Operating profit/Sales	18.2	14.9	13.1	11.9	10.9	6.1	7.6	3.1	3.8	10.9
3. Sales/Operating assets (times)	1.11	1.20	1.09	1.12	1.04	1.30	0.98	1.25	0.81	1.11
Departmental costs (as a percentage of sales)										
4. Production costs	71.3	77.1	77.4	79.6	79.4	84.2	82.5	89.5	84.3	79.6
5. Distribution and marketing costs	4.9	3.7	4.1	2.2	3.3	2.9	4.4	3.3	3.6	3.6
6. Administrative costs	5.6	4.3	5.4	6.3	6.4	6.8	5.7	4.1	8.3	5.7
Production costs (as a percentage of sales value of production)										
7. Materials cost	46.9	53.0	51.0	50.8	56.2	55.3	56.3	56.5	51.7	53.0
8. Works labour cost	10.4	9.8	7.3	10.1	9.2	12.3	8.2	16.1	14.7	10.1
9. Production overheads	14.0	14.3	19.1	18.7	14.0	16.6	18.0	16.9	17.9	16.9
Asset utilisation (£'s per £1,000 of sales)										
3a. Total operating assets	899	833	918	893	960	770	1,019	798	1,233	899
10. Current assets	328	384	400	351	379	404	589	423	430	400
11. Fixed assets	571	449	518	542	581	366	430	375	803	518
Current asset utilisation (£'s per £1,000 of sales)										
12. Material stocks	58	73	43	58	86	65	129	80	68	68
13. Work in progress	51	90	104	63	44	114	164	122	135	104
14. Finished stocks	66	94	123	63	118	77	147	60	84	84
15. Debtors	153	127	130	167	131	148	149	161	143	148
Fixed asset utilisation (£'s per £1,000 of sales)										
16. Land and buildings	240	87	102	143	156	88	47	73	299	102
17. Plant and machinery	316	343	407	389	413	267	363	289	486	363
18. Vehicles	15	19	9	10	12	11	20	13	18	13

*The median is the middle figure for each ratio

SUMMARY: THE SCOPE FOR IMPROVEMENT, MEASURED IN RATIOS AND ABSOLUTE FIGURES

If you were able to achieve materials and labour cost ratios equal to the medians, whilst retaining your present production overheads ratio and the same ratios for your other departmental costs, your profit to sales ratio would improve to 10.6 per cent.

In order to achieve your improved labour cost ratio, you might have to spend more on new plant. Supposing you increased your plant value (which at the moment is £267 per £1,000 of sales) by 50 per cent, then your fixed assets ratio would increase to £499. However, you should be able to improve your work in progress figure to the median, giving a lower current asset ratio (ratio 10) of £394. Your rate of turnover of operating assets (ratio 3) would then become 1.12 times. Because of your increased investment in plant and machinery, your depreciation would go up, and the effect of this would be to increase your production overheads ratio to 17.6 per cent; your profit margin on sales would then become 9.6 per cent and your return on assets 10.8 per cent – i.e. nearly three percentage points higher than it is now.

In terms of absolute figures: your present sales volume is £2 millions. At the same volume of sales, your new profit ratio would mean a profit of £192,000 – an improvement of £70,000 on your present profits.

©Centre for Interfirm Comparison Ltd. 1969

Table 2-10   Example of interfirm comparison

WHAT THE COMPARISON SHOWS FIRM 6

Suppose you are the managing director of firm 6 in the table opposite, what does the comparison show you?

1. First and most important, the comparison gives you for the first time an objective yardstick of your firm's overall success – as indicated by the standing of your operating profit/operating assets ratio against that of other firms.
   The comparison of this primary ratio shows that your firm's overall success and effectiveness is *less* than that of the majority of the others, since your return on assets is only 7.9 per cent against the median of 11.3 per cent.

2. What is the cause of your low operating profit/operating assets? Comparison of ratios 2 and 3 shows that the reason is your low operating profit/sales – your figure of 6.1 per cent is the third lowest of the figures shown. On the other hand, your turnover of assets, ratio 3, is the fastest of any firm. It therefore seems that you should first of all investigate the cost ratios which determine your operating profit/sales.

3. Looking at the departmental cost ratios, you find that your production cost, ratio 4, is high; your distribution and marketing cost, ratio 5, is below-average; and your administration cost, ratio 6, is above-average.

4. The causes of your high ratio 4 are shown by ratios 7 and 8 to be your high materials and labour costs. In the actual comparison, you have access to more detailed comparative data which throws further light on these points – it shows (a) that your high materials cost is related to your high materials waste ratio, and (b) that your high works labour cost is caused, not by high wages, etc. costs per employee, but by low volume of output per employee.

5. Turning to the asset utilisation ratios you see that your fast turnover of total operating assets (ratio 3) is expressed in a different way by ratio 3a, which shows that you have the lowest figure of total operating assets per £1,000 of sales. You will see from ratio 11 that this is because you have the lowest figure of fixed assets in relation to sales. This is, in turn, mainly due to your low plant and machinery ratio (ratio 17). Incidentally, the fixed asset figures used in this comparison are based upon comparable valuations.
   The more detailed data available (not shown in this table) indicate that the average age of your plant is greater than that of most other firms; and that your value of plant and machinery per works employee is below the average. The comparison therefore suggests that your low labour productivity (a major cause of your high production costs) may be due to the fact that your plant is not sufficiently up-to-date.

6. Your current asset utilisation ratios (ratios 12 to 15) show that most of your current asset items are about average – with the exception of your work in progress, ratio 13, which is above the average. This seems to provide another indication of the need for altering your production arrangements so as to allow a faster throughput.

Measurement (MTM) is one of the principal PMT systems.

5 *Estimating*—assessing the time for a job based on knowledge and experience of similar types of work but without breaking the job down into elements as is done when synthesising from standard data.

6 *Analytical estimating*—a half way house between estimating and synthesising from standard data. The job is broken down into elements and the standard time for these is found partly from knowledge and practical experience and partly by reference to standard data from time studies of other jobs.

7 *Comparative estimating*—arriving at a time for a job by comparing the work in it with the work in a series of similar, bench mark jobs, the work content of which has been measured.

All the above methods lead to a standard time in which a job should be completed by a qualified and motivated worker using the specified method and taking the appropriate relaxation allowance.

Anyone wanting detailed information should refer to one of the many books on the subject. One which may be recommended is: *Introduction to Work Study*. International Labour Office, Geneva 1969. Two other sources of information are the Institute of Work Study Practioners, 9/10 River Front, Enfield, Middlesex, and Method-Time Measurement Association Limited, P.O. Box 20, 31 Battersby Lane, Warrington, Lancashire.

2.4 Composite Standards: Internal plus External

There are some standards which are a mixture of internal and external, for example:

Performance of other subsidiaries or units.

If a company operates through a number of subsidiaries or divisions or units it is always possible to obtain standards of performance by organising comparisons between them. Such a comparison shares a disadvantage with the process of a firm comparing itself with its own past, because all the units may be equally bad. As this is always a possibility this method is no real substitute for an external comparison with other companies.

On the other hand such a comparison has some of the advantages of an organised interfirm comparison, namely the larger amount of data that can be obtained and the fact that it is possible to ensure that it has been arrived at in a uniform manner.

How much information can be compared depends on how similar the activities of the units are. But however dissimilar they are they should all be comparable to the extent that they are all being run to make a profit out of good use of their assets.

It is often useful to compare dissimilar subsidiaries, because the very process of asking questions as to why ratios should or should not be similar between different units leads management to reconsider assumptions about practices, processes, and so on, with the result that these may be improved or changed rather than their existence and 'rightness' remaining unchallenged. The sort of question which management should ask itself is: 'Bearing in mind our similarity/dissimilarity to unit X would we expect our ratios for A, B, C, etc. to be highter than/lower than/the same as those of unit X and why?' This question should be asked preferably before the comparative data is available. When it is, management should discuss why their predictions were or were not right (particularly bearing in mind the degree and/or trend of difference) and what action or further investigation this suggests.

Other people

It is nearly always possible to establish some yardstick of performance within a firm by making a comparison between employees. Such a process may have the same advantages and disadvantages as a comparison between subsidiaries. For example, workers may have been operating under different conditions or salesmen in different territories. However, if they were, management should know and should ask itself whether the differences in environment were enough (or perhaps more than enough) to account for differences in performance. This should help them to set realistic targets for, and provide equitable rewards to, their employees.

2.5 Constraints

While considering standards against which a firm's ratio should be compared it should be recognised that the possible magnitude of a number of ratios is affected by various external constraints to which a firm's management is subject.

1 *Legal/Social* The size of some ratios is determined for a firm by the legal and social framework in which it operates. For example:
   (*a*) The speed on roads
   (*b*) Minimum wages (National Agreements)
   (*c*) Maximum hours of work (Factories Act).

2 *Physical* It is possible that the magnitude of some ratios might be limited by the physical properties of matter such as the boiling point of water, the conductivity of copper, and so on.

3 *Suppliers/Customers* The specifications of machines (such as rate of operation), the prices of raw materials and the specifications of products made to customers' order are all factors which limit the size of some of the ratios which management must watch.

2.6 Summary

There are many standards available to management against which to measure current performance. The standards vary in their availability, reliability and applicability. Probably no one standard is best for all purposes, but if a budget is composed with due regard to a firm's performance in the past, and the performance of competitors and, to a lesser extent, fellow subsidiaries (if any), and if the budget for the appropriate ratios is based on work measurement, then such a budget will form a useful yardstick against which management can monitor its performance and control its business.

Appendix 2.1

Sources of Published Information

Other firms' accounts direct from the firm's company secretary.
Other firms' accounts and other documents may be inspected at Companies House, 55 City Road, London, E.C.1.
Summaries of individual firms' results for past years may be obtained from:

Extel Statistical Services Limited
37-45 Paul Street, London, E.C.2.
Moodies Services Limited,
6, 7 & 8 Bonhill Street,
London E.C.2.

Aggregates and averages of the results of firms in a range of industries are published by:

Inter Company Comparisons Limited, 81 City Road, London, E.C.1.
Duns Review and Modern Industry, 99 Church Street, New York.
Economist Intelligence Unit Limited (Last issue October to December 1970), 27 St James's Place, London S.W.1.
Business Ratios, (last issue Spring 1970), Adelaide House, London Bridge, London E.C.4.

Other sources of information include:

Times 1000, published by The Times, Printing House Square, London E.C.4.
Stock Exchange Official Year Book published by Thomas Skinner and Company (Publishers) Limited, RAC House, Lansdowne Road, Croydon, Surrey, CR9 2HH.
Commercial Motor's tables of operating costs for goods and passenger vehicles, Hamlyn Publishing Group, Hamlyn House, Feltham, Middlesex.
Fortune published by Time Incorporated, 541 North Fairbanks Court, Chicago, Illinois 60611.
Management Today, published by Haymarket Publishing Limited, Gillow House, 5 Winsley Street, London W1N 8AD.
Financial Times, published by Financial Times Limited, Bracken House, Cannon Street, London E.C.4.
Surveys published by various firms of stockbrokers for their clients.

Prices have not been quoted as these tend to get out of date rapidly and may be obtained from the organisations concerned at the addresses given.

Appendix 2.2

How To Trace UK Company Information (see Diagram 2-1)

Companies registration office

The prime source of information on companies is the companies registration office, 55 City Road, London EC1 to which every limited company is required to make returns under the various Companies Acts. The file of any company may be seen for the statutory fee of five pence. Much of this information for public companies and certain private companies is published by a number of commercial organisations, perhaps in a more digestible form for reference and comparison. A considerable amount of information about companies is outside the scope of the companies registration office and the sources of this information are indicated below.

Business names

An individual carrying on a business under a name other than his own, must register the business name, together with the general nature and principal place of business, at the above address. There is no published register of business names and it must be stressed that many of these businesses are not registered companies. There is often confusion between business names and registered trade marks.

Staff

Financial directories normally include only the names of the board of directors and the secretary of a company. Executives responsible for fields such as advertising, personnel, research, sales and production can often be traced in appropriate trade directories.

Directors

Biographical details of directors and other executives are frequently available in specialised 'who's who's', local yearbooks or trade directories.

Sources

Moodies British Company Service—Moodie Cards

Each of the 5,000 public quoted companies covered is represented by a large card which is issued once a year, after publication of the accounts, and a small card reissued

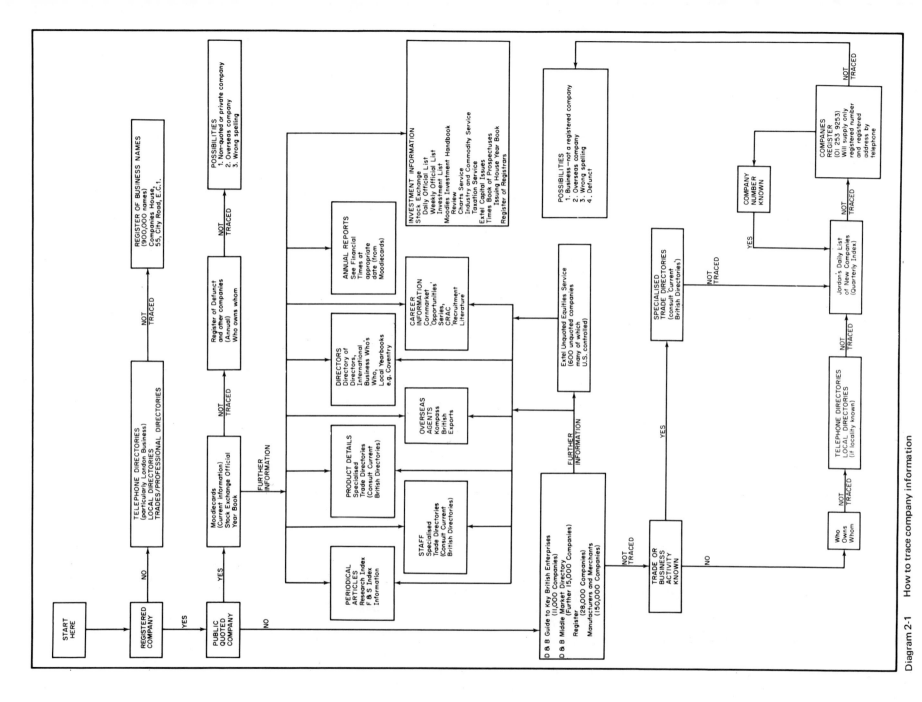

Diagram 2-1   How to trace company information

cumulatively as soon as there is any news about the company to keep the large card up-to-date. The large card provides background information and a detailed analysis of figures measuring growth efficiency and performance over a number of years. The small card includes earnings and dividends adjusted for new issues, balance sheet figures, tabulated details of dividends, a table of new issues, news items and the chairman's speech. (A similar service is provided by Extel Statistical Services.)

Extel Unquoted Equities Service

This is a card service, covering over 1,200 unquoted companies. These include many US controlled companies as well as some of the larger private firms.

Information given for most companies includes date of registration, address of registered office, brief history, business activity, directors, secretary, bankers, auditors, authorised capital, capital changes, voting rights of shares, whether a close company, directors' holdings, other large holdings, borrowing powers, consolidated accounts (issued ordinary shares, turnover, value of exports, net pre-tax profit, corporation tax, cost of ordinary dividend, retained profit, depreciation, interest, directors' charges, total payroll, number employed), consolidated balance sheet, capital commitments, ratio of current assets to current liabilities, net asset value.

Jordan's Company Service (Daily)

Includes—name, date of registration, registration number, names and addresses of directors and, in some cases, the purpose of the company. Indexes of company names, each covering a period of three months, are available.

The Stock Exchange Official Year-book (Annual)

Gives details of directors, history, structure, capital and dividends of quoted companies. The index of about 30 000 company names refers to parent companies where appropriate.

Register of Defunct and Other Companies (Annual)

Contains 23 000 notices of companies removed from the *Stock Exchange Official Year book* since 1875.

Dun and Bradstreet's Guide to Key British Enterprises (Alternate Years)

A selection of approximately 11 000 of the most important firms engaged in the primary, manufacturing and distributive trades, incorporating also the fields of transport and communication and a number of specialist service organisations. Information provided includes reference to parent company or group, factory locations, line of business, trade names, markets, number of employees, date of formation, directors. A list of parent companies, showing their constituent companies, with an index to the latter, is provided.

Dun and Bradstreet's *British Middle Market Directory* (Alternate Years)

As above, with a further 15 000 firms covered.

Kompass *Register of British Industry and Commerce* (Annual)

The company volume contains almost 30 000 companies arranged geographically. Information provided—name, address, bank, office hours, location, directors, share capital, product groups, number of employees, related companies. The companion product volume contains a detailed arrangement of products and indicates which companies are manufacturers or agents.

Kelly's Manufacturers and Merchants Directory: Including Industrial Services, volume 1 'Great Britain, Northern Ireland, Republic of Ireland' (Annual)

150 000 firms listed alphabetically with address, telephone number and product. There is also an alphabetical arrangement by products.

Who Owns Whom: U.K. Edition (Annual)

Current edition contains 92 700 entries. Main sequences (1) parent and associate companies showing subsidiary and associate companies (2) subsidiary and associate companies showing parent and associate companies.

Current British Directories (Sixth Edition 1970-71)

Detailed list of both local and specialised directories. Includes a very useful analytical index. Annotations indicate detail of company information in each directory.

Directory of Directors (Annual)

Alphabetical arrangement of the names of 40 000 directors with their companies.

Kompass *British Exports* (Fourth Edition, 1971)
Overseas agents of 10 000 companies.

Research index. Business Surveys Ltd. (Fortnightly)

Indexes articles in 120 British business, economic and trade periodicals. Section one covers industrial and commercial news and reports not dealing specifically with a particular company under almost 200 subject headings. Section two is arranged alphabetically under names of companies. About 3000 references are given in each issue. Issues are not cumulated.

F & S Index International (Monthly, annual cumulation)

Indexes 250 periodicals from various countries. Each month issue is divided into three sections: 1. Industries and products. 2. Countries other than USA. 3. Companies. About 6000 references are given in each monthly issue.

Careers for school leavers, guide to British employers, directory of opportunities for qualified and experienced men, directory of opportunies for graduates (Cornmarket Press).

Although primarily intended to provide facts on careers, reveal much useful information on individual companies.

Appendix 2.3

Trade Associations and Economic Development Councils in the U K.

The following organisations carry out comparative surveys and/or exchanges of information in their industries or trades.

Trade Associations

Institute of Practitioners in ADVERTISING
Scottish AGRICULTURAL Colleges
Ministry of AGRICULTURE, Fisheries and Food
Ministry of AGRICULTURE for Northern Ireland
British BRUSH Manufacturers' Research Association
National Federation of BUILDERS' and Plumbers' Merchants
Institute of BUILDING
British CAST Iron Research Association

CHEMICAL Industries Association
COAL Tar Research Association
British CONSTRUCTIONAL Steelwork Association
National Association of DROP Forgers and Stampers
DYERS and Cleaners Research Organisation
Institute of FOOD Distribution
FURNITURE Development Council/Furniture Industry Research Association
British GLASS Industry Research Association
GLASS Manufacturers' Federation
Scottish GROCERS' Federation
HEATING and Ventilating Contractors' Association
National HOSIERY Manufacturers' Federation
HOT Dip Galvanisers Association
Institute of IRON and Steel Wire Manufacturers
National Federation of IRONMONGERS
Association of JUTE Spinners and Manufacturers
LEAD Development Association
LINEN Industry Research Association
MACHINE Tool Trades Association
MILK Marketing Board
MOTOR Agents' Association
NEWSPAPER Society
PIRA: Research Association for the PAPER Board, Printing and Packaging Industries
PIG Industry Development Authority
National PORTS Council
British Federation of Master PRINTERS
Society of Master PRINTERS of Scotland
Scottish RETAIL Drapers' Association
National Association of RETAIL Furnishers
RUBBER and Plastics Research Association of Great Britain
SCIENTIFIC Instrument Manufacturers' Association of Great Britain
SIRA (British SCIENTIFIC Instrument Research Association)
British SHIP Research Association
SHOE and Allied Trades Research Association
British SPINNERS' and DOUBLERS' Association
British STATIONERY and Office Equipment Association
TEXTILE Council Productivity Centre
TIMBER Trade Federation of the United Kingdom
Scottish TOURIST Industry Consultancy Service
Institute of Road TRANSPORT Engineers
British VALVE Manufacturers' Association

WELDING Institute
British WOODWORK Manufacturers' Association
WOOL (and allied) Textile Employers' Council
ZINC Development Association

Economic Development Councils

1 Clothing
   Financial league tables
   Financial information on companies in the clothing industry
   NEDO free (1969)
2 Electronics
   Annual statistical survey of the electronics industry
   Statistics of output, trade, employment, research and development for 1968
   and 1969.
   NEDO free (1969 and 1970)
3 Hosiery and knitwear
   A Study of profitability in the hosiery and knitwear industry
   NEDO 45p (1971)
4 Mechanical Engineering
   Company financial results 1963/64-1968/69
   Profit and cash flow from the accounts of 275 mechanical engineering
   companies
   NEDO free (1970)
5 Wool Textiles
   Manpower productivity comparisons
   A pilot project comparing manpower productivity in the fine worsted
   manufacturing section of the industry
   NEDO free (1968)

Appendix 2.4

**Organised interfirm comparisons: list of industries and trades in which the Centre for
Interfirm Comparison has prepared IFC schemes**

Bedding manufacture
Biscuit manufacture
Blanket manufacture
Book publishers distribution
Building and civil engineering
Cable trunking manufacture

Carpet manufacture
Chemical manufacture*
Clothing manufacture
Cold rolled sections manufacture
Colour makers
Computer Services Bureau

Confectionery manufacture
Corn and agricultural merchants
Cotton spinning
Crane manufacture
Decorators merchants
Domestic central heating equipment
   manufacture
Drop forgers
Electrical contractors
Electrical/electronic (small firms)
Engineers' tool manufacture
English woollen and worsted industry
Estate agents
Flexible packaging manufacture
Food distribution
Food manufacture and marketing
Forgemasters
Footwear manufacture
Fork lift truck manufacture
Furniture warehousing and removing
Gauge and tool manufacture
General medium/heavy engineering*
Glass container manufacture
Hand tool manufacture
Hire purchase finance houses
Insurance brokers
Iron foundries
Joinery manufacture
Leather dressing
Light engineering*
Machine tools manufacture
Mains cable manufacture
Maltsters
Motor component manufacture
Narrow fabric manufacture
Nylon hose dyeing
Painting and decorating contractors
Paintmakers
Paper manufacture
Paper sack manufacture: (a) UK (b) Europe

Pharmaceutical manufacture
Pipework contractors
Plastics moulding
Publishing: (a) books (b) periodicals
Pump manufacture
Quarrying (limestone)
Radio and electronic component
   manufacture
Rayon weaving
Road haulage: (a) bulk liquid haulage
   contractors (b) express carriers
Road Haulage: R H A 'Cost and
   Productivity Scheme' for general
   haulage; long-distance haulage; agri-
   cultural haulage and tipping vehicle
   operators
Rubber manufacture*
Sand and gravel pits
Scientific instrument manufacture
Scottish woollen industry
Secondary aluminium ingots
Shirt manufacture
Soft drinks manufacture
   and distribution
Solicitors
Steel stockholders
Stockbrokers
Structural steelwork (fabrication and
   erection)
Synthetic resin manufacture
Tank and industrial plant contractors
Throwsters
Timber engineers
Timber importers
Timber merchants
Timber pallet manufacture
Tufted carpet manufacture
Valve manufacture (mechanical)
Warp knitting

*Covering various types and size groups

Chapter 3

Principles of ratio definition and calculation

3.1 General Principles

Consistency. It is most important that there should be consistency between the numerator and the denominator of a ratio, and between the method of calculating a ratio and the standard with which it is being compared.

For example, if income from a particular activity is included in one part of a ratio, the cost of obtaining that income, or the value of the asset employed to bring that income in, should be in the other part of the ratio.

Further, if a firm that you are comparing your results with has arrived at its profit after valuing stock and calculating depreciation in certain ways, it may be necessary to recalculate your profit in the same ways in order to make an accurate comparison. It is worth bearing in mind when making any comparison based on figures either in your own accounts or in those of other firms that *accounts are not so much facts as a number of estimates and opinions clothed in the language of money.*

Inflation. If comparisons are being made over time involving money values, the effects of different amounts of inflation on these values at different times should be removed (see Chapter 5—the section on Growth). Equally important is the addition of inflation to asset and capital values of an earlier period when comparing them to sales, costs or profits of a later period.

Averages. When relating profits, costs or sales to assets or capital, the figure for assets or capital should be an average of its values over the period to which the profits, costs or sales relate. Similarly, the number of staff who have left in a period should be related to the average number present during the same period, not to the number at either the beginning or the end of the period.

Time Lag. There is always a time lag between incurring expenditure and receiving the benefit from it. Calculations of ratios that relate benefit to expenditure must take account of this lag and how a firm's accountant has dealt with it, if at all. There are two accounting devices for dealing with the problem of lag. If the expenditure has produced a physical object which has not yet been sold, the expenditure is diverted into 'stock' and only the balance is left to be related to sales. If the expenditure has not produced a physical object, it may be treated as 'expenditure in advance' and not deducted in arriving at this year's profits (but it will be deducted from a future year's profit) or it may be written off straightaway. Examples of items usually treated as expenditure in advance are rent and rates. Items usually written off when incurred are advertising and research expenditure.

It is because of differences in treatment such as the above that accounts need to be used with caution, as do any ratios calculated from them. It is desirable where there is significant lag between expenditure and benefit to correct for it, using one of the accountant's devices mentioned above or to offset the items in time, for example by relating advertising expenditure for one period to the sales of another period ending (say) six months later.

3.2 Main Accounting Terms

A number of terms in general use have been given a more precise meaning in this book. For the convenience of the reader they have all been set out here. The relationship between the principal ones is shown in Diagrams 3-1 and 3-2.

Fixed assets include those assets which it is not the intention of the firm to trade in but to use for the purpose of producing goods or services for sale. This means that the

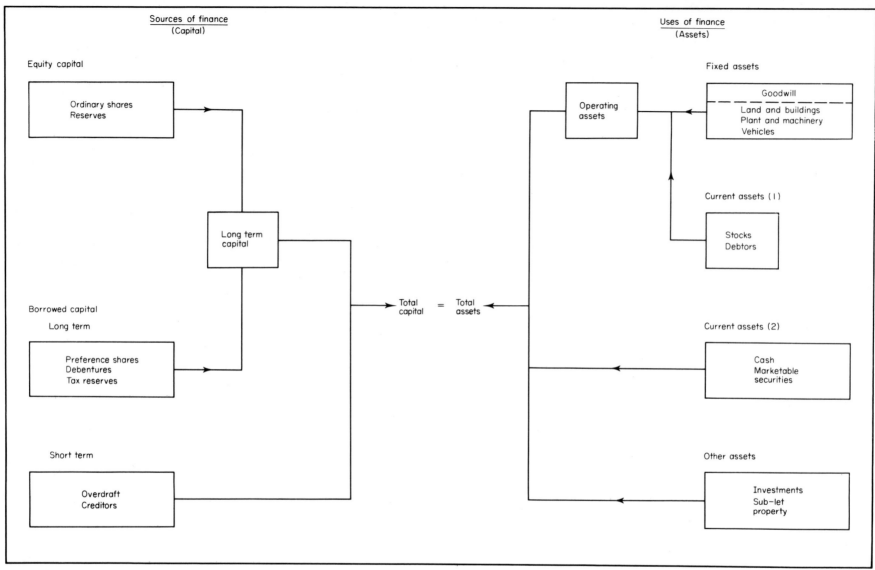

Sources of finance
(Capital)

Uses of finance
(Assets)

Equity capital

Fixed assets

Ordinary shares
Reserves

Goodwill

Land and buildings
Plant and machinery
Vehicles

Operating assets

Long term capital

Current assets (1)

Stocks
Debtors

Borrowed capital

Long term

Preference shares
Debentures
Tax reserves

Total capital = Total assets

Current assets (2)

Cash
Marketable securities

Short term

Overdraft
Creditors

Other assets

Investments
Sub-let property

Diagram 3-1   Sources and uses of finance

following are normally included: land, buildings, plant, machinery and vehicles. Goodwill, patents and other intangible assets are normally excluded because, more than for the other items, they are the result of bookkeeping entries. Fixed assets should be valued, if possible, at their estimated current values taking into account the effects of age, obsolescence and inflation.

Current assets (1) include the firm's trading assets, that is stocks and debtors. If possible average values for these items should be used, because the value at the balance sheet date may well be untypical of the period as a whole.

Current assets (2) When related to current liabilities, current assets includes stocks, debtors, cash, and marketable securities (that is those that can be easily converted into cash).

Other assets include those assets of a firm not being used in its main operations, for example sub-let property (which would then be excluded from fixed assets) investments (which should be taken at their market value—shown in a note to the balance sheet) and cash.

Operating assets is the sum of fixed assets and current assets (1).

Total assets is the sum of operating assets and other assets.

Borrowed capital includes all sources of finance other than that provided by the owners or ordinary shareholders of a company. It can be subdivided into long-and short-term borrowed capital.

Long-term borrowed capital includes debentures, preference shares, and long-term loans. It should also include tax reserves and tax equalisation accounts. For convenience minority interests in the company can be included.

Short-term borrowed capital includes overdrafts, trade and expense creditors, short-term loans, tax provisions.

Equity capital includes ordinary shares, capital and revenue reserves (except for tax) and undistributed profits (balance on profit and loss account plus proposed dividends on ordinary shares) plus or minus any surplus or deficit on the revaluation and/or averaging of fixed, current and other assets less the value of intangible assets. Another way of arriving at the same result is to subtract borrowed capital from total assets.

Total capital is the sum of borrowed capital and equity capital. By definition total capital equals total assets.

Long-term capital is the sum of long-term borrowed capital and equity capital.

Operating profit is the profit derived from the main operation of the business, that is, from the employment of operating assets. Basically it will be sales less operating costs including depreciation but excluding interest and tax.

Other income is the income derived from other assets. It should be gross before deduction of tax.

Total profit equals the sum of operating profit and other income.

Interest paid equals all interest and/or dividends paid to the providers of borrowed

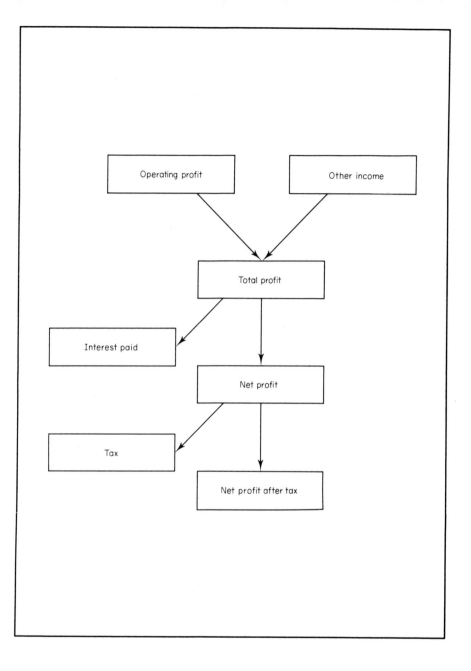

Diagram 3-2   Profits and Income

47

capital. The gross before-tax figure should be used. For convenience it will include the minority interest's share of profit.

Net profit equals total profit minus interest paid.

Tax includes corporation tax, capital gains tax, overseas tax, income tax deducted from dividends received, *less* double taxation relief and income tax retainable from dividends payable.

Net profit after tax equals net profit minus tax.

3.3 Use of Data Assembly and Ratio Calculation Work Sheets

At the end of each of Chapters 4 to 11 will be found data assembly sheets and ratio calculation work sheets. The former provide a handy place to assemble all the information required to calculate the ratios described in the preceding chapter.

Each data assembly sheet has a number of columns; they can be used for:

1   The actual figures for a number of periods for the company concerned
2   The budgeted (target or forecast) figures for one or more periods
3   The figures of other companies (where available)
4   The figures of fellow subsidiaries or divisions or departments depending on the standards against which the ratios are being compared.

In Chapter 4 the first column of each data assembly sheet has had the figures of an imaginary company inserted in it as a guide to the calculation of the ratios.

The ratio calculation work sheets contain:

1   The name of each ratio
2   The formula for calculating it (this is keyed by a letter reference to the relevant item in the data assembly sheet)
3   Columns to enter the ratios calculated from the corresponding figures in the data assembly sheet (that is any of the possibilities listed in the previous paragraph).

In Chapter 4 the first column of each ratio calculation work sheet contains ratios calculated from the figures of the imaginary firm given in the first column of the corresponding data assembly sheet.

PART TWO

Chapter 4

Priority ratios for the chief executive

Before considering what ratios the chief executive should examine, the long-term objectives of the firm must be defined. Naturally, in the short term, there will be subsidiary objectives and it may sometimes be necessary to give a sub-objective priority in the short term. For example it may be necessary to grant a wage increase which reduces profit in the short term because not to do so would have very damaging effects on the firm's long-term profitability.

What should be the primary objective of the board of directors of a company? The philosophy of this book is founded on the belief that the answer to this question is 'the maximisation over the medium to long term of the return to the ordinary shareholder on his investment'. This means that short-term improvements in profitability must not be sought if they will be achieved at the expense of greater long-term decreases in profit. It also means that the directors are primarily concerned with the ordinary shareholder. Other providers of capital will need consideration but only to the extent that they are contributing to the profit for the ordinary shareholder. The return on the ordinary shareholder's investment is made up of dividends and capital gains. Neither should be neglected at the expense of the other.

Finally, the ordinary shareholder is concerned with the return on his investment, not just the figure of profit but the profit in relation to the money he has put into the company by initial subscription, by purchase of the shares on the market and by additional injections of capital during the life of the company.

The remainder of this chapter deals with secondary objectives, which have to be achieved if the primary one is to be met, and as the ratios will, of necessity, be looked at and action taken in the short term, it will be useful if the chief executive also considers from time to time the long-term effects of his colleagues' plans and action on the primary objective of their company.

The twenty-eight ratios that the chief executive of every company should monitor are described. This may seem a large number of ratios but they do not all need examining at the same time. While some may need to be monitored every month, others need be looked at only once a year or every six months.

These ratios are related to the key areas which are common to nearly all businesses and with which the top man must be concerned—although in broad terms only. These key areas will fluctuate in relative importance over the course of time, and the amount of energy devoted to them and the frequency with which they are studied will correspondingly change. The order in which they are described here should not therefore be taken as in any way an order of importance.

All firms are the meeting point of a number of economic forces. It would be oversimplifying the business world to pretend that any one of these forces has priority over the others. All must be satisfied in the long run, or at the least have their demands palliated in the short term. It is the task, by no means an easy one, of the chief executive constantly to balance the demands of one force against the needs of the others.

The areas that a chief executive must consider are the relationship between his firm and:

1   Its markets
2   The providers of its capital, both risk and loan
3   Its suppliers
4   Its employees.

He must also watch:

5   How well it is using its assets
6   How well it is providing for the future.

The ratios in this chapter are numbered as follows. The number before the decimal point refers to the key area listed above. (For example 1.1 is a marketing ratio.) The number after the decimal point is the number of the ratio within the area. (For example 1.3 is the third ratio in the marketing area.) Ratios which are alternatives are indicated by (a), (b), (c), etc.

At the end of the chapter there are data assembly sheets and ratio calculation sheets to facilitate the calculation of the ratios described.

These ratios should be graphed over time. It is even more helpful if the same graph is used to show the firm's budget or target for the ratio, and the performance of competitors' ratios (if obtainable). Needless to say, budget, target and competitors' figures must be worked out on the same basis as the firm's current, actual figures. The data assembly sheets can be used for all of the figures mentioned.

4.1 The Firm and its Markets

How well the market likes a firm's products is indicated by the rate of growth of its sales, which can be measured by:

1.1(a)
$$\frac{\text{Sales this year}}{\text{Sales last year}}$$

or by

1.1(b)
$$\frac{\text{Sales this month}}{\text{Sales last month}}$$

or by

1.1(c)
$$\frac{\text{Sales this month}}{\text{Sales same month last year}}$$

Ratio 1.1(b) is obviously more sensitive to changes in demand than ratio 1.1(a). In any business where demand is seasonal ratio 1.1(c) is more useful than ratio 1.1(b).

If there have been price changes during the period between last year (month) and this, it is desirable to reduce the apparent growth shown by ratios 1.1(a), 1.1(b), or 1.1(c) to growth in real terms by measuring both numerator and denominator at the same prices. This may be too time consuming to be practicable. An alternative method, if it is known that prices have on average increased by x per cent, is to reduce ratios 1.1(a), (b) or (c) by that percentage.

Simple growth is usually not enough. A firm will want to increase, or at least maintain, its share of the market. If figures are available (perhaps from the firm's trade association or from government sources) as to the size of the market then the chief executive can also monitor

1.2
$$\frac{\text{Share of the market now}}{\text{Share of the market (last year/last month/same month last year)}}$$

The size of the order book is of importance to all firms. How large or how small they want it to be depends on whether they are in a heavy engineering or other long-term contracting business, or aim to provide an 'off the shelf', 'by return' service.

1.3
$$\frac{\text{Value of orders outstanding}}{\text{Average value of sales per day}}$$

It is probably a universal tendency for the range of products a firms sells to grow. Almost equally universal is the tendency for this to lead to a reduction in profitability. Every year, or thereabouts, the chief executive should have the following exercise carried out:

1   Products should be listed in descending order of their annual turnover.
2   Starting from the top of the list the turnover of each item should be added until 80 per cent of the annual turnover is reached. At this point a line should be drawn
3   The number of items below the line should be expressed as a percentage of the total number of items (this is market ratio 1.4)
4   The ratio calculated in (3) should be compared with the same ratio calculated a year ago. If there has been an increase, then almost certainly the range has grown too wide and items below the line, starting at the bottom of the list, should be considered for removal from the range.

In this process of consideration it may be useful to use Drucker's classification* of products into:

1   Today's breadwinners
2   Tomorrow's breadwinners
3   Productive specialities
4   Development products
5   Failures
6   Yesterday's breadwinners
7   Repair jobs
8   Unnecessary specialities
9   Unjustified specialities
10 Investments in managerial ego
11 Cinderellas

The last ratio to be monitored under this heading is

1.5
$$\frac{\text{Debtors} \times \text{Number of days in period}}{\text{Credit sales}}$$

* P.F. Drucker, *Managing for Results*, Heinemann, 1964, page 48 and following.

The number of days to use for this ratio is the number of calendar days. Interest is payable on an overdraft for every day of the year! For ratio 1.3 the number of days should be the number of selling days taken to achieve the relevant sales figure. Ratio 1.3 is then the number of selling or working days required to work off the order book.

Ratio 1.5 shows how much credit a firm's customers are taking. The more this can be reduced the more profitable will be the business; and the greater the risk that it will lose customers to competitors who are prepared to give longer credit! It is very much a matter of judgement where the line should be drawn. But no judgement can be exercised unless this and other ratios are first monitored.

This subject is dealt with more fully in Chapters 5 and 6.

To calculate ratios 1.1 to 1.5 use data assembly and ratio calculation sheet 4-1 at the end of this chapter.

4.2 The Firm and the Providers of Capital

The return that the providers of risk capital are getting is best measured by the ratio

$$2.1 \quad \frac{\text{Net profit after tax}}{\text{Equity capital}}$$

If this ratio declines and/or remains depressed for any length of time, the chief executive, and perhaps his fellow board members, must be prepared for:

1   A move by shareholders to replace them at the next AGM
2   A takeover bid from another company whose board consider they can run the firm more profitably.

The chief executive can gauge the opinion of the stock market of his company (if it is quoted) by the size of its P/E ratio.

$$2.2 \quad \frac{\text{Price per share}}{\text{Earnings after corporation tax per share}}$$

This ratio reflects the view of the stock exchange not only of the company, but of the industry in which it operates and of the economy as a whole. Any changes in this ratio need therefore to be looked at in the context of changes in the P/E ratios of competitors. Within this limitation the higher his firm's P/E ratio is the happier should the chief executive be, unless:

1   It has been pushed up as the result of a takeover bid or the rumours of one, or
2   He thinks it is unreasonably high in the light of his knowledge of any likely future growth in profits.

The ratio of

$$2.3 \quad \frac{\text{Interest paid}}{\text{Borrowed capital}}$$

tells us how much a firm is having to pay for the finance obtained from sources other than the providers of risk capital. This ratio needs to be compared with:

1   The market rate for such finance (on debentures and overdrafts)
2   The return on risk capital (2.1 above)
3   The return being earned on the assets of the business (ratio 5.1 below).

The market rate will be particularly relevant if the firm has a debenture whose redemption date(s) is/are near or if it wants to increase its gearing (see below).

The return on risk capital and the return on assets should obviously both be higher than ratio 2.3. If they are lower the firm is in a very unhealthy situation.

While on this pessimistic note 'interest cover' should be looked at. This measures a firm's ability to go on paying its interest commitments.

$$2.4 \quad \frac{\text{Total profit}}{\text{Interest paid}}$$

Gearing enables the ordinary shareholder to get a higher return on his investment than management is obtaining from the use of the firm's assets. Gearing can be measured by

$$2.5 \quad \frac{\text{Borrowed capital}}{\text{Equity capital}}$$

This is a ratio which management has to keep in balance. The higher it is then the bigger the return to the equity shareholders, but the risk to them and the fixed interest lenders will be greater as indicated by a decline in ratio 2.4 above.

This subject is dealt with more fully in Chapter 8.

To calculate ratios 2.1 to 2.5 use data assembly and ratio calculation sheet 4-2 at the end of this chapter.

4.3 The Firm and its Suppliers

There are three aspects of the performance of his firm's suppliers which a chief executive should monitor: price, delivery and quality.

Changes in price are best measured by index numbers. It may be uneconomic to monitor the price of all items used but a practical compromise would be to list purchases in descending order of value and measure changes in all items that account for the top 80 per cent (say) by value, and of a sample of the rest. This price index is the buyer's first ratio:

$$3.1 \quad \frac{\text{Suppliers' prices now}}{\text{Suppliers' prices at the base date}}$$

Increases in price of products used may require improved purchasing by the buying department, more productivity from the work force, perhaps a change in the materials used, or an increase in the price charged to customers.

Suppliers' lead times can be measured by the ratio of

3.2
$$\frac{\text{Value of orders outstanding with suppliers}}{\text{Average daily purchases}}$$

Perhaps more significant than lead times is the (un)reliability of suppliers. The ratio to use to monitor this is

3.3
$$\frac{\text{Value of orders overdue from suppliers}}{\text{Average daily purchases}}$$

Any increase in either of these two ratios means that management must decide whether to quote longer deliveries to customers, accept a lower level of service to customers, increase its stock holding, or alter its buying pattern.

The credit given by suppliers is a useful source of finance for all firms and should be used to the limit, that is, the point where the supplier threatens to stop deliveries, or the rate of discounts not obtained becomes higher than the interest paid on other available sources of finance, or than the rate of profit earned on assets.

3.4
$$\frac{\text{Creditors}}{\text{Average daily purchases}}$$

measures the length of credit the firm is taking.

It is at this point that the chief executive must consider liquidity—the ability of the business 'to pay its way'. He is best advised to use a variant of the 'acid test' ratio for this

3.5
$$\frac{\text{Cash} + \text{Debtors} + \text{Marketable securities}}{\text{Current liabilities plus an appropriate part of capital expenditure to which the firm is committed.}}$$

This should not be allowed to fall below unity.

An indication of the quality of the goods bought from suppliers is the percentage that have to be returned.

3.6
$$\frac{\text{Value of goods returned or credited}}{\text{Purchases}}$$

An increase in this ratio might indicate the need to look for new sources of supply. A decrease might indicate that the company's quality control standards were slipping. In either case changes in this ratio should lead to investigation and remedial action.

This subject is dealt with more fully in Chapter 7.

To calculate ratios 3.1 to 3.6 use data assembly and ratio calculation sheet 4-3 at the end of this chapter.

4.4 The Firm and its Employees

In times of full employment, if a firm does not satisfy its work force, it may have started on the road to bankruptcy. Dissatisfied employees, if they can, vote with their feet. A chief executive should therefore keep his eye on the turnover of his employees

4.1
$$\frac{\text{Number of leavers}}{\text{Average number of employees}}$$

Like many ratios this must be kept in balance. Too high a figure can obviously be disastrous. Too low a figure can indicate stagnation, so it is suggested that the chief executive should also look at

4.2
$$\frac{\text{Average age of senior staff now}}{\text{Average age of senior staff five years ago}}$$

Is arteriosclerosis setting in?

Businesses are not charitable institutions, however, and they will only want to keep employees if their output is satisfactory. This can be measured in three ways

4.3(a)   Sales per employee

or, better,

4.3(b)   Value added (sales minus materials cost) per employee

or, best,

4.3(c)   Profit per employee

It is also necessary to know how much the firm's employees are costing, so the chief executive should look at

4.4   Wages and salaries per employee

This subject is dealt with more fully in Chapter 10.

To calculate ratios 4.1 to 4.4 use data assembly and ratio calculation sheet 4-4 at the end of this chapter.

4.5 Use of Assets

As well as getting the best out of its employees, and suitably rewarding them, a firm needs to use its assets profitably in order to pay its employees and the providers of its capital. There are four ratios worth examining here. The first is

5.1
$$\frac{\text{Operating profit}}{\text{Operating assets}}$$

Operating profit is arrived at after deducting depreciation but before subtracting interest payments or tax and it does not include income from sources outside the mainstream of the business, such as investments. The two main factors which influence the size of this ratio are:

1   The balance between cost and income, best measured by

$$5.2 \quad \frac{\text{Operating profit}}{\text{Sales}}$$

2   The balance between investment in assets and the volume of business obtained, most easily measured by

$$5.3 \quad \frac{\text{Sales}}{\text{Operating assets}}$$

This ratio is usually called a firm's 'turnover of assets' and is described as being 'so many times per year'.

If some measure of the maximum output a plant is capable of can be obtained, either in physical or financial terms, ratio 5.3 is most usefully supplemented by

$$5.4 \quad \frac{\text{Actual output}}{\text{Maximum output}}$$

To avoid hair-splitting arguments over how much maintenance time and changeover time should be provided for and how long is the working week/year, it is a good idea to arrive at the maximum output assuming that production can be maintained twenty-four hours a day, seven days a week, 365 days a year.

To calculate ratios 5.1 to 5.4 use data assembly and ratio calculation sheet 4-5 at the end of this chapter.

4.6 The Future

All the ratios described so far in this chapter deal with the company as it is at the present time. Equally important is the subject of how well it is providing for the future. There are three main divisions of this subject:

1   Product innovation
2   Staff training and development
3   Asset renewal and expansion.

On product innovation the firm's record over the immediate past can be looked at by using the ratio

$$6.1 \quad \frac{\text{Sales of products introduced in the past five (?) years}}{\text{Total Sales}}$$

The trend of this ratio over the past ten (or more) years will indicate any tendency for the firm to rest on its laurels.

Obviously it is not enough to introduce new products to the market, they must be profitable. In fact, they should be more profitable than the old ones have become, as competition has forced down margins over the course of time. The ratio

$$6.2 \quad \frac{\text{Profit (or contribution) from products introduced in the past five (?) years}}{\text{Sales of these products}}$$

should therefore be higher than the same ratio for the rest of the firm's products.

At this stage it is useful to introduce a new concept, namely 'discretionary cash flow'. There are some items of expenditure over which management has a greater degree of choice as to how much to spend and when to spend it. A firm must buy the raw materials and pay the employees if it is to remain in business at all. How much it spends on such items as research, staff training, the purchase of new equipment, consultancy advice, advertising, etc; and the timing of such expenditure, is much more a matter for managerial discretion. Moreover the items listed have two other features in common:

1   They are for the benefit of the future rather than the present
2   They are more likely to be affected by the amount of cash available than by the volume of sales.

Discretionary cash flow (dCF to avoid confusion with DCF—discounted cash flow) is therefore the sum of:

1   Profit after tax, depreciation and interest payments.
2   Depreciation (an item of cost which does not cause an outflow of cash).
3   Dividends on ordinary shares (their size is within the absolute discretion of directors).
4   All items mentioned above which are considered to be discretionary by the management of the firm.
5   Any money received from new share issues or new loans obtained.
6   Any money received as the result of reducing the amount invested in net current assets or from selling fixed assets.

The ratios which the chief executive needs to monitor are then

$$6.3(a) \quad \frac{\text{Research and development expenditure}}{\text{dCF}}$$

$$6.3(b) \quad \frac{\text{Training expenditure}}{\text{dCF}}$$

plus ratios relating to any other item of discretionary expenditure of importance, and

$$6.4 \quad \frac{\text{Fixed asset expenditure}}{\text{dCF}}$$

In connection with the last it is also useful to measure

$$6.5 \quad \frac{\text{Fixed asset expenditure}}{\text{Depreciation}}$$

Because of the 'lumpiness' of fixed asset expenditure it is better to measure both numerator and denominator over a number of years (say three or more). If this ratio falls below unity then a firm is running down its fixed assets.

Two notes of caution need to be sounded in connection with this ratio:

1   If a firm depreciates its assets faster than it really believes they are going to wear out or become obsolete for reasons of prudence or accounting conservatism, this ratio can fall below unity without it meaning that the assets are being run down. If this is the case, it is suggested that, whatever the firm shows in its accounts, it makes a realistic assessment of the true figure of depreciation and uses this for management purposes.

2   Because of inflation it will nearly always cost more to replace an asset than it originally cost. But depreciation is based in virtually all firms on original cost. This ratio can then be above unity while fixed assets are being run down. What the firm should do, as a matter of sound business sense, irrespective of what it does in its accounts, is to calculate depreciation on the basis of an estimate of what the assets would cost to replace.

To calculate ratios 6.1 to 6.5 use data assembly and ratio calculation sheet 4-6 at the end of this chapter.

4.7 Summary

The priority ratios for the chief executive are summarised below:

1   *Markets*
1.1   Growth of sales
1.2   Growth of market share
1.3   Length of order book
1.4   Proportion of items in bottom 20 per cent of turnover
1.5   Debtors/Sales

2   *Providers of capital*
2.1   Net profit after tax/Equity capital
2.2   P/E ratio
2.3   Interest paid/Borrowed capital
2.4   Total profit/Interest paid
2.5   Borrowed capital/Equity capital

3   *Suppliers*
3.1   Suppliers' prices index
3.2   Suppliers' lead time
3.3   Days orders overdue
3.4   Creditors/Purchases
3.5   Cash, debtors, marketable securities/Current liabilities and capital expenditure
3.6   Value of goods returned or credited/Purchases

4   *Employees*
4.1   Number of leavers/Average numbers employed
4.2   Average age of senior staff: now/Five years ago
4.3   'Output' per employee
4.4   Remuneration per employee

5   *Assets*
5.1   Operating profit/Operating assets
5.2   Operating profit/Sales
5.3   Sales/Operating assets
5.4   Actual output/Maximum output

6   *Future*
6.1   Sales of products introduced in last five years/Total sales
6.2   Profit from above sales/Sales of these products
6.3a R & D/dCF
6.3b Training/dCF, etc
6.4   Fixed asset expenditure/dCF
6.5   Fixed asset expenditure/Depreciation

4.8 Data Assembly and Ratio Calculation Work Sheets

In the pages that follow forms have been provided to assemble the necessary data, and to calculate and tabulate the ratios described in this chapter. Imaginary figures have been inserted in the first column of the data sheet and these have been used to calculate the ratio shown in the corresponding column of the ratio sheet. It is hoped that this will be an aid to readers in calculating their own ratios.

Appendix 4.1
The Weinstock Yardsticks of Efficiency

The selection of priority ratios for the chief executive described in this chapter reflects the views and experience of the author. Readers may like to compare it with those that Arnold Weinstock uses as described in an article by Anthony Vice in *The Times* Business News of 29 November 1968.

Arnold Weinstock now chief executive of GEC, English Electric and Associated Electrical Industries, has built an outstanding reputation as a revitaliser of companies. The basis for his takeover of AEI and for the subsequent merger with English Electric is based on the seven years since 1961 during which he has transformed GEC from the sick man of the electrical industry into one of the most efficiently run of all large companies in Britain.

Financial control lies at the heart of Weinstock's operations, and in recent conversations he set out the seven key criteria which he uses to assess possible acquisitions and, above all, to control the performance of divisions within his own group. These seven criteria form the basis of the reports which are sent every month to Weinstock at the group's headquarters in Stanhope Gate, London. It is on the basis of these reports, and what they disclose, that Weinstock bases his control of GEC–AEI–English Electric operations.

Weinstock has built up these seven criteria partly from his own experience, and partly by sending teams to examine the methods used by General Electric and Texas Instruments in the United States—two companies which Weinstock believes to be among the most efficient in his own world-wide industry. (GEC's summary accounts, interestingly, are made up so as to show the results of the seven criteria comparison.) The seven criteria, whose results are set out in the accompanying table, are as follows

1. Profits on capital employed. This is probably the most widely used financial criterion in the private sector of industry. In the last resort this measures the earning power of capital which is used to make electrical equipment rather than buying gilt-edged, investing abroad or going into another line of business. GEC's 23 per cent compares with a United Kingdom industrial average of about 15 per cent; ICI's low figure of 13 per cent probably understates the company's performance, as it reflects assets which are not yet fully profit-earning. But a massive group like GE of America was able to earn nearly double the United Kingdom average, and even GE's figure is after allowing for nuclear power and computer losses. (Comparative figures may be affected to some extent by companies' different treatment of loan capital.)

2. Profits on sales—This is another widely used test indicating profit margins, but the figure tends to vary markedly between different industries. GEC's emerges higher than GE's while English Electric's is unusually low, probably reflecting the size of their business in heavy electrical goods.

3. Sales as a multiple of capital employed—This shows the productivity of the company's net capital; comparisons should be made between companies of roughly comparable financial structure and similar capital intensity, for an unusually capital-intensive group like ICI will tend to show a low ratio. But overall, the ratio of sales to total capital probably represents a fair measure of a company's efficiency through its ability to generate business from a given volume of assets. GE stands out in this comparison, and a broad contrast of British and American companies illustrates, for example, the differences in trade unions' attitudes towards the use of capital equipment.

4. Sales as a multiple of fixed assets—This is a major subdivision of the previous criterion. The ability of fixed assets to generate sales is probably the best measure of their real worth, often one of the most difficult problems in analysing company performance. Here again, a basic guide for management is that companies in the same sort of business should tend to show a similar sale/fixed asset ratio. GEC come out well ahead of both GE and Texas Instruments.

5. Sales as a multiple of stocks—This is one area where both the United States companies show up much better than their British opposite numbers. One reason is the much wider use in America of computer techniques for stock and production control, allied to the higher level of general education among middle management—which means that specialist techniques can be widely employed to control the level of working capital. United States companies also tend to receive better service from their suppliers.

Even with an efficient company like GEC the ability to sustain GE's stock/sales ratio would enable it to cut inventories by some £25 000 000. For United Kingdom industry as a whole, this would imply an inventory saving of perhaps £1 750 000 000, a massive once-for-all gain for the balance of payments and bank financing. Just under a decade ago the United States achieved a substantial reduction in imports following the introduction of computer control techniques.

6. Sales per employee. This is the broad measure of the productivity of a work force, and should indicate the number of non-productive personnel—whose elimination has been one of the main aims of Weinstock's planning. But both the sales and profit/employee ratios emerge as secondary pieces of evidence. They are essentially a by-product of the other five Weinstock ratios; if those are showing well, then the sales and profit/employee ratios will come right. From the employee's side, this also points to the value of the product generated by each man. An international comparison of sales per employee is thus the first step towards a comparison of relative industrial wealth.

7. Profits per employee. This a closer examination of the previous criterion, to which it is related by the basic profit/sales ratio. The size of profits related to work force remains, after all, the ultimate justification for workers' employment in industry while from the employees' side this sets the area of bargaining for increases in wages. For management, this figure is a fundamental tool in assessing how far, and in which areas, a work force should be expanded.

These seven rules form a basic framework for assessing a company or a self-contained division within a company. In general terms, one can only say that if all seven criteria are showing the right results, then the company will be working successfully. In general policy terms—as opposed to a specific situation—no one of the criteria is fundamental to the others. The time to apply specific judgements, in which Arnold Weinstock has been outstandingly successful, is when one of the criteria starts to show danger. The seven rules are also valuable for making comparisons between companies which are broadly similar in their operations, as in Table 4-1 which shows two American electrical companies, GE and Texas along with GEC and English Electric. A comparison with ICI, which operates in a different sector of industry, shows ICI's low ratio of sales to capital employed and its high ratio of sales to employees.

An international comparison of these figures brings out one striking contrast between Britain and American industry. While profit margins are roughly the same, British industry uses twice the amount of capital to produce a given quantity of sales or profits. In other words, a British company will tend to spend twice as much on human or real capital to reach the American level of profits—by the same logic, British firms can be said to be working only half as efficiently. This is a measure of United States industrial power, which also highlights the British problem: how to make the best use of human and material capital. Arnold Weinstock has raised GEC to the level where it can begin to compare with the most efficient in American industry; the task in Britain is for the other 100 or more major industrial companies to do the same.

	G.E.C.	English Electric	General Electric(US)	Texas Instruments	I.C.I.
1. Profits as per cent of capital employed	23	14	29	17	12.9
2. Profits as per cent of sales	11	4.8	8.8	7.2	10.3
3. Sales as a multiple of capital employed	2.1	2.8	3.3	2.4	1.3
4. Sales as a multiple of fixed assets	6.1	4.1	5.2	4.1	1.0
5. Sales as a multiple of stocks	3.6	2.8	5.3	6.2	4.3
6. Sales per employee (£)	3,000	3,285	9,600	6,120	5,570
7. Profits per employee (£)	330	160	840	440	595

Table 4-1   How major companies measure up to the Weinstock yardsticks of efficiency

Data assembly sheet 4-1 (a)

Markets

Code letter	Item	Month or quarter to (date)					
		30 Sept					
		£'000					
A	Our sales last year	£70					
B	Our sales this year	£80					
C	Percentage price increase	5%					
D	Total industry sales: Last year	£750					
E	This year	£970					
F	Value of orders from customers outstanding	£ 20					
G	Debtors	£150					
H	Credit sales if different from B	£ 75					
K	Number of working days in period	20					
L	Number of calendar days in period	28					

Markets

Ratio	Formula for calculation of ratio	Unit of measurement	Month or quarter to (date)					
			30 Sept					
1.1 (a) Growth of sales	$(B \times 100 \div A) - 100$	%	14					
1.1 (b) Growth of sales in real terms	$[(B \times 100 \div A) \times 100 \div (100 + C)] - 100$	%	8					
1.2 Change in share of market	$(B \div E) \times 100 \div (A \div D) - 100$	%	−11.3					
1.3 Length of order book	$F \div B \div K$	days	5					
1.4 Length of tail of range	See sheet 4-1(b)	%	80					
1.5 Credit taken by customers	$G \div H \div L$	days	48					

Data assembly sheet and Ratio calculation sheet 4-1(b)
Analysis of turnover within product range

Item description		Turnover(£)	Cumulative turnover(£)
1	A	1,000	1,000
2	B	800	1,800
3	C	700	2,500
4	D	650	3,150
20	T	5	3,940
Total turnover for period			3,940

As £3,150 is 80% of £3,940

Ratio 4 is $\dfrac{20 \text{ minus } 4}{20}$ =80%

i.e. 80% of the range (items E to T) are producing only 20% of the turnover

Data assembly sheet 4-2
Providers of capital

Code letter	Item	Month or quarter to (date)					
		30 Sept					
A	Equity capital	£2,200,000					
B	Borrowed capital	£1,550,000					
C	Number of ordinary shares	£1,800,000					
D	Price of ordinary shares	£1.50					
E	Total profit	£449,000					
F	Total interest paid	£88,000					
G	Corporation tax	£161,000					
H	Net profit after tax (E—F—G)	£200,000					
K	Number of calendar days in period	365					

Providers of capital

Ratio	Formula for calculation of ratio	Unit of measurement	Month or quarter to (date)					
			30 Sept					
2.1 Return on equity capital Net profit after tax/Equity capital	H x 365 ÷ K x 100 ÷ A	% pa	9.1					
2.2 P/E ratio Price per share/ Net profit after tax per share	D ÷ (H x 365 ÷ K ÷ C)	times	13.5					
2.3 Rate of interest paid on borrowed capital Interest paid/ Borrowed capital	F x 365 ÷ K x 100 ÷ B	% pa	5.7					
2.4 Interest cover Total profit/ Interest paid	E ÷ F	times	5.10					
2.5 Gearing Borrowed capital/ Equity capital	B ÷ A	times	0.71					

Data assembly sheet 4-3(a)
Suppliers

Code letter	Item	Month or quarter to (date)					
		30 Sept					
	Information from buying department						
A	Value of orders outstanding with suppliers	£142,000					
B	Value of orders overdue from suppliers	£14,000					
C	Purchases	£71,000					
D	Value of goods returned	£1,400					
	Information from balance sheet						
E	Creditors	£500,000					
F	Cash at bank and in hand	£44,000					
G	Debtors	£497,000					
H	Marketable securities	£177,000					
K	Current liabilities (e.g. creditors, overdraft, etc.)	£600,000					
L	Number of working days in period	20					
M	Number of calendar days in period	28					
N	Capital expenditure committed	£50,000					

Ratio	Formula for calculation of ratio	Unit of measurement	Month or quarter to (date)					
			30 Sept					
3.1 Suppliers' price index	See sheet 4-3 (b)		128					
3.2 Suppliers' lead time	$A \div C \div L$	days	40					
3.3 Days orders overdue	$B \div C \div L$	days	10					
3.4 Credit taken	$E \div C \div M$	days	196					
3.5 Acid test (variant)	$(F + G + H) \div (K + N)$	times	1.1					
3.6 Returns percentage	$D \times 100 \div C$	%	2					

Data assembly sheet and Ratio calculation sheet 4-3 (b)

Calculating a price index for purchases

Major products used	Quantity used	Price Date(a)	Date(b)
A	1000 lb	£1.50	£1.70
B	500 dozen	£2.40	£3.60
C	1600 gallons	£1.00	£1.25

Calculation of price index   Cost

Item	Date(a)	Date(b)
A	1000 x 1.50 = 1,500	1000 x 1.70 = 1,700
B	500 x 2.40 = 1,200	500 x 3.60 = 1,800
C	1600 x 1.00 = 1,600	1600 x 1.25 = 2,000
	4,300	5,500

Index at date (b) = $\frac{5,500}{4,300} \times \frac{100}{1} = 128$

(date (a) = 100)

Data assembly sheet 4-4(a)

Employees

Code letter	Item	Month or quarter to (date)					
		30 Sept					
A	Number employed at beginning	870					
B	Plus numbers joining during	150					
C	Minus numbers leaving during	90					
D	Equals numbers at end	930					
E	Average numbers employed $(A + D) \div 2$	900					
F	Sales	£2,985,000					
G	Materials cost	£1,261,000					
H	Value added $(F - G)$	£1,724,000					
K	Wages and salaries	£1,155,000					
L	All other costs	£133,000					
M	Profit $(H - K - L)$	£436,000					
N	Number of calendar days in period	365					

Ratio	Formula for calculation of ratio	Unit of measurement	Month or quarter to (date)					
			30 Sept					
4.1 Turnover of employees	C x 365 ÷ N ÷ E	% pa	10					
4.2 Age of senior staff, change in	See sheet 4-4(b)	years	−3.9					
4.3 (a) Sales per employee	F x 365 ÷ N ÷ E	£ pa	33,200					
(b) Value added per employee	H x 365 ÷ N ÷ E	£ pa	19,200					
(c) Profit per employee	M x 365 ÷ N ÷ E	£ pa	4,850					
4.4 Wages and salaries per employee	K x 365 ÷ N ÷ E	£ pa	1,280					

Data assembly sheet and Ratio calculation sheet 4-4(b)

Calculation of average age of senior staff

Senior staff*	Age	
	Date (a)	Date (b)†
Able	45	50
Baker	55	—
Charlie (Baker's replacement)	—	38
Dog	40	45
Easy	42	—
Fox (Easy's replacement)	—	40
George (a new post)	—	35
TOTAL	182	208
Average ((a) ÷ 4; (b) ÷ 5)	45.5	41.6
Average age date (a)	45.5	
Average age date (b)	41.6	
Change in average age	$\overline{3.9}$	

*Can be defined as convenient. A suggestion for a small firm is MD, those who report to him, and those who report to them. †(b) is 5 years later than (a)

Data assembly sheet 4-5
Use of assets

Code letter	Item	Month or quarter to (date)					
		30 Sept					
	Fixed assets*	£000 2,723					
	Stocks	309					
	Debtors	497					
A	Operating assets+	3,529					
B	Sales	2,985					
	Profit as shown in accounts						
	Add back						
	Subtract						
C	Operating profit ‡	436					
D	Actual output	6,000,000 units					
E	Maximum output	9,500,000 units					
F	Number of calendar days in period	365					

* Preferably at their current value, i.e. what they could be bought or sold for, not at their book value.

+ N.B. operating assets does *not* include goodwill, investments or cash or any other assets not used in the main business of the company, e.g. sublet property.

‡ Operating profit is defined as the profit earned from the normal operations of the business (e.g. excluding investment income) after deducting depreciation but before charging tax or interest payments. It may be necessary, therefore, to adjust the figure of profit shown in the accounts and space has been left for this in the work sheet.

Use of assets

Ratio		Formula for calculation of ratio	Unit of measurement	Month or quarter to (date)						
				30 Sept						
5.1	Operating profit/ Operating assets	$C \times F \div 365 \times 100 \div A$	% pa	12.4						
5.2	Operating profit/ Sales	$C \times 100 \div B$	%	14.6						
5.3	Turnover of assets Sales/Operating assets	$B \times F \div 365 \div A$	times per year	0.85						
5.4	Capacity utilis- ation Actual output/ Maximum output	$D \times 100 \div E$	%	63						

Data assembly sheet 4-6(a)
The future

Product	Date of introduction	Within last years*			More than years* ago		
		Sales	Costs†	Profit or contribution ‡	Sales	Costs†	Profit or contribution ‡
Total		1,300	460	840	1,685	801	884
Code letter		A		B	C		D

* The number of years to use to separate new from old products must be decided by the individual firm. Five years is a suggestion.

† Costs can be either full costs from an absorption costing system or only those which would not have been incurred if the product had not been made or marketed.

‡ Profit = sales less full costs. Contribution = sales less marginal costs.

Ratio	Formula for calculation of ratio	Unit of measurement	Year to					
			30 Sept					
6.1 Proportion of turnover from new products	A x 100 ÷ (A + C)	%	43.5					
6.2(a) Contribution from new products	B x 100 ÷ A	%	64.5					
(b) Contribution from old products	D x 100 ÷ C	%	52.5					
6.3(a) R & D/ Discretionary cash flow	F x 100 ÷ H	%	3.9					
(b) Training/ Discretionary cash flow	G x 100 ÷ H	%	0.8					
6.4 Fixed asset expenditure/ Discretionary cash flow	K x 100 ÷ H	%	15.5					
6.5(a) Fixed asset expenditure/ Depreciation	K x 100 ÷ E	%	75					
(b) Fixed asset expenditure/ 'True' depreciation	K x 100 ÷ (h)	%						

Data assembly sheet 4-6(b)

The future

Code letter	Item	Year to					
		30 Sept					
		£,000					
	Profit after tax, depreciation and interest	200					
	Add back						
E	Depreciation	80					
	Dividend on ordinary shares	90					
F	R & D expenditure	15					
G	Training expenditure	3					
	Consultancy expenditure						
	Advertising expenditure						
	New money raised						
	Reduction in net current assets						
	Sale of fixed assets						
H	Discretionary cash flow	388					
K	Expenditure on fixed assets	60					

Data assembly sheet 4-6(c)
Calculation of 'true depreciation'

Class of asset							Total
Fixed assets at cost or valuation (a) Less depreciation to date (b)							
Net book value (a)−(b) (c)							
Number of years company has owned asset (d) Number of years before asset wears out or becomes obsolete (e)							
Total life of asset (d)+(e) (f)							
Estimated cost to replace asset with new equivalent (g)							
'True' depreciation for one year (g) ÷ (f) (h) to date (g) ÷ (f) x (d) (k)							
Amount needed to be set aside for asset replacement in addition to depreciation provision in balance sheet (k)−(b) (l)							

Chapter 5

Ratios for overall control

5.1 Investment in Subsidiaries and/or Divisions

If the organisation is divided into a number of subsidiaries or divisions, the board will want to monitor the performance of each. The best ratio to use is

$$\frac{\text{Profit from subsidiary}}{\text{Investment in subsidiary}}$$

How the terms are defined depends on the nature of the subordinate organisation. (It may be helpful to refer back to Chapter 3 while reading the next few paragraphs.)

If the board are dealing with a subsidiary with powers to raise some of its own finance (particularly from creditors or banks), and perhaps even with minority shareholders of its own, investment is best defined as the parent company's holding in the subsidiary's equity capital. Profit is then what remains after deducting interest payments and the minority's share of profits.

If the parent company's investment is partly in the subsidiary's ordinary shares and partly by way of loans to the subsidiary, the investment must include the loan and the profit must have added back to it the loan interest. The interest cannot be ignored because it will affect the size of profit available to the minority.

If the board are dealing with an operating division the profit is the profit from its operations and the investment is the value of its operating assets.

In both cases the parent company or head office will have assets and expenses of its own. One way of dealing with these is to allocate them to the subsidiaries and divisions: the former being added to their investment and the latter being subtracted from their profit. It is preferable however not to do this because the local management has little or no control over the size of these items (though it may benefit from them). Instead, use a system of ratios as in Diagram 5-1 (which is based on operating divisions—subsidiaries would be slightly different).

Ratios A2, A3 and A4 show how much of the company's capital is invested in each division; ratio A5 the amount in head office assets. Ratios A6, A7 and A8 can be used by the board to monitor the performance of each division.

The board should control head office by requiring to be convinced that any growth in ratio A5 (Head office assets/Total capital) or in ratio A9 (Head office costs/Head office assets), will still lead to an increase in ratio A1 (Total profit/Total capital). Depending on whether group sales or total group employees are better measures of the need for head office then it will be useful to monitor also either ratios A10 (Head office costs/Group sales) and A11 (Group sales/Head office assets) or ratios A12 (Head office costs/Total group employees) and A13 (Head office assets/Total group employees).

Ratios A6, A7 and A8 are useful for monitoring the performance of divisions. The higher these ratios are the more favourably will the board regard requests for further capital. However, decisions on the allocation of capital should be taken on the basis of the rate of return of the particular project being canvassed which may be either higher or lower than the average rate of return on past projects which is measured by ratio A6, A7 and A8. No doubt the board's view of the credibility of the proposal will be influenced by the division's past performance as shown by ratios A6, A7 and A8.

How high should the rate of return on a project be for the board to authorise it? (The relevant rate of return will be the 'after-tax-discounted-cash-flow' rate of return.*) The answer depends on where the money for the project is coming from. If it is to come from new finance which has not yet been raised, the return on the project must be higher than the rate of interest on the new finance. In theory it need be only just higher; in practice a reasonable margin is needed to cover the risks and inaccuracies associated with the estimated return on the project.

* See, for example, A.J. Merrett & Allen Sykes, *Capital Budgeting and Company Finance,* Longmans, 1966. A.M. Alfred & J.B. Evans, *Discounted Cash Flow,* Chapman & Hall, Third Edition 1971, prepared by J. Connor & R. Cooper of Courtaulds.

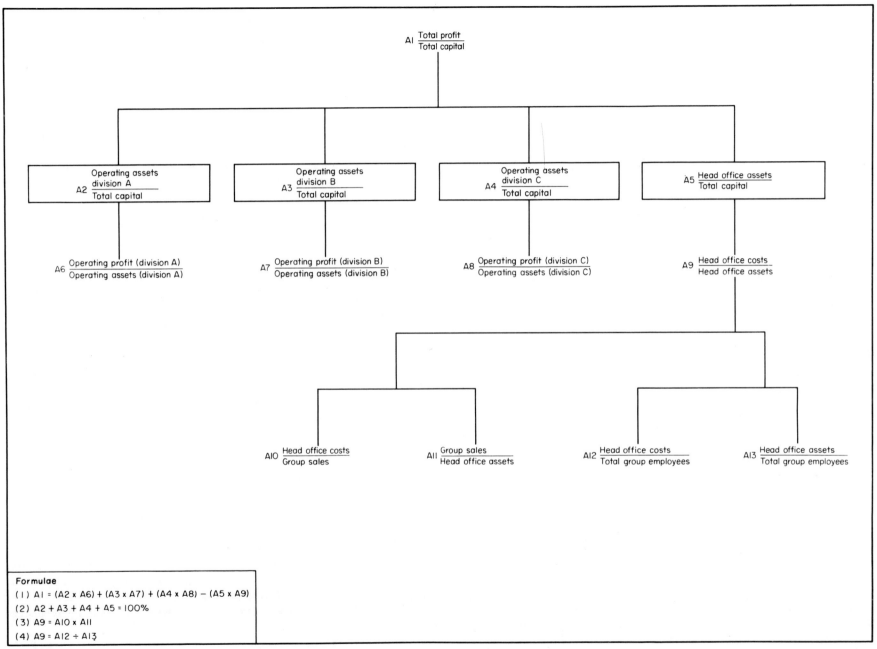

Diagram 5-1   Investment in divisions

If the firm already has the money, the return on the project must be higher than the return on any other alternative use for the money. Broadly speaking there are three classes of alternative to be considered:

1   Other investment projects
2   Investments in marketable securities
3   Repayment of borrowed capital

For example, if a new project is estimated to yield 10 per cent, it would take second place to:

1   Another investment proposal yielding 15 per cent
2   Investment on the stock exchange also yielding 15 per cent
3   Repayment of borrowed capital with an interest rate of 15 per cent

'Opportunity cost' is a useful concept when analysing many problems requiring managerial decision. 'Cost' normally refers to the cost of *doing* something. However, if a company (or individual) does one thing, it (or he) is often automatically precluded from doing some other thing. The income or profit that would have been derived from doing that 'other thing' is the 'opportunity cost' of doing the first thing.

For example, if a company decides to finance a new project from the sale of investments, the project must yield a return higher than the likely future yield from those investments. The likely future yield of the existing investments is one of the 'opportunity costs' of the new project to be considered in evaluating it. Other opportunity costs of the new project would be other new projects with even higher yields.

To sum up this part of the chapter: the board, when considering investment in projects, must always consider:

1   The marginal return from the project, not the average return of the division, and either
2   The marginal cost of the new money, not the average cost of borrowed capital, or
3   The 'opportunity cost' of alternative uses for the money.

This may seem a statement of the obvious but it is surprising how often these principles are forgotten in the midst of discussions and elaborate calculations.

To calculate ratios A1 to A13 use data assembly and ratio calculation sheet 5-1 at the end of this chapter.

5.2 Product Policy

Most firms sell a range of products and/or services. This section applies equally to products and to services, but, to avoid monotonous repetition, only products are specifically referred to.

Some products are more profitable than others; some may even lose money. It is useful therefore for the board to review from time to time the profitability of items or groups of items in the range. In doing so there are two pitfalls to avoid. One is to look at profitability only in relation to sales and ignore the asset investment involved. The other is to allocate all costs (and all assets) to specific products on the conventional absorption costing basis rather than to use the more relevant marginal approach. How to avoid these pitfalls is described in detail in the following paragraphs.

The firm's costs and assets should be divided between product costs and product assets on the one hand, and non product costs and non product assets on the other and between different products or product groups by asking the question: If we were to stop selling this product or product group would we be able to reduce costs and/or assets and, if so, by how much? It is probable that, while some costs and assets will be reduced in proportion to the reduction in sales, others will not. For an equal value of sales, some products may use more materials or labour, may require higher stocks, or discounts to distributors o‌r transportation than others. One aspect which often repays attention is the number of pieces of paper associated with the sale of a product. Clerical costs and salesmen's costs tend to vary with the number of transactions, not with their value.

Once this division of costs and assets has been made, and if 'product contribution' is defined as the difference between a product's sales and its costs arrived at on the above basis, the ratios of Diagram 5-2 can be calculated.

Ratios B2 and B3 are both indicators of the value of a product profitability exercise. If

1   Product assets are a small part of total operating assets (ratio B2), or if
2   Product costs are a small part of total operating costs (ratio B3)

the exercise may not be worth carrying out. Conversely, the larger either B2 or B3 are, the more useful will be the results of the analysis. Non-product costs and non-product assets should be regarded with the same suspicion as head office costs and head office assets (see ratios A5 and A9 to A13). Any tendency of ratios B2 and B3 to decline should give rise to searching questions as to the usefulness of the non-product costs and assets which are growing.

Ratio B4 shows total product contribution in relation to product assets. By 'total product contribution' is meant total sales of all products less total product costs—the

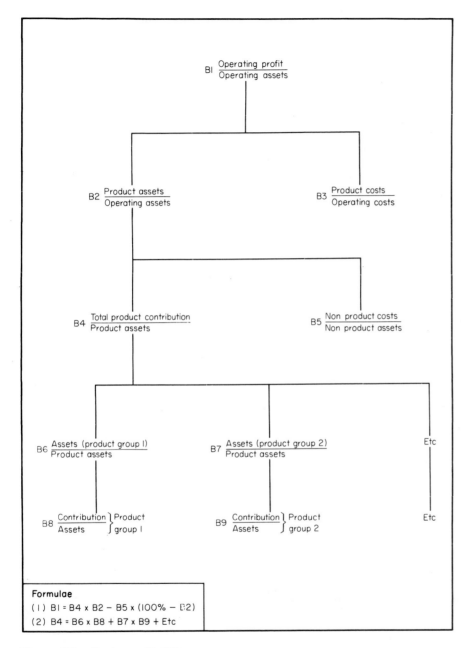

Formulae
(1) $B1 = B4 \times B2 - B5 \times (100\% - B2)$
(2) $B4 = B6 \times B8 + B7 \times B9 + Etc$

Diagram 5-2   Product profitability

costs which are identifiable with specific product groups. Ratio B4 can be improved by:

1   Increasing the profitability of the less profitable product groups (increasing B8, B9, and so on).
2   Deploying more assets in the product groups which *are* more profitable (changing ratios B6, B7, and so on).

There are two constraints to the above process:

1   The alleged necessity of maintaining a complete range
2   The definite need to consider the likely future profitability and growth of new and less profitable ranges

To calculate ratios B1 to B9 use data assembly and ratio calculation sheet 5-2 at the end of this chapter.

5.3 Capacity Utilisation

The board monitors the performance of its divisions, and a smaller company measures its own performance by the ratio:

$$\frac{\text{Operating profit}}{\text{Operating assets}}$$

What ratios should be used to measure reasons for changes in this ratio?

The two main factors affecting the ratio are respectively the profit margin on sales and the rate of turnover of assets. Ratios devised by the du Pont company and by the Centre for Interfirm Comparison, measure these factors. The Centre's ratios are shown in Diagram 5-3; this analysis together with variations and developments of it has been extensively used by the Centre in recent times. Ratio C2 shows the profit margin on sales of the company. If this is too low, it indicates that there is a lack of balance between the size of the business and the volume of sales it is achieving.

To calculate ratios C1 to C3 use data assembly and ratio calculation sheet 5-3 at the end of this chapter.

In some companies, a better measure of the volume of its business than sales in money terms is given by some physical measure of output (such as square yards of cloth woven, pounds of bread baked, gallons of drink botled). In these companies a variant of the basic analysis can be used (see Diagram 5-4).

To calculate ratios C1, C4 and C5 use data assembly and ratio calculation sheet 5-4 at the end of this chapter.

Another variant of the basic analysis is to use value added instead of sales. Value added is sales less all purchases of goods and services from third parties. A convenient approximation to value added is sales less materials costs. This variant is shown in Diagram 5-5.

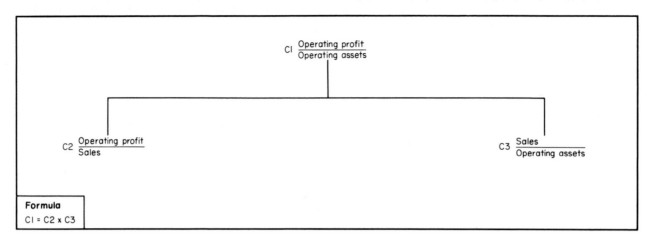

Diagram 5-3   Basic analysis of factors affecting operating profit/operating assets.
With acknowledgements to the Centre for Interfirm Comparison.

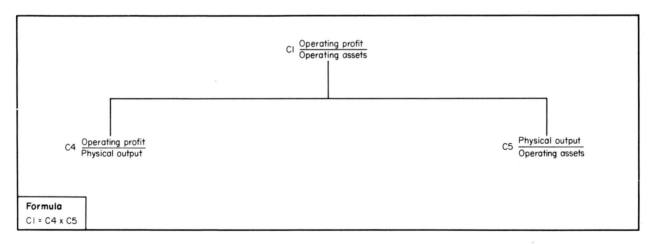

Diagram 5-4   The same analysis using the physical output variant developed at the Centre for Interfirm Comparison.

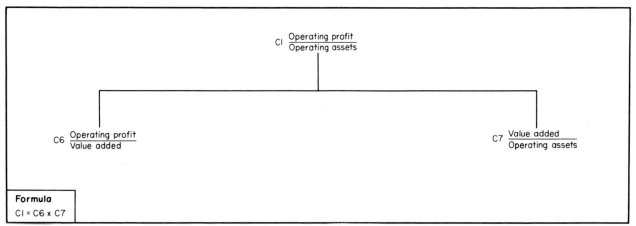

Diagram 5-5   The same analysis using the value-added variant developed at the Centre for Interfirm Comparison.

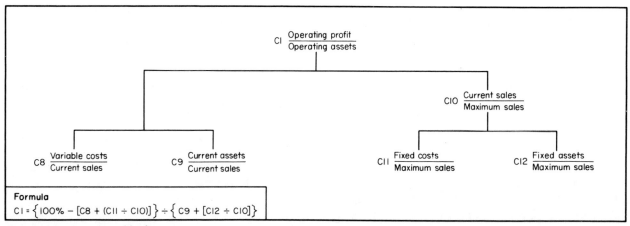

Diagram 5-6   Capacity utilisation

To calculate ratios C1, C6 and C7 use data assembly and ratio calculation sheet 5-5 at the end of this chapter.

A disadvantage of the du Pont analysis is that it does not take into account the fact that in most companies part of the costs and part of the assets are fixed. This has the result that both ratios C2 and C3 (or C4 and C5, or C6 and C7) vary as a consequence of changes in sales volume alone. This disadvantage is overcome by using the ratios in Diagram 5-6.

The denominator of ratios C10, C11 and C12 is maximum sales—the maximum that can be achieved with current capacity. The numerator of ratio C10 and the denominator of ratios C8 and C9 is current sales—the sales actually being achieved in the period currently being analysed. If sales volume fluctuates and efficiency does not change, only ratios C1 and C10 will alter—ratios C8, C9, C11 and C12 should remain unchanged. Increases in ratios C8, C9, C11 or C12 are signals of possible inefficiency, whether ratio C10 is changing or not, and pointers to the areas requiring remedial action. To be able to use these ratios a firm must be able to:

1   Divide its costs between fixed and variable
2   Divide its assets between fixed and current
3   Arrive at a figure for maximum sales.

No firm should find 2 difficult. More effort will be involved in doing 1 and 3. However, 100 per cent accuracy is not needed and the improved usefulness of the analysis should easily outweigh the labour involved.

To calculate ratios C1, and C8 to C12 use data assembly and ratio calculation sheet 5-6 at the end of this chapter.

5.4 Planning for the Future—Discretionary Cash Flow

While monitoring the present or immediate past, the board must always have an eye to the future. It is with this important aspect of a firm that the ratios in this section are concerned.

There are some items of expenditure about which management has a greater degree of choice than others. A firm must buy its raw materials and pay its work people but, within limits, it may choose how much, and when, to spend on such items as research, advertising, staff training, consultancy and the purchase of new equipment. One thing that these items have in common is that they are for the benefit of the future; they are unlikely to contribute to the sales or profits of the current period. Another thing which they have in common is that their level is likely to be influenced more by the availability of cash than by the level of sales.

How much cash is available? What are the sources of a firm's discretionary cash flow? (This term is used because a wider field is being considered than in the traditional definition of cash flow and in order to emphasise the element of management discretion which is involved.) The sources are:

1   The firm's sales and other income less all items of cost (including taxation and interest payments) other than those which either do not involve a cash flow (such as depreciation) or management classes as discretionary. It is suggested that the following should be considered as candidates: research, advertising, staff training, consultancy, dividends on ordinary shares, directors' remuneration in owner managed companies.
2   A reduction in current assets other than cash, such as stock, debtors.
3   An increase in current liabilities.
4   New loans or other finance obtained.

The uses to which this discretionary cash flow can be put are:

1   Expenditure on revenue items for the benefit of the future (research, advertising, staff training, consultancy)
2   Expenditure on capital items for the benefit of the future (investment in buildings, equipment, and so on)
3   Build-up of stocks and debtors to increase the service to customers
4   Rewards to the risk takers and/or entrepreneurs (dividends on ordinary shares, directors' remuneration, senior staff bonuses)
5   Repayment of loans and other debts
6   Build-up of cash reserves.

The board will find it useful to express each source and each use of discretionary cash flow as a percentage of the total flow and to calculate these ratios for a number of years in order to get the trends. The questions to ask are: Has the balance between investment in the future (1, 2 and 3) and reward in the present (4) been right? Has the investment in the future paid off, and if not why not? What are the future flows likely to look like and is this what management wants?

To calculate ratios D1 to D17 use data assembly and ratio calculation sheet 5-7 at the end of this chapter.

5.5 Planning for the Future—Research and Development

While on the subject of payoff, it is worth considering how to decide how much to spend on research and development (R and D) and how to monitor the effectiveness of the expenditure.

R and D can be set at a certain percentage of sales and this percentage can be compared with competitors' figures, if available. This is not very satisfactory because there is no cause and effect linkage between this year's research (which it is hoped will benefit future years' sales) and this year's sales (which have benefited from the research of previous years). To allocate a certain percentage of discretionary cash inflow (item 1 only, i.e. excluding the more capital-like items 2, 3 and 4) may be more meaningful.

It is difficult to measure the effectiveness of R and D. However, two ratios are suggested:

E1   *Rate of new product innovation*

$$\frac{\text{Sales of products introduced in the past five (?) years}}{\text{Total sales}}$$

E2   *Profitability of new products*

$$\frac{\text{Profit (or contribution) from products introduced in the past five (?) years}}{\text{Total profit (or contribution)}}$$

Ratio E1 should be compared with a similar ratio for competitors if this can be obtained, deduced or guessed. Too great a divergence in either direction may be cause for concern. Although no firm wants to have a range of products which is tending to economic obsolescence, money can be equally lost by a too rapid introduction of too many new products in relation to the market's capacity to absorb them.

Ratio E2 should be compared with the profitability of the rest of the range. It is not enough to introduce new products; they must, in the early stages of their career, make more profit than the less troublesome bread and butter lines which are feeling the effects of competitive pressure and may be on the way out. The profit/time profile of a product is well known to be of the shape shown in Diagram 5-7.

To calculate ratios E1 and E2 use data assembly and ratio calculation sheet 5-8 at the end of this chapter.

5.6 Growth and Stability

As well as making profit, firms want to grow. It is growth of profits that enables a firm to pay higher dividends to the ordinary shareholder. It is expectation of the growth of dividends that increases a share's price and gives its holder his capital gains. Growth is best measured by index numbers—in the case of sales by dividing each year's sales by the value of sales at some chosen base year (see ratio F2 in Diagram 5-8).

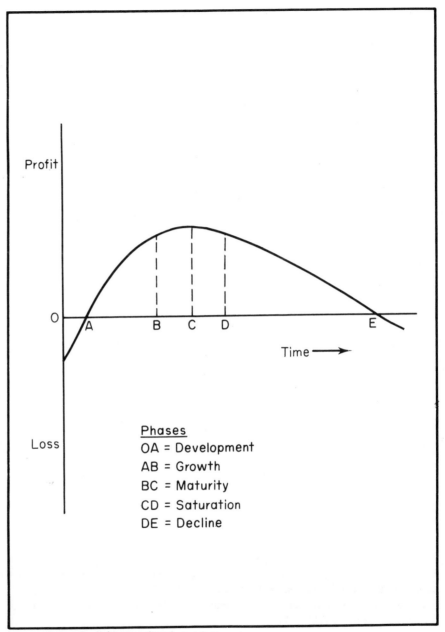

Phases
OA = Development
AB = Growth
BC = Maturity
CD = Saturation
DE = Decline

Diagram 5-7   Profit/time profile of a product

Crude Growth Indices	Adjusted Growth Indices
F1 $\dfrac{\text{Profit this year}}{\text{Profit in base year}}$	$F4 = F1 \div \dfrac{\text{Suitable price index now}}{\text{Suitable price index in base year}}$
F2 $\dfrac{\text{Sales this year}}{\text{Sales in base year}}$	$F5 = F2 \div \dfrac{\text{Suitable price index now}}{\text{Suitable price index in base year}}$
F3 $\dfrac{\text{Assets this year}}{\text{Assets in base year}}$	$F6 = F3 \div \dfrac{\text{Suitable price index now}}{\text{Suitable price index in base year}}$

Share of the Market

F7 $\dfrac{\text{Our sales this year}}{\text{Our and our competitors' sales this year}}$

Diagram 5-8   Growth ratios

It is desirable that profit should grow faster than sales and sales faster than assets (ratios F1, F2 and F3).

Part of a firm's apparent growth is the result of inflation. The effects of inflation can be removed by applying suitable price indices derived from government statistics to the crude growth indices (ratios F4, F5 and F6).

As well as having its sales grow, a firm will want to increase its share of the market. This should, therefore, also be measured (ratio F7).

Most people prefer a reasonably stable rate of growth to one that fluctuates violently. Techniques to measure stability of growth are however outside the scope of this book.

To calculate ratios F1 to F7 use data assembly and ratio calculation sheet 5-9 at the end of this chapter.

Appendix 5.1

Worked example of Calculation of Growth Indices

The following is a worked example of the calculation of index numbers to measure growth, both in money terms and in real terms. The example shows how to deal with a number of problems encountered in practice.

It is desired to measure the growth of Marks and Spencer's turnover and profit for the last ten years (see Table 5-1).

Columns 2 to 5 were completed from Marks and Spencer's Moodies card. For simplicity, the overseas turnover has been included in the clothing turnover because it is small, is unlikely to be food, and because no break-down of it is available as between food and clothing.

From the data in columns 2 to 5 it is possible to see that both categories of turnover, and profits, are all growing. It is difficult however to form a clear impression of the rate of growth of each item, how this is changing over time, and how each item is growing in relation to the other items. Converting the absolute money figures into the type of ratio called an index number will make all of these points clearer.

The conversion is very simple. The figures for each year are divided by the figure for that item for the base year (the first year in the table—the year to 31 March 1961). For example, the 1962 index number for the growth of food sales of 115.8 was arrived at by dividing the food sales for the year to 31 March 1962 (£33.0m) by the food sales for the year to 31 March 1961 (£28.5m). In a similar manner all the figures in columns 13 to 16 were arrived at.

From columns 13 and 14 it will now be seen that food sales have grown much faster than clothing sales. The food sales index for each year is higher than the clothing sales index, and by 1970 they were standing at 341.1 and 191.1 respectively.

The figures in column 15 show that total sales have grown each year and that by 1970 they were over double (216.8 per cent) the 1961 level. The rate of growth of total sales is between that of food and clothing. It is much nearer to the clothing figure because of the high proportion of clothing sales in the total. In the early years of the period profit did not grow so fast as sales but after 1966 the position was reversed and by 1970 the ordinary shareholder's profits were nearly 2½ times (246.5 per cent) what they were in 1961.

However the indices in columns 13 to 16 have a disadvantage. They all measure growth in money terms; part of that growth will have been real growth (for example, more shirts will have been sold) and part will have been apparent growth resulting from the growth of prices (inflation). It is more useful to measure growth in real terms rather than in money terms and this is done by dividing the money growth index by a suitable index of price increases.

A suitable index for food sales is the retail food price index. A convenient index for clothing sales is the index of clothing and footwear prices. An appropriate index for the growth of profits is the index of all retail prices. This index is used *not* because Marks and Spencer's is a retailer but because the cost of living of the ordinary shareholders to whom the profit belongs is most easily measured by the index of all retail prices. If profits do not grow at least as fast as this index, the real income (or standard of living) of these shareholders will decline to the extent that their income comes from Marks and Spencer's shares.

The price indices were extracted from the *Annual Abstract of Statistics* and were entered in columns 6 to 9. Marks and Spencer's figures relate to years to 31 March. The price indices are for calendar years. For simplicity we have taken the calendar year 1960 as being equivalent to the year to 31 March 1961, and so on for subsequent

Data from accounts					Index of retail prices				Revised index of retail prices			Marks & Spencer Indices							
												Money				Real			
Year to 31 March	Turnover			Earned for Ordinary	Year	All	Food	Clothing & Footwear	All	Food	Clothing & Footwear	Food	Cloth-ing	Total	Earned for Ordinary	Food	Cloth-ing	Total	Earned for Ordinary
	Food	Clothing	Total																
	← £ millions →			(£ 000)															
1	2	3	4	5	6	7	8	9	10	11	12	13	14	15	16	17	18	19	20
1961	28.5	138.0	166.5	10,080	1960	110.7	107.4	103.9	100.0	100.0	100.0	100.0	100.0	100.0	100.0	100.0	100.0	100.0	100.0
1962	33.0	139.8	172.8	10,321	1961	114.5	109.1	105.6	103.4	101.6	101.6	115.8	101.3	103.8	102.4	114.0	99.7	102.4	99.0
					16 Jan 1962	117.5	110.7	106.6	106.1	103.1	102.6								
1963	39.0	145.9	184.9	10,891	1962	101.6	102.3	102.0	107.8	105.5	104.7	136.8	105.7	111.1	108.0	129.7	101.0	107.1	100.2
1964	45.0	156.5	201.5	12,006	1963	103.6	104.8	103.5	109.9	108.0	106.2	157.9	113.4	121.0	119.1	146.2	106.8	115.6	108.4
1965	50.0	169.8	219.8	12,642	1964	107.0	107.8	104.9	113.6	111.1	107.6	175.4	123.0	132.0	125.4	157.9	114.3	124.2	110.4
1966	56.0	182.0	238.0	18,206	1965	112.1	111.6	107.0	118.9	115.1	109.8	196.5	131.9	142.9	180.6	170.7	120.1	132.0	151.9
1967	65.6	190.2	255.8	18,854	1966	116.5	115.6	109.9	123.6	119.2	112.8	230.2	137.8	153.6	187.1	193.1	122.2	140.4	151.4
1968	76.4	205.9	282.3	20,016	1967	119.4	118.5	111.7	126.7	122.2	114.6	268.1	149.2	169.5	198.6	219.4	130.2	154.3	156.7
1969	86.8	230.5	317.3	21,668	1968	125.0	123.2	119.1	132.6	127.0	122.2	304.6	167.0	190.6	215.0	239.8	136.7	164.9	162.1
1970	97.2	263.7	360.9	24,850	1969	131.8	131.0	123.9	139.8	135.1	127.1	341.1	191.1	216.8	246.5	252.5	150.4	177.9	176.3

Sources

    Columns 1 to 5 Moodies Cards
    Columns 6 to 9 Annual Abstract of Statistics, Central Statistical Office, 1970
    1960, 1961 and 16 Jan 1962 are based on 17 Jan 1956 = 100
    1962 and onwards are based on 16 Jan 1962 = 100

Formulae (numbers are column numbers)

    10 = 7 x 100 ÷ 7 for base year (=110.7) and, for 1962 and onwards, multiplied by index number at change of base (=117.5) and ÷ 100
    11 = 8 x 100 ÷ 8 for base year (=107.4) and, for 1962 and onwards, multiplied by index number at change of base (=110.7) and ÷ 100
    12 = 9 x 100 ÷ 9 for base year (=103.9) and, for 1962 and onwards, multiplied by index number at change of base (=106.6) and ÷ 100
    13 = 2 x 100 ÷ 2 for base year (=28.5)
    14 = 3 x 100 ÷ 3 for base year (=138.0)
    15 = 4 x 100 ÷ 4 for base year (=166.5)
    16 = 5 x 100 ÷ 5 for base year (=10,080)
    17 = 13 ÷ 11 x 100
    18 = 14 ÷ 12 x 100
    19 = 17 x (2 ÷ 4) + 18 x (3 ÷ 4)
    20 = 16 ÷ 10 x 100

Table 5-1   Calculation of index numbers to measure growth

years. For greater accuracy it would have been possible to have taken a weighted average of two calendar years' index numbers (¾ of 1960 plus ¼ of 1961) to arrive at an index number for the Marks and Spencer's year (1960/61), but this degree of accuracy was not considered to be necessary.

The price indices as extracted are not usable for our purposes without two arithmetic manipulations first being performed.

The index numbers for 1960 and 1961 are based on the figure for 17 January 1956 being 100; those for 1962 and onwards are based on the figure for 16 January 1962 being 100. It is more convenient for us to have one continuous index. This is achieved by multiplying the second series of index numbers by the figure which the first index had reached at the transition date (117.5 for the all price index) and dividing by 100.

The second change is to bring this new continuous index to the same base date as our Marks and Spencer's growth-in-money-terms index (the year to 31 March 1961 or the calendar year 1960). This is achieved by dividing the new continuous index by its value at the base date (110.7 for the all price index) and multiplying by 100.

The above two changes produce the revised price indices shown in columns 10, 11 and 12.

We are now in a position to change the Marks and Spencer's indices of growth in money terms to indices of growth in real terms by dividing the money index by the price index for the same year (for example, by dividing the money index for food for 1962/1963 of 136.8 by the price index for food for 1962 of 105.5) and multiplying the result by 100.

This process is satisfactory for the indices of growth of food and clothing sales and of profit but it cannot be applied to the index of growth of all sales as there is not a corresponding price index. (The all price index includes more items than just food and clothing, which are the constituents of total sales.) The solution to this problem is to construct the total sales real growth index from a weighted average of the real growth indices for food and clothing. The weights used are the proportion of food and clothing sales respectively to total sales in the year in question.

The real growth indices are shown in columns 17 to 20. It will be seen that whereas, in money terms, food sales had increased from 1961 to 1970 to 341.1 per cent, in real terms the growth was *only* 252.5 per cent. Similarly whilst in money terms clothing sales had nearly doubled, in real terms they had increased by only 50 per cent.

Column 20 shows that in 1962 and 1963, while profits were growing in money terms, they were declining or stagnant in real terms.

The ordinary shareholder's profits had grown in money terms from 1961 to 1970 2½ times, in real terms *only* 1¾ times.

The word *only* has been emphasised in the above sentences because these growth rates are obviously very satisfactory; the point being made is the difference between growth in money terms and in real terms.

Data assembly sheet 5-1
Investment in divisions

Code letter	Item	Month or quarter to (date)					
A	Operating profit (division A)						
B	Operating profit (division B)						
C	Operating profit (division C)						
D	(A + B + C)						
E	Head office costs						
F	Total profit (D − E)						
G	Average operating assets (division A)						
H	Average operating assets (division B)						
K	Average operating assets (division C)						
L	Average head office assets						
M	Average total capital (G + H + K + L)						
N	Group sales						
P	Average total group employees						
Q	No of working days in period						
R	No of working days in year						

Ratio		Formula for calculation of ratio	Unit of measurement	Month or quarter to (date)					
A1	Total profit/ Total capital	F x 100 ÷ M x R ÷ Q	% pa						
A2	Operating assets division A/ Total capital	G x 100 ÷ M	%						
A3	Operating assets division B/ Total capital	H x 100 ÷ M	%						
A4	Operating assets division C/ Total capital	K x 100 ÷ M	%						
A5	Head office assets/ Total capital	L x 100 ÷ M	%						
A6	Operating profit (division A)/ Operating assets (division A)	A x 100 ÷ G x R ÷ Q	% pa						
A7	Operating profit (division B)/ Operating assets (division B)	B x 100 ÷ H x R ÷ Q	% pa						
A8	Operating profit (division C)/ Operating assets (division C)	C x 100 ÷ K x R ÷ Q	% pa						
A9	Head office costs/ Head office assets	E x 100 ÷ L x R ÷ Q	% pa						
A10	Head office costs/ Group sales	E x 100 ÷ N	%						
A11	Group sales/ Head office assets	N ÷ L x R ÷ Q	times per year						
A12	Head office costs/ Total group employees	E ÷ P x R ÷ Q	£'s pa per head						
A13	Head office assets/ Total group employees	L ÷ P	£'s per head						

Data assembly sheet 5-2
Product profitability

Code letter	Item	Month or quarter to (date)					
A	Sales (product group 1)						
B	Costs (product group 1)						
C	Contribution (product group 1) (A − B)						
D	Sales (product group 2)						
E	Costs (product group 2)						
F	Contribution (product group 2) (D − E)						
G	Total product costs (B + E)						
H	Total product contribution (C + F)						
K	Non product costs						
L	Operating profit (H − K)						
M	Average assets (product group 1)						
N	Average assets (product group 2)						
P	Average product assets (M + N)						
	Average non product assets						
R	Average operating assets (P + Q)						
S	No of working days in period						
T	No of working days in year						

Ratio	Formula for calculation of ratio	Unit of measurement	Month or quarter to (date)					
B1 Operating profit/ Operating assets	L x 100 ÷ R x T ÷ S	% pa						
B2 Product assets/ Operating assets	P x 100 ÷ R	%						
B3 Product costs/ Operating costs	G x 100 ÷ (G + K)	%						
B4 Total product contribution/ Product assets	H x 100 ÷ P x T ÷ S	% pa						
B5 Non product costs/ Non product assets	K x 100 ÷ Q x T ÷ S	% pa						
B6 Assets (product group 1)/ Product assets	M x 100 ÷ P	%						
B7 Assets (product group 2)/ Product assets	N x 100 ÷ P	%						
B8 Contribution (product group 1)/ Assets (product group 1)	C x 100 ÷ M x T ÷ S	% pa						
B9 Contribution (product group 2)/ Assets (product group 2)	F x 100 ÷ N x T ÷ S	% pa						

Data assembly sheet 5-3

Basic analysis

Code letter	Item	Month or quarter to (date)					
A	Operating profit						
B	Average operating assets						
C	Sales						
D	No of working days in period						
E	No of working days in year						

Ratio	Formula for calculation of ratio	Unit of measurement	Month or quarter to (date)					
C1 Operating profit/ Operating assets	$A \times 100 \div B \times E \div D$	% pa						
C2 Operating profit/ Sales	$A \times 100 \div C$	%						
C3 Sales/Operating assets	$C \div B \times E \div D$	times per year						

Data assembly sheet 5-4
Basic analysis in physical terms

Code letter	Item	Month or quarter to (date)					
A	Operating profit						
B	Average operating assets						
C	Physical output						
D	No of working days in period						
E	No of working days in year						

Basic analysis in physical terms

	Formula for calculation of ratio	Unit of measurement	Month or quarter to (date)					
C1 Operating profit/ Operating assets	A x 100 ÷ B x E ÷ D	% pa						
C4 Operating profit/ Physical output	A ÷ C	£'s per unit						
C5 Physical output/ Operating assets	C ÷ B x E ÷ D	Units per year per £						

Data assembly sheet 5-5

Basic analysis using value added

Code letter	Item	Month or quarter to (date)					
A	Sales						
B	Materials cost *						
C	Value added (A — B)						
D	Costs other than materials						
E	Operating profit (C — D)						
F	Average operating assets						
G	No of working days in period						
H	No of working days in year						

* If stock changes are significant this should be materials cost content of sales ie purchases adjusted for changes in raw materials stock and in the materials content of work in progress and finished goods stock.

Ratio	Formula for calculation of ratio	Unit of measurement	Month or quarter to (date)					
C1 Operating profit/ Operating assets	E x 100 ÷ F x H ÷ G	% pa						
C6 Operating profit/ Value added	E x 100 ÷ C	%						
C7 Value added/ Operating assets	C ÷ F x H ÷ G	times per year						

Capacity utilisation

Code letter	Item	Month or quarter to (date)					
A	Maximum sales for period						
B	Current sales						
C	Variable costs						
D	Fixed costs						
E	Total costs (C + D)						
F	Operating profit (B − E)						
G	Average current assets						
H	Average fixed assets						
K.	Average operating assets (G + H)						
L	No of working days in period						
M	No of working days in year						

Capacity utilisation

Ratio		Formula for calculation of ratio	Unit of measurement	Month or quarter to (date)					
C1	Operating profit/ Operating assets	$F \times 100 \div K \times M \div L$	% pa						
C8	Variable costs/ Current sales	$C \times 100 \div B$	%						
C9	Current assets/ Current sales	$G \times 1000 \div (B \times M \div L)$	$^0\!/\!_{00}$ pa						
C10	Current sales/ Maximum sales	$B \times 100 \div A$	%						
C11	Fixed costs/ Maximum sales	$D \times 100 \div A$	%						
C12	Fixed assets/ Maximum sales	$H \times 1000 \div (A \times M \div L)$	$^0\!/\!_{00}$ pa						

Discretionary cash flow

Code letter	Item	Month or quarter to (date)					
	Sources of discretionary cash flow						
A	Profit after tax and minorities						
B	Add back depreciation						
C	Sub total (A + B)						
D	Research						
E	Advertising						
F	Staff training						
G	Consultancy						
H	Dividend on ordinary shares						
I	Directors' remuneration						
J	Other 'discretionary payments'						
K	Profit before depreciation and discretionary payments (the sum of items C to J)						
L	Reduction in stock						
M	Reduction in debtors						
N	Increase in current liabilities						
P	New loans obtained						
Q	Total discretionary cash flow (the sum of items K to P)						

Data assembly sheet 5-7: *continued*

Discretionary cash flow

Code letter	Item	Month or quarter to (date)					
	Uses of discretionary cash flow						
R	Research						
S	Advertising						
T	Staff training						
U	Consultancy						
V	Dividend on ordinary shares						
W	Directors' remuneration						
Y	Other 'discretionary payments'						
Z	Increase in stocks						
AA	Increase in debtors						
AB	Senior staff bonuses						
AC	Repayment of loans						
AD	Increase in cash reserves						
AE	Total discretionary cash flow (the sum of items R to AE)						

NB   Item Q should equal item AE

Discretionary cash flow

Ratio	Formula for calculation of ratio	Unit of measurement	Month or quarter to (date)					
Sources of discretionary cash flow								
D1 Profit before depreciation and discretionary payments/Total discretionary cash flow	K x 100 ÷ AE	%						
D2 Reduction in stock/Total discretionary cash flow	L x 100 ÷ AE	%						
D3 Reduction in debtors/Total discretionary cash flow	M x 100 ÷ AE	%						
D4 Increase in current liabilities/Total discretionary cash flow	N x 100 ÷ AE	%						
D5 New loans obtained/ Total discretionary cash flow	P x 100 ÷ AE	%						
Use of discretionary cash flow								
D6 Research/Total discretionary cash flow	R x 100 ÷ AE	%						
D7 Advertising/Total discretionary cash flow	S x 100 ÷ AE	%						
D8 Staff training/ Total discretionary cash flow	T x 100 ÷ AE	%						

Ratio		Formula for calculation of ratio	Unit of measurement	Month or quarter to (date)					
D9	Consultancy/Total discretionary cash flow	U x 100 ÷ AE	%						
D10	Dividend on ordinary shares/Total discretionary cash flow	V x 100 ÷ AE	%						
D11	Directors' remuneration/Total discretionary cash flow	W x 100 ÷ AE	%						
D12	Other 'discretionary payments'/Total discretionary cash flow	Y x 100 ÷ AE	%						
D13	Increase in stocks/Total discretionary cash flow	Z x 100 ÷ AE	%						
D14	Increase in debtors/Total discretionary cash flow	AA x 100 ÷ AE	%						
D15	Senior staff bonuses/Total discretionary cash flow	AB x 100 ÷ AE	%						
D16	Repayment of loans/Total discretionary cash flow	AC x 100 ÷ AE	%						
D17	Increase in cash reserves/Total discretionary cash flow	AD x 100 ÷ AE	%						

Research and development

Code letter	Item	Month or quarter to (date)					
A	Sales of products introduced in the last 5 years						
B	Total sales						
C	Profit (or contribution) from products introduced in the last 5 years						
D	Total profit (or contribution)						

Research and development

Ratio	Formula for calculation of ratio	Unit of measurement	Month or quarter to (date)					
E1 Rate of new product innovation. Sales of products introduced in the last 5 years/ Total sales	A x 100 ÷ B	%						
E2 Profitability of new products. Profit (or contribution) from products introduced in the last 5 years / Total profit (or contribution)	C x 100 ÷ D	%						

Growth ratios

Code letter	Item	Month or quarter to (date)					
	Base year figures						
A	Profit						
B	Sales						
C	Assets						
D	Price index for profits						
E	Price index for sales						
F	Price index for assets						
	This period figures						
G	Profit						
H	Sales						
K	Assets						
L	Price index for profits						
M	Price index for sales						
N	Price index for assets						
P	Our competitors' sales (estimated)						

Growth ratios

Ratio	Formula for calculation of ratio	Unit of Measurement	Month or quarter to (date)					
Crude growth indices								
F1 Profit this year/ Profit in base year	G x 100 ÷ A	%						
F2 Sales this year/ Sales in base year	H x 100 ÷ B	%						
F3 Assets this year/ Assets in base year	K x 100 ÷ C	%						
Adjusted growth indices								
F4 Growth of profit in real terms	Ratio F1 x D ÷ L	%						
F5 Growth of sales in real terms	Ratio F2 x E ÷ M	%						
F6 Growth of assets in real terms	Ratio F3 x F ÷ N	%						
Share of the market								
F7 Our sales this period/ Our and our competitors' sales this period	H x 100 ÷ (H + P)	%						

Chapter 6

Ratios for marketing management

6.1 Marketing Ratios in a Manufacturing Business

In Chapter 1 it was stated that it is desirable to provide each manager with a single key ratio which measures the degree of his success. Such a ratio relates the results achieved by the marketing management to the resources available.

The result that marketing management is trying to achieve is an optimum balance between:

1 Maximisation of profitable sales
2 Minimisation of marketing costs
3 Minimisation of assets used.

A ratio that measures the combined result of achieving a balance between all three of the above objectives is

$$\frac{\text{Marketing contribution}}{\text{Marketing assets}}$$

Marketing contribution is defined as sales less marketing costs less variable manufacturing costs. The reason for subtracting marketing costs is obvious; less so that for deducting variable manufacturing costs. It is as follows: no firm wants just to maximise sales; it also wants to sell proportionally more of the more profitable items and proportionally less of the less profitable ones. A useful measure of profit in this case is sales less variable manufacturing costs, that is, those costs which would not have been incurred if the product had not been made and sold.

Marketing costs will include warehousing, distribution, advertising, selling and sales office costs, plus discounts given and bad debts. It is obviously up to each firm to decide which member of management should be responsible for which item of

expenditure so some firms may wish to add to or subtract from this list. A few comments on some of them may be helpful.

Discounts given may be fairly obvious—there is a limit to the price reduction it is worth giving to achieve a sale—but it is surprising how many firms do not record discounts given but only net sales.

Bad debts are often on the budget of financial management because it is responsible for collecting the money from customers. In this book both marketing and financial management have bad debts as part of their responsibility because this seems better to reflect the reality of the situation. Salesmen must take some of the responsibility for selling to a customer who does not pay. The accounts department must also be alert to get money in quickly, particularly if there is a risk that a customer might go bankrupt.

Sales office costs covers all the clerical costs involved in a sale: invoices, advice and delivery notes, statements, receipts, entries in the sales ledger, sales analysis and statistics, and so on. These costs are obviously caused by the activities of marketing although some of the people may well be supervised by other managers in the organisation. Including these costs may help to emphasise the relative profitability of small and large orders.

Marketing assets will include:

1 Finished goods stock (likely to be a joint responsibility with production management)
2 Debtors (likely to be a joint responsibility with finance management)
3 Selling and distribution vehicles.

The main subsidiary ratios that marketing management should have are shown in Diagram 6-1. To improve his key ratio (G1) the marketing manager can take action in three broad fields. He can:

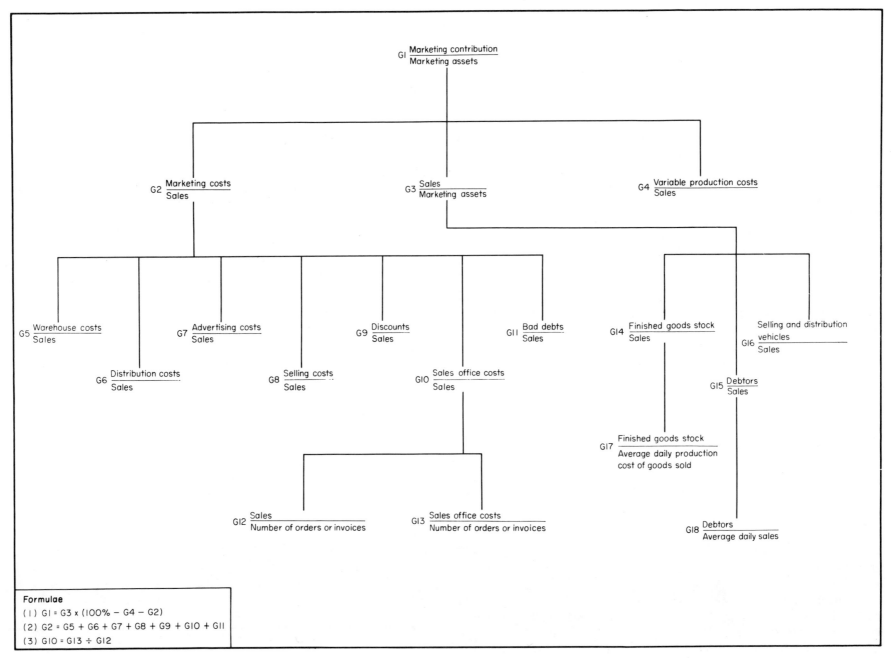

Diagram 6-1   Ratios for marketing management

113

1   Increase sales with a less than proportionate increase in marketing costs
     (ratio G2 will fall)
2   Increase sales with a less than proportionate increase in marketing assets
     (ratio G3 will rise)
3   Increase the proportion of sales which are of items with a higher profit
     margin (ratio G4 will fall).

The above tends to assume an expanding economy. If marketing management is faced
with a contracting economy, the necessary action becomes:

4   To cut marketing costs with a less than proportionate drop in sales (ratio
     G2 will fall)
5   To cut marketing assets with a less than proportionate drop in sales (ratio
     G3 will rise)
6   To reduce the proportion of sales which are of items with a low profit
     margin (ratio G4 will fall)

Obviously action may be taken in more than one of the fields 1 to 3 or 4 to 6 at a time.
Part of the job of marketing management is to balance the activities in these fields in
order to optimise the result on the ratio of marketing contribution to marketing
assets.

To calculate ratios G1 to G18 use data assembly and ratio calculation sheet 6-1 at
the end of this chapter.

6.2 Advertising

As the benefit of this period's advertising expenditure may well not be felt until a later
period and as, conversely, this period's sales may be benefiting from an earlier period's
advertising, it may be useful to marketing management to have a lagged ratio for this
expenditure, as:

$$\frac{\text{Advertising for a previous period}}{\text{Sales for this period}}$$

It may be possible to estimate the length of the lag from past experience by graphing
advertising expenditure and sales over time and measuring the time distance between
successive peaks on the two lines (see Diagram 6-2).

If a firm does much export business and if, as is usual, its home and export selling
and distribution costs are different, marketing management will probably want to
have ratios H1 to H5 (Diagram 6-3), in addition to those in Diagram 6-1.

Using these ratios will quickly show whether a change in the ratios of selling costs to
sales and/or distribution costs to sales is due to a change in the proportion of home to

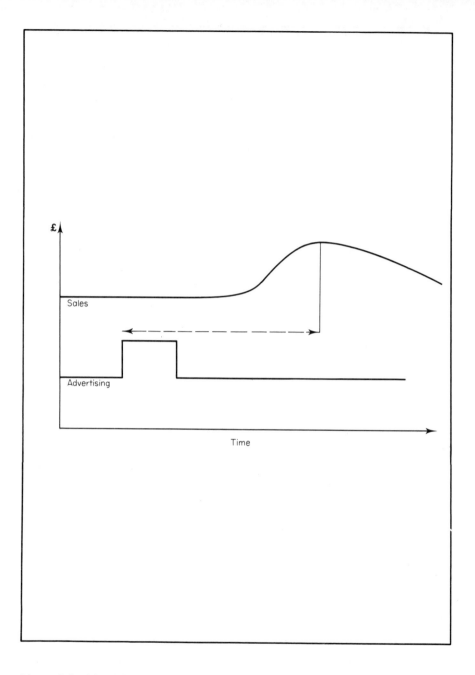

Diagram 6-2   Advertising and sales over time

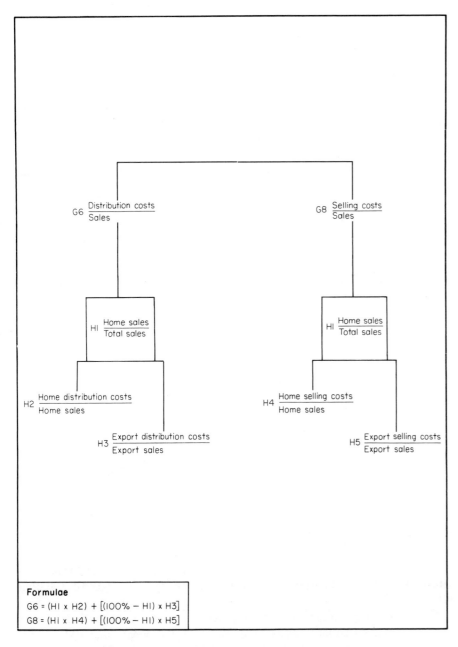

G6 $\dfrac{\text{Distribution costs}}{\text{Sales}}$

G8 $\dfrac{\text{Selling costs}}{\text{Sales}}$

HI $\dfrac{\text{Home sales}}{\text{Total sales}}$

HI $\dfrac{\text{Home sales}}{\text{Total sales}}$

H2 $\dfrac{\text{Home distribution costs}}{\text{Home sales}}$

H4 $\dfrac{\text{Home selling costs}}{\text{Home sales}}$

H3 $\dfrac{\text{Export distribution costs}}{\text{Export sales}}$

H5 $\dfrac{\text{Export selling costs}}{\text{Export sales}}$

Formulae

G6 = (HI x H2) + [(100% − HI) x H3]
G8 = (HI x H4) + [(100% − HI) x H5]

Diagram 6-3   Distribution and selling costs; home and export analyses.
Based on the scheme developed by the Centre for Interfirm Comparison.

export business (ratio H1) or to a change in the costs of selling or distributing one pound's worth of home or export sales (ratios H2 to H5) and thus indicate more precisely where action is called for.

To calculate ratios H1 to H5 use data assembly and ratio calculation sheet 6-2 at the end of this chapter.

6.3 Three Dimensions in Marketing

It is sometimes useful for marketing management to regard its responsibilities as being in three dimensions. These are illustrated in Diagram 6-4. They are:

1   Activities, such as distributing, advertising
2   Products or product groups
3   Markets, either in the geographical sense (such as the European market) or the demographic sense (such as the teenage market).

The ratios described in this chapter so far are all activity ratios. They analyse one dimension of marketing managment's responsibilities. But management will also find it useful to analyse its own key ratio of marketing contribution/marketing assets by products or by markets. The start of a product analysis is shown in Diagram 6-5.

Unallocated marketing costs and assets are those costs and assets which are not sufficiently identified with a particular product group to warrant attributing them to that group. A market analysis would be very similar to a product analysis and is therefore not separately illustrated here.

Marketing management must decide for itself how far to pursue its analysis along each of the three dimensions. Moreover, with changes in the company's fortunes, in the economic climate and so on, management may well, and indeed should, change the pattern of analysis it receives. In a small business, ratios G1 to G4 in Diagram 6-1 may be adequate for control by marketing management; a medium-sized firm's marketing management may wish to add some or all of ratios G5 to G17; a large firm's marketing management will almost certainly need all of these ratios, plus those shown in Diagrams 6-7 and 6-8. All this is giving greater detail but in only one of the dimensions in which marketing functions. Even the smaller firm will soon want to add the other two dimensions of its marketing operations.

Wherever possible it is desirable that the majority of the marketing ratios of Diagrams 6-1, 6-3, 6-7 and 6-8 should be subdivided by product group and/or market. It is probably preferable to do this at the expense, if necessary, of cutting down on the number of activity ratios provided.

To calculate ratios I1 to I12 use data assembly and ratio calculation sheet 6-3 at the end of this chapter.

115

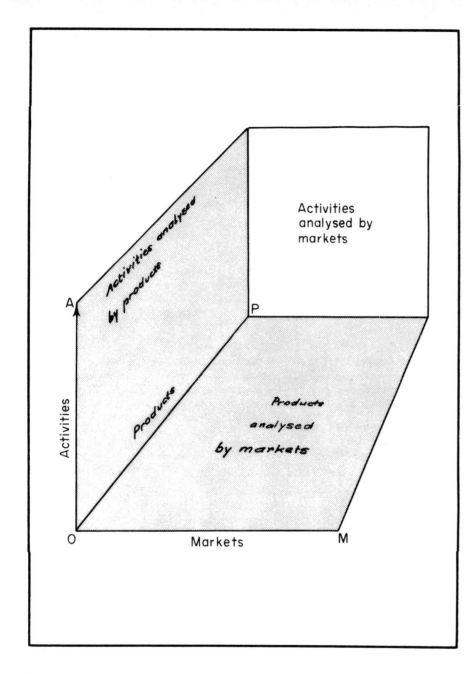

Activities
analysed by
markets

A

P

Activities analysed by products

Activities

products

Products analysed by markets

O

Markets

M

Diagram 6-4   Three dimensions in marketing

6.4 Marketing in a Business with Long-Term Contracts

The ratios in Diagram 6-1 are suitable for most manufacturing firms. If the firm manufactures on contract, however, particularly if the contracts tend to be long term, a different set of ratios is needed. In this situation marketing effort is related to obtaining orders which may not be delivered and invoiced, and hence appear in the firm's sales figure, for some months or years.

The key ratio remains the same but marketing contribution is defined as the value of orders obtained less marketing costs, less estimated variable contract costs. The set of ratios for this situation is shown in Diagram 6-6. Marketing management can improve its key ratio by:

1   Obtaining more profitable contracts; ratio J2 will then increase
2   Cutting the costs of getting an order; ratio J3 will then fall
3   Cutting the money tied up in marketing assets in relation to sales; ratio J4 will then increase
4   Increasing the volume of business being obtained now in relation to that obtained in the past; ratio J5 will increase.

The cost of getting an order (ratio J3) can be reduced by:

1   Improving the quotation success rate (ratio J5) by more effective tendering
2   Cutting the cost of making a quotation (ratio J6) by improving the efficiency of the tendering department.

Marketing assets are related to sales because there is more relationship between them and sales (the value of the work being done by the production side of the business) than between them and the orders being obtained. The investment in these assets in relation to sales volume can be reduced:

1   By prompt billing of progress claims; this will reduce ratio J8
2   By quicker debt collection; this will reduce ratio J9.

Retentions are a different problem to debtors but every effort needs to be made to satisfy the client and get the retention released. Maximum use of sales and distribution vehicles will help to keep ratio J11 down.

If the marketing management is helping the business to expand, ratio J5 (orders obtained during the period/sales during the period) will be greater than 100 per cent. Unfortunately a figure for ratio J5 greater than 100 per cent is ambiguous because as well as having the favourable meaning just mentioned it could also mean that sales for

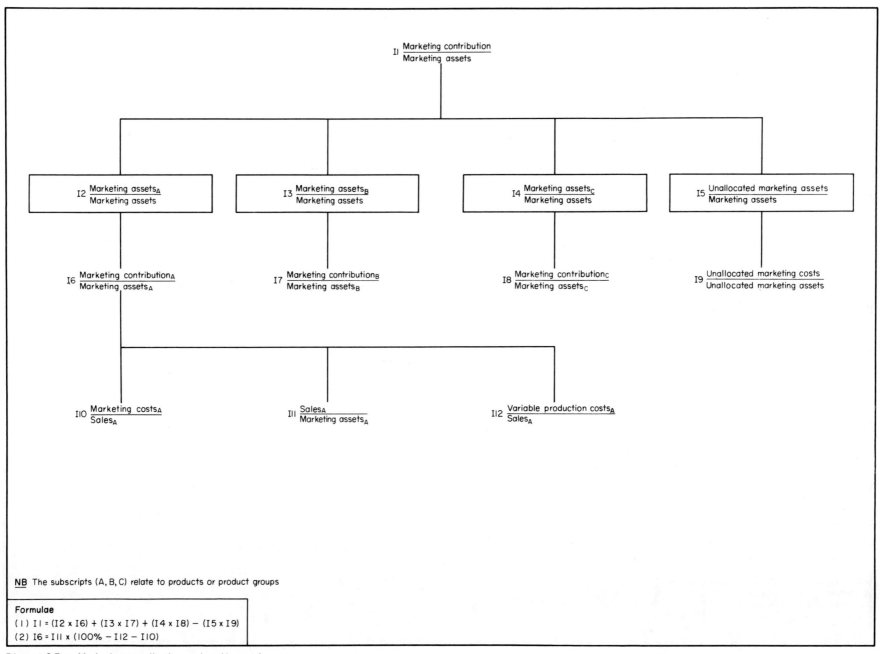

NB The subscripts (A, B, C) relate to products or product groups

Formulae

(1) I1 = (I2 x I6) + (I3 x I7) + (I4 x I8) − (I5 x I9)

(2) I6 = I11 x (100% − I12 − I10)

Diagram 6-5   Marketing contribution analysed by products

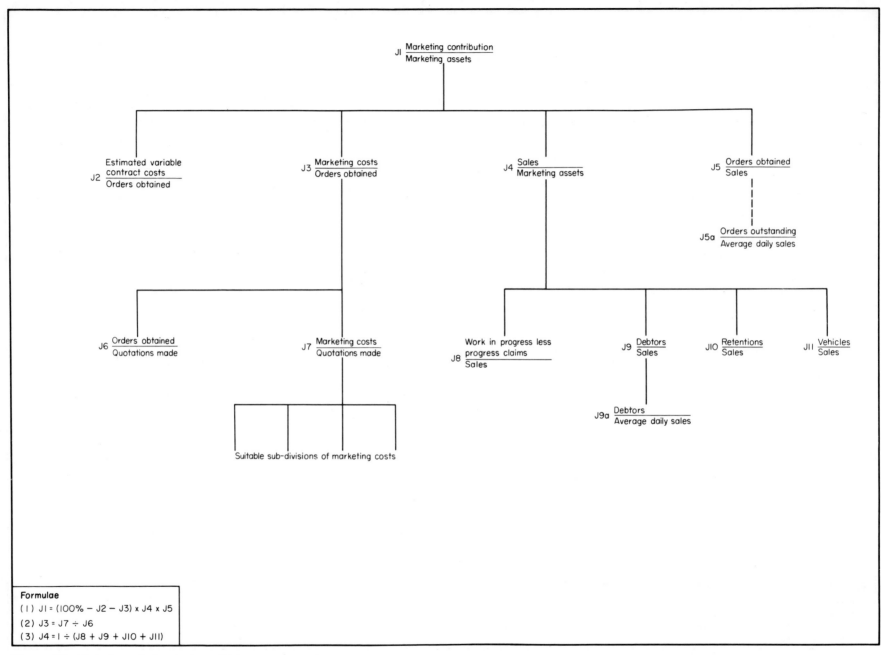

J1 $\dfrac{\text{Marketing contribution}}{\text{Marketing assets}}$

J2 $\dfrac{\text{Estimated variable contract costs}}{\text{Orders obtained}}$

J3 $\dfrac{\text{Marketing costs}}{\text{Orders obtained}}$

J4 $\dfrac{\text{Sales}}{\text{Marketing assets}}$

J5 $\dfrac{\text{Orders obtained}}{\text{Sales}}$

J5a $\dfrac{\text{Orders outstanding}}{\text{Average daily sales}}$

J6 $\dfrac{\text{Orders obtained}}{\text{Quotations made}}$

J7 $\dfrac{\text{Marketing costs}}{\text{Quotations made}}$

J8 $\dfrac{\text{Work in progress less progress claims}}{\text{Sales}}$

J9 $\dfrac{\text{Debtors}}{\text{Sales}}$

J9a $\dfrac{\text{Debtors}}{\text{Average daily sales}}$

J10 $\dfrac{\text{Retentions}}{\text{Sales}}$

J11 $\dfrac{\text{Vehicles}}{\text{Sales}}$

Suitable sub-divisions of marketing costs

Formulae

(1) J1 = (100% − J2 − J3) x J4 x J5

(2) J3 = J7 ÷ J6

(3) J4 = 1 ÷ (J8 + J9 + J10 + J11)

Diagram 6-6   Marketing ratios for a business with long-term contracts

the period had dropped because the production side of the business was falling down on deliveries. Such a state of affairs would be indicated by ratio J5a (orders outstanding/average daily sales) rising. This ratio measures the length of the order book in terms of the number of days' production. It also shows marketing management the average delivery date it can quote when giving rough estimates.

Ratio J5a is useful for liaison between production and sales in a contracting business. If it rises too high it may be very difficult to get orders unless and until production can be expanded. If it falls too low selling effort must be increased and/or thoughts turned to cutting back production.

What is too high or too low depends to some extent on the industry and the too high mark varies over the course of time with competitors' figures for delivery dates.

To calculate ratios J1 to J11 use data assembly and ratio calculation sheet 6-4 at the end of this chapter.

6.5 Selling

If the organisation is large enough it may be worth providing a further set of ratios to measure reasons for changes in ratio G8 in Diagram 6-1. This further set is shown in Diagram 6-7. It has been assumed that selling costs are partly representatives' remuneration and expenses and partly agents' commission. Agents will most probably be operating in territories where it is uneconomic to have representatives. There are three broad factors which would cause the ratio of selling costs/sales (ratio K1) to change:

1   Representatives' performance (that is the value of sales they obtain in relation to their own costs) might change, indicated by a change in ratio K5.
2   Agents' rate of commission might be altered; this would be shown up by a change in ratio K6.
3   The proportion of sales through representatives or agents might change, shown up by a movement in ratios K2 or K3. (These two ratios are complementary; if one goes down, the other must go up so that their sum is always 100 per cent.)

It will probably be worth having a separate set of ratios K1 to K6 for each major territory as an aid to controlling performance in different geographical areas. It is also worth keeping a comparative eye on the relative sizes of K5 and K6 so as to make sure that selling is being conducted by the most economical means for a territory.

It is dangerous to look at K5 and K6 in isolation, however. The growth of sales in the various representatives' and agents' territories must also be considered. Low costs

may not be enough to compensate for stagnating, or worse, declining sales. Representatives' performance is affected by three factors:

1   Average cost of a call (ratio K7)
2   Call success rate (ratio K8)
3   Average value of the order obtained from successful calls (ratio K9).

The sales manager will look at these ratios not only for his force overall but for individual representatives as well. Furthermore, he may well want to sub-divide ratios K7, K8 and K9 between calls made on new customers and repeat business.

A firm may well need to have a policy on how much of its representatives' time should be spent with existing customers and how much with potential customers. Too much on either could be equally fatal. Some firms' representatives may need to make 'keeping warm' calls not so much to obtain an order as to avoid losing the next one. This fact will need to be taken into account in interpreting the size of ratio K8.

To achieve overall success a sales manager and his representatives must maintain a balance between:

1   The desire to minimise the cost of a call by making more calls per day
2   The desire to maximise the call success rate by taking small value orders in large numbers and/or only calling on easy customers
3   The desire to maximise the value of orders by neglecting the smaller customer.

That is why all three ratios (K7 to K9) should be used, preferably for each representative.

To calculate ratios K1 to K9 use data assembly and ratio calculation sheet 6-5 at the end of this chapter.

6.6 Distribution

Only in the very largest businesses or in a firm where distribution costs are a very high proportion of sales income is it necessary to provide many ratios to monitor performance in this field. Nevertheless distribution is becoming increasingly important and a full set of ratios has been provided in Diagram 6-8, broken up by a number of horizontal lines. Managers in this area of a firm's operations can literally 'draw the line' at one of these lines and use the ratios above it and omit those below it.

These ratios assume that the distribution manager reports to the marketing manager, who monitors his performance by the ratio of distribution costs to sales (ratio G6 in Diagram 6-1 and L1 in Diagram 6-8).

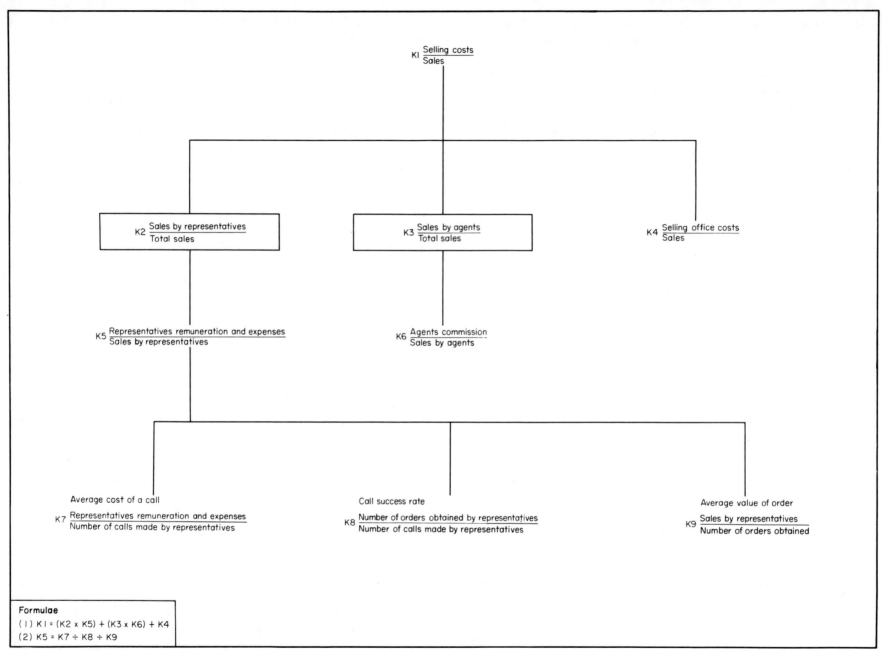

KI $\dfrac{\text{Selling costs}}{\text{Sales}}$

K2 $\dfrac{\text{Sales by representatives}}{\text{Total sales}}$

K3 $\dfrac{\text{Sales by agents}}{\text{Total sales}}$

K4 $\dfrac{\text{Selling office costs}}{\text{Sales}}$

K5 $\dfrac{\text{Representatives remuneration and expenses}}{\text{Sales by representatives}}$

K6 $\dfrac{\text{Agents commission}}{\text{Sales by agents}}$

Average cost of a call

K7 $\dfrac{\text{Representatives remuneration and expenses}}{\text{Number of calls made by representatives}}$

Call success rate

K8 $\dfrac{\text{Number of orders obtained by representatives}}{\text{Number of calls made by representatives}}$

Average value of order

K9 $\dfrac{\text{Sales by representatives}}{\text{Number of orders obtained}}$

Formulae

(1) $KI = (K2 \times K5) + (K3 \times K6) + K4$

(2) $K5 = K7 \div K8 \div K9$

Diagram 6-7   Ratios for sales management

120

The distribution manager is providing a service related to the distance he transports the firm's goods. The first two ratios he looks at are therefore ratios L2 and L3. These show him how many miles (or ton miles) of transport he is providing for each pound of sales (ratio L2) and what his costs per mile are (ratio L3). If ratio L2 rises so, obviously, does ratio L1 which is used to monitor his performance. Yet the number of miles the firm's goods are carried is largely outside his control. It is arguable, therefore, that ratio L2 should be part of the marketing manager's set of ratios and the distribution manager's responsibility should start at ratio L3.

If the distribution manager uses a number of different types of transport (such as British Rail, British Road Services and the company's own fleet) he needs suitable switching ratios (L4, L5 and L6) to measure how much is being transported by each method. Ratios L7, L8 and L9 show the cost of the different forms of transport.

The magnitude of the ratio of standing charges to miles run (ratio L10) is affected by the ratio of these charges to the maximum number of miles the fleet could run in the year (ratio L12)—to some extent a subjective judgement—and how much the fleet's capacity was used (ratio L13).

It is useful to divide running costs between wages, which are paid largely on a time basis, and other running costs (petrol, oil) which vary largely with distance run. This gives ratios L14 and L15. Ratio L16 (average speed of vehicle) completes the picture. The average wage rate (ratio L14) depends on:

1   Basic wage rate (L17)
2   Overtime rate (L18)
3   Amount of overtime put in (L19).

The average speed of the vehicles (ratio L16) is a function of:

1   Time spent on loading (L20)
2   Time spent on unloading (L21)
3   Time spent on running (L22)
4   Speed of the vehicle when running (L23).

Loading and unloading time depends on the efficiency of both the firm's staff and of its customers' staff. It also depends on the frequency of deliveries (or drops) and the value of each drop must also be borne in mind. The running speed of the vehicle depends on the law, traffic congestion and the time of day. Only the last of these three is in the transport manager's control.

Ratios L7, L8 and L9 show average *total* cost. When deciding whether to use his own or an outside fleet the transport manager has to consider in the short run his own fleet's *marginal* cost if it is operating below capacity. This marginal cost is shown by ratio L11. The costs of the firm's own fleet can be broken down into standing charges (ratio L10) and running costs (ratio L11). The former are incurred irrespective of the miles run (licence fees, garage rent and so on), the latter vary with the distance covered.

To calculate ratios L1 to L23 use data assembly and ratio calculation sheet 6.6 at the end of this chapter.

The ratios described above draw on analysis of the distribution function carried out at the Centre for Interfirm Comparison, and readers wishing to obtain standards for these ratios are advised to consider participation in the comparison schemes run by the Centre relating to the distribution operations of manufacturers in various industries, and also relating to commercial road haulage.

6.7 Stock Turnover and Customers' Creditworthiness

There are two further subjects with which marketing management should be concerned. They are stock turnover and customers' creditworthiness. The former is dealt with in Chapter 7, the latter in Chapter 8.

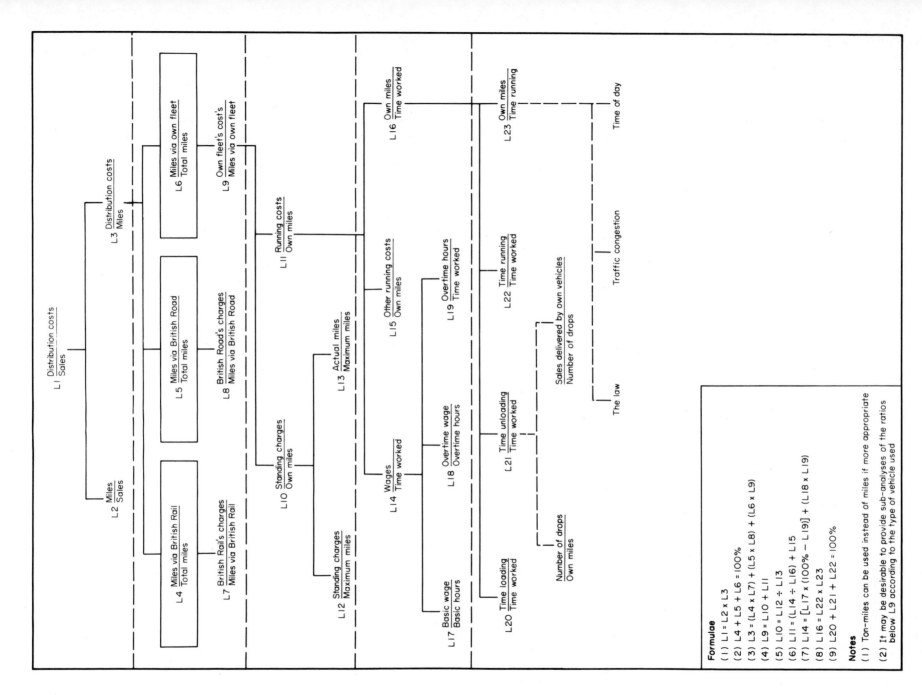

$L1 \dfrac{\text{Distribution costs}}{\text{Sales}}$

$L2 \dfrac{\text{Miles}}{\text{Sales}}$

$L3 \dfrac{\text{Distribution costs}}{\text{Miles}}$

$L4 \dfrac{\text{Miles via British Rail}}{\text{Total miles}}$

$L5 \dfrac{\text{Miles via British Road}}{\text{Total miles}}$

$L6 \dfrac{\text{Miles via own fleet}}{\text{Total miles}}$

$L7 \dfrac{\text{British Rail's charges}}{\text{Miles via British Rail}}$

$L8 \dfrac{\text{British Road's charges}}{\text{Miles via British Road}}$

$L9 \dfrac{\text{Own fleet's cost's}}{\text{Miles via own fleet}}$

$L10 \dfrac{\text{Standing charges}}{\text{Own miles}}$

$L11 \dfrac{\text{Running costs}}{\text{Own miles}}$

$L12 \dfrac{\text{Standing charges}}{\text{Maximum miles}}$

$L13 \dfrac{\text{Actual miles}}{\text{Maximum miles}}$

$L14 \dfrac{\text{Wages}}{\text{Time worked}}$

$L15 \dfrac{\text{Other running costs}}{\text{Own miles}}$

$L16 \dfrac{\text{Own miles}}{\text{Time worked}}$

$L17 \dfrac{\text{Basic wage}}{\text{Basic hours}}$

$L18 \dfrac{\text{Overtime wage}}{\text{Overtime hours}}$

$L19 \dfrac{\text{Overtime hours}}{\text{Time worked}}$

$L20 \dfrac{\text{Time loading}}{\text{Time worked}}$

$L21 \dfrac{\text{Time unloading}}{\text{Time worked}}$

$L22 \dfrac{\text{Time running}}{\text{Time worked}}$

$L23 \dfrac{\text{Own miles}}{\text{Time running}}$

$\dfrac{\text{Number of drops}}{\text{Own miles}}$

$\dfrac{\text{Sales delivered by own vehicles}}{\text{Number of drops}}$

The law

Traffic congestion

Time of day

Formulae

(1) L1 = L2 × L3

(2) L4 + L5 + L6 = 100%

(3) L3 = (L4 × L7) + (L5 × L8) + (L6 × L9)

(4) L9 = L10 + L11

(5) L10 = L12 ÷ L13

(6) L11 = (L14 ÷ L16) + L15

(7) L14 = [L17 × (100% − L19)] + (L18 × L19)

(8) L16 = L22 × L23

(9) L20 + L21 + L22 = 100%

Notes

(1) Ton-miles can be used instead of miles if more appropriate

(2) It may be desirable to provide sub-analyses of the ratios below L9 according to the type of vehicle used

Diagram 6-8   Ratios for the distribution manager

Ratios for the marketing director

Code letter	Item	Month or quarter to (date)					
A	Warehouse costs						
B	Distribution costs						
C	Advertising costs						
D	Selling costs						
E	Discounts						
F	Sales office costs						
G	Bad debts						
H	Marketing costs (A + B + C + D + E + F + G)						
K	Variable production costs						
L	Sub total (H + K)						
M	Sales						
N	Marketing contribution (M − L)						
P	Finished goods stock						
Q	Debtors						
R	Selling and distribution vehicles						
S	Marketing assets (P + Q + R)						

Data assembly sheet 6-1: *continued*

Ratios for the marketing director

Code letter	Item	Month or quarter to (date)					
T	No of orders or invoices						
W	Production cost of goods sold						
Y	No of working days in period						
Z	No of working days in year						
AA	No of calendar days in period						

Ratios for the marketing director

Ratio	Formula for calculation of ratio	Unit of measurement	Month or quarter to (date)					
G1 Marketing contribution/ Marketing assets	$N \times 100 \div S \times Z \div Y$	% pa						
G2 Marketing costs/ Sales	$H \times 100 \div M$	%						
G3 Sales/Marketing assets	$M \div S \times Z \div Y$	times per year						
G4 Variable production costs/Sales	$K \times 100 \div M$	%						
G5 Warehouse costs/ Sales	$A \times 100 \div M$	%						
G6 Distribution costs/Sales	$B \times 100 \div M$	%						
G7 Advertising costs/Sales	$C \times 100 \div M$	%						
G8 Selling costs/ Sales	$D \times 100 \div M$	%						
G9 Discounts/ Sales	$E \times 100 \div M$	%						
G10 Sales office costs/Sales	$F \times 100 \div M$	%						
G11 Bad debts/ Sales	$G \times 100 \div M$	%						
G12 Sales/ No of orders or invoices	$M \div T$	£ per order or invoice						
G13 Sales office costs/No of orders or invoices	$F \div T$	£ per order or invoice						

Ratios for the marketing director

Ratio		Formula for calculation of ratio	Unit of measurement	Month or quarter to (date)					
G14	Finished goods stock/Sales	P x 1000 ÷ (M x Z ÷ Y)	% pa						
G15	Debtors/Sales	Q x 1000 ÷ (M x Z ÷ Y)	% pa						
G16	Selling and distribution vehicles/ Sales	R x 1000 ÷ (M x Z ÷ Y)	% pa						
G17	Finished goods stock/Average daily production cost of goods sold	P x Z ÷ W	days						
G18	Debtors/Average daily sales	Q x AA ÷ M	days						

Distribution and selling costs: home and export analysis

Code letter	Item	Month or quarter to (date)					
A	Home distribution costs						
B	Export distribution costs						
C	Distribution costs (A + B)						
D	Home selling costs						
E	Export selling costs						
F	Selling costs (D + E)						
G	Home sales						
H	Export sales						
K	Sales (G + H)						

Distribution and selling costs: home and export analysis

Ratio		Formula for calculation of ratio	Unit of measurement	Month or quarter to (date)					
G6	Distribution costs/ Sales	C x 100 ÷ K	%						
G8	Selling costs/Sales	F x 100 ÷ K	%						
H1	Home sales/Total sales	G x 100 ÷ K	%						
H2	Home distribution costs/Home sales	A x 100 ÷ G	%						
H3	Export distribution costs/Export sales	B x 100 ÷ H	%						
H4	Home selling costs/ Home sales	D x 100 ÷ G	%						
H5	Export selling costs/ Export sales	E x 100 ÷ H	%						

Marketing contribution analysed by products

Code letter	Item	Total	Product group A	Product group B	Product group C	Unallocated
		(1)	(2)	(3)	(4)	(5)
A	Sales					
B	Variable production costs					
C	Marketing costs					
D	Subtotal (B + C)					
E	Marketing contribution (A − D)					
F	Average marketing assets					
G	No of working days in period					
H	No of working days in year					

Marketing contribution analysed by products

Ratio	Formula for calculation of ratio	Unit of measurement	Month or quarter to (date)					
I1 Marketing contribution/Marketing assets	E1 x 100 ÷ F1 x H ÷ G	% pa						
I2 Marketing assets (A)/Marketing assets	F2 x 100 ÷ F1	%						
I3 Marketing assets (B)/Marketing assets	F3 x 100 ÷ F1	%						
I4 Marketing assets (C)/Marketing assets	F4 x 100 ÷ F1	%						
I5 Unallocated marketing assets/Marketing assets	F5 x 100 ÷ F1	%						
I6 Marketing contribution (A)/Marketing assets (A)	E2 x 100 ÷ F2 x H ÷ G	% pa						
I7 Marketing contribution (B)/Marketing assets (B)	E3 x 100 ÷ F3 x H ÷ G	% pa						
I8 Marketing contribution (C)/Marketing assets (C)	E4 x 100 ÷ F4 x H ÷ G	% pa						
I9 Unallocated marketing costs/Unallocated marketing assets	C5 x 100 ÷ F5 x H ÷ G	% pa						
I10 Marketing cost (A)/Sales (A)	C2 x 100 ÷ A2	%						
I11 Sales (A)/Marketing assets (A)	A2 ÷ F2 x H ÷ G	times per year						
I12 Variable production costs (A)/Sales (A)	B2 x 100 ÷ A2	%						

Data assembly sheet 6-4

Marketing ratios for a business with long-term contracts

Code letter	Item	Month or quarter to (date)					
A	Orders outstanding at beginning of period						
B	Orders obtained during the period						
C	Sub total (A + B)						
D	Sales						
E	Orders outstanding at the end of the period (C − D)						
F	Estimated variable contract costs						
G	Marketing costs						
H	Sub total (F + G)						
K	Marketing contribution (B − H)						
L	Work in progress						
M	Progress claims						
N	Work in progress less progress claims (L − M)						
P	Debtors						
Q	Retentions						
R	Vehicles						
S	Marketing assets (N + P + Q + R)						

Marketing ratios for a business with long-term contracts

Code letter	Item	Month or quarter to (date)					
T	Quotations made						
W	No. of working days in period						
Y	No. of working days in year						
Z	No. of calendar days in period						

Marketing ratios for a business with long-term contracts

Ratio	Formula for calculation of ratio	Unit of measurement	Month or quarter to (date)					
J1 Marketing contribu-tion/ Marketing assets	$K \times 100 \div S \times Y \div W$	% pa						
J2 Estimated variable contract costs/Orders obtained	$F \times 100 \div B$	%						
J3 Marketing costs/ Orders obtained	$G \times 100 \div B$	%						
J4 Sales/Marketing assets	$D \div S \times Y \div W$	times per year						
J5 Orders obtained/ Sales	$B \times 100 \div D$	%						
J5(a) Orders outstanding/ Average daily sales	$E \times W \div D$	days						
J6 Orders obtained/ Quotations made	$B \times 100 \div T$	%						
J7 Marketing costs/ Quotations made	$G \times 100 \div T$	%						
J8 Work in progress less progress claims/Sales	$N \times 1000 \div (D \times Y \div W)$	‰ pa						
J9 Debtors/Sales	$P \times 1000 \div (D \times Y \div W)$	‰ pa						
J9(a) Debtors/Average daily sales	$P \times Z \div D$	days						
J10 Retentions/Sales	$Q \times 1000 \div (D \times Y \div W)$	‰ pa						
J11 Vehicles/Sales	$R \times 1000 \div (D \times Y \div W)$	‰ pa						

Data assembly sheet 6-5

Ratios for the sales manager

Code letter	Item	Month or quarter to (date)					
A	Representatives remuneration and expenses						
B	Agents' commission						
C	Selling office costs						
D	Selling costs (A + B + C)						
E	Sales by representatives						
F	Sales by agents						
G	Total sales (E + F)						
H	Number of calls made by representatives						
K	Number of orders obtained by representatives						

Ratios for the sales manager

Ratio	Formula for calculation of ratio	Unit of measurement	Month or quarter to (date)					
K1 Selling costs/ Sales	D x 100 ÷ G	%						
K2 Sales by representatives/ Total sales	E x 100 ÷ G	%						
K3 Sales by agents/ Total sales	F x 100 ÷ G	%						
K4 Selling office costs/ Sales	C x 100 ÷ G	%						
K5 Representatives' remuneration and expenses/Sales by representatives	A x 100 ÷ E	%						
K6 Agents' commission/ Sales by agents	B x 100 ÷ F	%						
Average cost of a call								
K7 Representatives' remuneration and expenses/No. of calls made by representatives	A ÷ H	£'s per call						
Call success rate								
K8 No of orders obtained by representatives/ No. of calls made by representatives	K x 100 ÷ H	%						
Average value of order								
K9 Sales by representatives/No. of orders obtained	E ÷ K	£'s per order						

Ratios for the distribution manager

Code letter	Item	Month or quarter to (date)					
A	Time loading						
B	Time unloading						
C	Time running						
D	Time worked (A + B + C)						
E	Basic hours						
F	Overtime hours						
G	Time worked (E + F) NB D should equal G						
H	Basic wage						
K	Overtime wage						
L	Wages (H + K)						
M	Other running costs						
N	Running costs (L + M)						
P	Standing charges						
Q	Own fleet's costs (N + P)						
R	British Rail's charges						
S	British Road's charges						
T	Distribution costs (Q + R + S)						

Ratios for the distribution manager

Code letter	Item	Month or quarter to (date)					
W	Own miles						
X	Miles via British Rail						
Y	Miles via British Road						
Z	Miles (W + X + Y)						
AA	Maximum miles per period						
AB	Sales						

Ratios for the distribution manager

Ratio	Formula for calculation of ratio	Unit of measurement	Month or quarter to (date)					
L1 Distribution costs/ Sales	T x 100 ÷ AB	%						
L2 Miles/Sales	Z ÷ AB	miles per £						
L3 Distribution costs/ Miles	T ÷ Z	£'s per mile						
L4 Miles via British Rail/Total miles	X x 100 ÷ Z	%						
L5 Miles via British Road/Total miles	Y x 100 ÷ Z	%						
L6 Miles via own fleet/Total miles	W x 100 ÷ Z	%						
L7 British Rail's charges/Miles via British Rail	R ÷ X	£'s per mile						
L8 British Road's charges/Miles via British Road	S ÷ Y	£'s per mile						
L9 Own fleet's costs/ Miles via own fleet	Q ÷ W	£'s per mile						
L10 Standing charges/ Own miles	P ÷ W	£'s per mile						
L11 Running costs/ Own miles	N ÷ W	£'s per mile						
L12 Standing charges/ Maximum miles	P ÷ AA	£'s per mile						

Ratio		Formula for calculation of ratio	Unit of measurement	Month or quarter to (date)					
L13	Actual miles/ Maximum miles	W x 100 ÷ AA	%						
L14	Wages/Time worked	L ÷ G	£'s per hour						
L15	Other running costs/ Own miles	M ÷ W	£'s per mile						
L16	Own miles/ Time worked	W ÷ G	miles per hour						
L17	Basic wage/ Basic hours	H ÷ E	£'s per hour						
L18	Overtime wage/ Overtime hours	K ÷ F	£'s per hour						
L19	Overtime hours/ Time worked	F x 100 ÷ G	%						
L20	Time loading/ Time worked	A x 100 ÷ D	%						
L21	Time unloading/ Time worked	B x 100 ÷ D	%						
L22	Time running/ Time worked	C x 100 ÷ D	%						
L23	Own miles/ Time running	W ÷ C	Miles per hour						

Chapter 7

Ratios for purchasing management

7.1 The Key Ratio

The key ratio which measures the success of the buyer is

$$M1 \qquad \frac{\text{Buying contribution}}{\text{Buying assets}}$$

Buying assets will probably consist of stocks of raw materials, bought-in parts and components, less creditors. Buying contribution is defined as sales value of production, less purchases, less buying costs.

Calculating the buying contribution is complicated, however, by the problem of the time lag between the purchase of an item and the eventual sale of the product incorporating that item. During that time lag, the item purchased is found successively in raw materials stock, work in progress, and finished goods stock. Thus, the purchases of one period are not necessarily related to the sales of that period and a ratio of purchases/sales is unlikely to be meaningful.

As the buyer is interested in the purchasing, rather than the selling end of the operation, it is preferable to adjust the sales figure rather than the figure for purchases. Ideally, purchases would be related to the estimated selling price of the product into which they are going to be manufactured. In practice this is unlikely to be possible. The best practical compromise is likely to be:

1   To adjust purchases for changes in raw materials stock and work in progress to get materials cost content of finished production, and

2   To use sales value of production (SVOP) instead of sales. SVOP is also needed for the ratios recommended for production management, so the one figure will serve two purposes. SVOP is defined as the estimated sales value of goods completed in a period. Details of how to calculate or to estimate it are given in Chapter 9.

7.2 Subsidiary Ratios

The subsidiary ratios which the buyer will want to monitor are shown in Diagram 7-1. He can improve his key ratio (ratio M1) by:

1   Obtaining lower prices from suppliers; ratio M2 will go down.
2   Reducing the cost of placing an order in relation to the value purchased; ratio M3 will go down.
3   Carrying less stock; ratio M4 will go down.
4   Obtaining longer credit from suppliers; ratio M5 will increase.

There are two ways of reducing the cost of buying in relation to the value of the itmes purchased (ratio M3):

1   Cut the costs of placing an order, measured by ratio M6 (but if less time is spent on shopping around a less favourable price may be paid and ratio M2 will go up)
2   Increase the amount purchased at any one time, measured by ratio M7 (but this will increase the amount of stock carried and ratio M4 will go up).

Similarly better prices may be obtained from quantity discounts and prompt payment but this will increase stock (ratio M4) and decrease credit taken (ratio M5) respectively.

The buyer must constantly weigh these pros and cons against each other. His success in doing so will be measured by his key ratio (M1) which combines the results of the various trade-offs he must make.

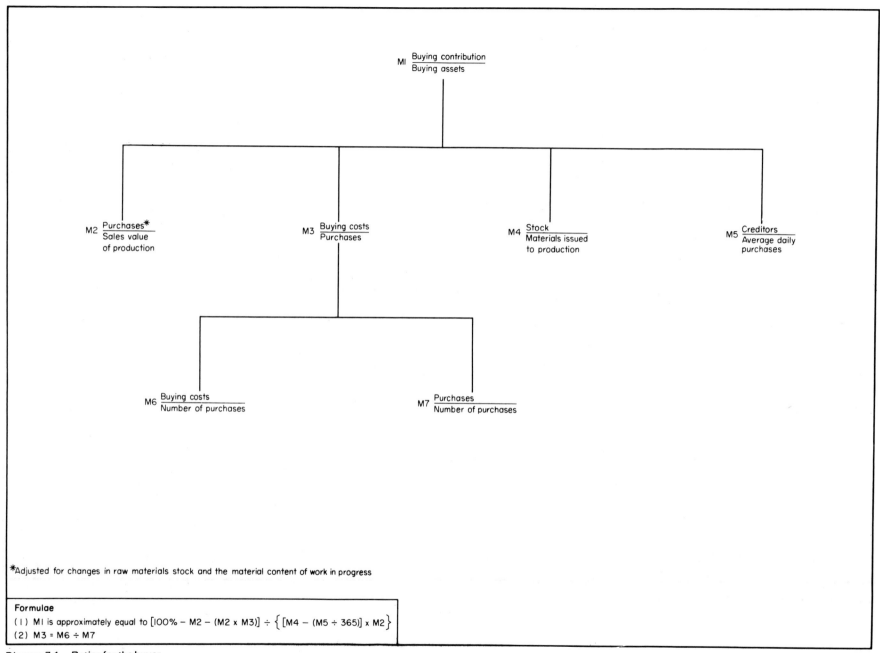

M1 $\dfrac{\text{Buying contribution}}{\text{Buying assets}}$

M2 $\dfrac{\text{Purchases*}}{\text{Sales value of production}}$

M3 $\dfrac{\text{Buying costs}}{\text{Purchases}}$

M4 $\dfrac{\text{Stock}}{\text{Materials issued to production}}$

M5 $\dfrac{\text{Creditors}}{\text{Average daily purchases}}$

M6 $\dfrac{\text{Buying costs}}{\text{Number of purchases}}$

M7 $\dfrac{\text{Purchases}}{\text{Number of purchases}}$

*Adjusted for changes in raw materials stock and the material content of work in progress

Formulae

(1) M1 is approximately equal to $[100\% - \text{M2} - (\text{M2} \times \text{M3})] \div \left\{ [\text{M4} - (\text{M5} \div 365)] \times \text{M2} \right\}$

(2) M3 = M6 ÷ M7

Diagram 7-1 Ratios for the buyer

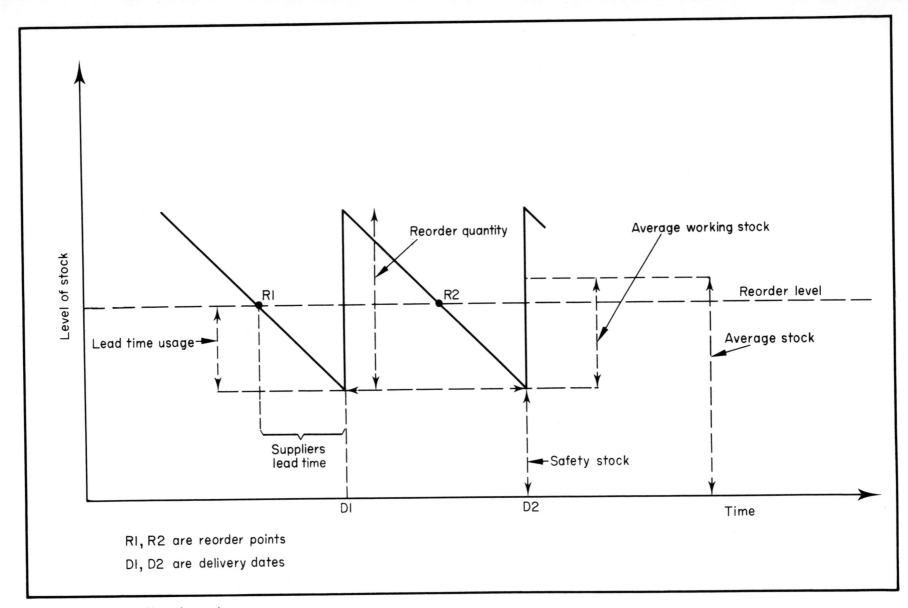

Diagram 7-2   Terms used in stock control

One item is missing, however. If the buyer cuts stock too low, production may be held up for the lack of some item and the money lost by production will outweigh any savings from lower stock. This is a difficult cost to measure—though a good system of labour cost control can quantify the cost of time waiting for materials—and even harder to attribute fairly. Did production control give the stores adequate warning? Could they, or the shopfloor superintendents, have reallocated work so that less time was lost? At this level, a quick meeting of all concerned, and a sensible prompt decision, is worth a multitude of ratios. It is suggested therefore that this cost should be left out of the system of ratio control.

To calculate ratios M1 to M7 use data assembly and ratio calculation sheet 7-1 at the end of this chapter.

7.3 Stock Control

It would not be appropriate to include in this book a long dissertation on stock control, but the subject is of such vital importance to most businesses, and concerns so many of the managers within a business, that it would seem desirable to include a few paragraphs on the subject and its associated ratios.

As with so many other aspects of management, stock control consists of balancing conflicting demands to arrive at the compromise which is optimum for the business as a whole. Because the demands are variable over time, as well as being conflicting, any optimum compromise will be only a temporary solution. A change in one of the factors will call for a new point of balanced compromise.

The buyer and the production manager will be concerned with the level of raw material stock. The production manager will also be involved in the amount of work in progress and finished goods stock. The sales manager is as concerned as the production manager with the level of finished stock available for delivery to the company's customers. Finally, the finance director is sure to want to keep the level of stock down as it is he who can see most clearly the problems associated with financing high levels of stock.

Diagram 7-2 shows the main terms used in stock control. The heavy black 'saw-tooth' line shows the level of stock dropping over time as it is consumed and then rising sharply as a delivery is received, only to drop again as consumption continues.

Stock is reordered at *reorder points* R1 and R2 when the level of stock falls to the *reorder level*. Between reordering and receipt of the goods is an interval of time called the *supplier's lead time* (measured by ratio N2, see page 147). Deliveries are received at D1 and D2.

Safety stock is held as an insurance against changes in usage, and deliveries taking longer than the expected lead time. *Average working stock* will be seen to be equal to half the *reorder quantity*. *Average stock* is equal to average working stock

plus safety stock. The *reorder level* is the lead time usage plus the safety stock.

The level of safety stock is related to the 'satisfaction levels' set by management (see below), the degree of unpredictability of demand, and the degree of unreliability of suppliers (measured by ratio N3, see page 147).

Stock control starts with the sales manager's forecast of demand for the range of products which the company supplies. At this point two policy decisions need to be taken:

1   In the light of the expected demand for each item in the range is it economical to continue to keep some items in the range at all?

2   What satisfaction level (the ratio of orders fulfilled without delay to orders received) is to be aimed at for different items? In arriving at a decision on this, it is necessary to bear in mind on the one hand the profit that might be lost if the item is out of stock, and on the other the cost of stocking and ordering it. It must also be remembered that the level of stock necessary to achieve different satisfaction levels rises steeply at the higher levels, Diagram 7-3 shows that it is uneconomic always to go for 100 per cent satisfaction levels.

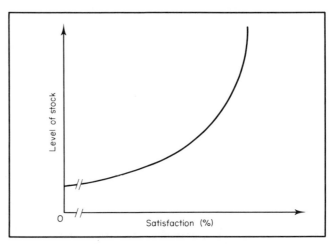

Diagram 7-3   Stock and satisfaction level

At this stage it is often useful to apply the 80/20 rule. This rule is also referred to as Pareto analysis, after the economist who invented it, and also as *ABC* analysis. It states that it is likely that 80 per cent by value of sales will be accounted for by 20 per cent of the items in the range and 80 per cent of the value of stock is likely to be accounted for by 20 per cent of the items in the stores. The *ABC* analysis is:

> *A* items are those which account for the top 80 per cent by value of turnover
>
> *B* items are those which account for the next 15 per cent by value of turnover
>
> *C* items are those which account for the bottom 5 per cent by value of turnover.

The first practical application of the rule and analysis is that the more sophisticated stock control techniques can be applied to the relatively few *A* items whilst the *B* and *C* items are dealt with by more rudimentary methods.

The essence of stock control theory is that the larger the quantity ordered at any one time:

1   The lower the ordering cost per item
2   The higher the holding cost per item.

A typical pattern for these costs and quantities is shown in Diagram 7-4.

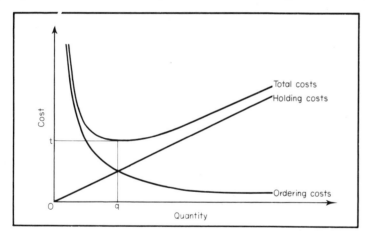

Diagram 7-4   Stock holding and ordering costs related to quantity

Holding costs rise steadily as the quantity ordered and held in stock increases. Ordering costs initially drop rapidly as quantity ordered increases but further increases in quantity cause only small decreases in cost. The total cost curve is the sum of the holding and ordering cost curves. It therefore drops rapidly to a minimum and thereafter rises gradually. The practical consequence of this cost/quantity pattern is

that, whereas orders for quantities *smaller* than that which minimises total cost (the economic order quantity—see below) cause a rapid increase in costs, orders for *larger* quantities have a less deleterious effect on costs. In other words, quantities equal to or slightly above the economic order quantity will minimise costs. Diagram 7-4 shows that there is an ordering quantity *q* at which total costs *t* are at a minimum. This quantity (*q*) can be divided into annual usage to get the optimum reordering frequency *f* in times per year. The actual values of *q, t* and *f* vary from item to item, from firm to firm, and over time. Nevertheless, as a generalisation, costs can be minimised if:

1   Items of small value are ordered in bulk at long intervals
2   Items of high value are ordered in small quantities at short intervals.

Books on stock control show that the economic ordering quantity (*q* in Diagram 7-4) is given by the formula

$$q = \sqrt{\frac{2AB}{CI}}$$

where

A = quantity needed per year
B = cost per order
C = value of one unit of the item
I = inventory holding cost per year as a decimal of the value of the inventory.

The application of the formula needs modification when there are price discounts for quantity orders.

Once the economic order quantity (*q*) has been calculated, the optimum reordering frequency (*f*) can be derived by dividing *q* into the quantity needed per year (*A*). There is then a choice between using:

1   A fixed order quantity system, based on *q*, or
2   A periodic review system, based on *f*.

To pursue this very important subject further would be outside the scope of this book. (Those interested are recommended to read *Stock Control in Manufacturing Industries,* A. B. Thomas, Gower Press, 1968). Space must be found however to mention one, relatively unsophisticated, method of stock control based on fixed order quantity, namely the 'two bin' or 'last bag' system.

This system is very suitable for the *C* items mentioned above. In it a quantity equal to the reorder level of the item is placed in a separate, second, bin or last bag, the remainder of the item being stored normally, (in the first bin etc.). Once the ordinary stock is exhausted and it is necessary to go to the second bin or last bag this is the signal to reorder the economic order quantity. When a delivery is received the second bin is topped up to the reorder level and the balance is placed in the first bin.

7.4 Further Subsidiary Ratios

In addition to his key ratio and the six subsidiary ratios shown in Diagram 7-1, the buyer will want some further ratio information on price, delivery, quality, the reliability and financial stability of his suppliers, and his degree of dependance on individual suppliers. The ratios which are suitable are discussed in the following paragraphs.

Changes in *price* can be measured in one or other of two ways. If a firm operates a standard costing system then the ratio to use would be

N1 $$\frac{\text{Price variance}}{\text{Budgeted purchases}}$$

the price variance being the difference between the budgeted price and the actual price, times the budgeted quantity.

If a firm does not have a standard costing system, price changes can be measured by an index number. Details of the method of calculating an index number are given in the work sheet at the end of this chapter. If a firm purchases a wide range of items, the work of calculating the index may be reduced by applying the 80/20 rule (see page 145-6). In this case the buyer would select the 20 per cent of the items that account for 80 per cent of the value of his purchases and measure all price changes for them and only measure the changes for a sample of the remaining 80 per cent of items which will only account for 20 per cent of the value.

A rise in prices is the signal for action on one or more of the following fronts:

1   Negotiation of price reductions/larger discounts
2   Consideration of larger purchases to get better prices
3   Consideration of alternative materials
4   Consideration of alternative suppliers
5   Improved efficiency within the firm
6   Consideration of price increases to customers.

Suppliers' lead time can be measured by dividing the value of orders outstanding at any one time by the average daily value of purchases.

N2 $$\frac{\text{Value of orders outstanding}}{\text{Average daily value of purchases}}$$

Any increase in this ratio will mean that:

1   The reorder level will need to be raised, and/or
2   The reorder review period will need to be shortened.

Suppliers' reliability can be measured by dividing the value of orders overdue at any one time by the average daily value of purchases.

N3 $$\frac{\text{Value of orders overdue}}{\text{Average daily value of purchases}}$$

Any increase in this ratio (i.e. an increase in *un*reliability) will mean that safety stock levels may need to be raised.

Increases in suppliers' lead time and/or unreliability may make it desirable:

1   To review sources of supply
2   To advise sales and production of the need to quote longer delivery dates to customers.

Quality can be measured by the ratio of

N4 $$\frac{\text{Value of goods returned and claims agreed}}{\text{Purchases}}$$

Any tendancy for this ratio to rise is a warning to:

1   Review suppliers to find a more reliable one
2   Query prices quoted. Is poor quality a by-product of too low a price?
3   Query delivery times quoted. Are the suppliers being given too little notice of requirements?

To calculate ratios N1 to N4 use data assembly and ratio calculation sheet 7.2 at the end of this chapter.

Financial stability of supplier

No buyer wants his suppliers suddenly to go out of business leaving him to get another supplier in a hurry with resulting uncompetitive prices. The buyer must therefore be aware of any adverse trends in his suppliers' financial standing. The main ratios to examine are the trends in

N5 $$\frac{\text{Current assets}}{\text{Current liabilities}}$$

N6 $$\frac{\text{Quick assets}}{\text{Current liabilities}}$$

N7 $\dfrac{\text{Net profit after tax}}{\text{Equity capital}}$

N8 $\dfrac{\text{Fixed costs}}{\text{Sales}}$

A decline in the first three, or a rise in the last one, are all warning signs either to start looking for alternate sources of supply or to offer assistance if the nature of the relationship between your firm and your supplier makes that appropriate or necessary.

These ratios, and others relating to the financial standing of a firm, are discussed more fully in Chapter 8.

It is usually wise to have more than one source of supply for any item. This spreads and therefore diminishes the risk of the failure of a supplier. It also helps to maintain a healthy bargaining position between purchaser and seller. Conversely it is unlikely to be desirable to spread purchases so widely as to be always buying in minimum quantities. This puts up both the price and the buying costs.

A balance needs to be struck between the two extremes. A useful set of ratios to have in this connection is

N9 $\dfrac{\text{Purchases from each supplier}}{\text{Total purchases}}$

If possible this ratio should be calculated both for separate items and for purchases as a whole. Cutting down the range of items purchased and/or stocked is likely to lead to a reduction both in purchasing costs and in stock carried. These are both courses of action where the application of the 80/20 rule is helpful.

To calculate ratios N5 to N9 use data assembly and ratio calculation sheet 7.3 at the end of this chapter.

Ratios for the buyer

Code letter	Item	Month or quarter to (date)					
A	Raw materials stock at beginning of period						
B	Purchases						
C	Sub total (A + B)						
D	Raw materials stock at end of period						
E	Materials issued to production (C—D)						
F	Work in progress at beginning of period						
G	Production cost (other than materials)						
H	Sub total (E + F + G)						
K	Work in progress at end of period						
L	Production cost of goods made (H — K)						
M	Finished goods stock at beginning of period						
N	Sub total (L + M)						
P	Finished goods stock at end of period						
Q	Production cost of goods sold (N — P)						
R	Sales						
S	Sales value of production (L x R ÷ Q)						
T	Buying costs						
W	Buying contribution (S — E — T — F + K)						

Ratios for the buyer

Code Letter	Item	Month or Quarter to (date)					
Y	Average creditors						
Z	Number of purchases						
AA	Average buying assets ([(A + D) ÷ 2] − Y)						
AB	No. of working days in period						
AC	No. of working days in year						
AD	No. of calendar days in period						

Ratios for the buyer

Ratio	Formula for calculation of ratio	Unit of measurement	Month or quarter to (date)					
M1 Buying contribution/ Buying assets	W x 100 ÷ AA x AC ÷ AB	% pa						
M2 Purchases/ Sales value of production	(E − F + K) x 100 ÷ S	%						
M3 Buying costs/ Purchases	T x 100 ÷ B	%						
M4 Stock/ Materials issued to production	[(A + D) ÷ 2] ÷ (E ÷ AB)	days						
M5 Creditors/ Average daily purchases	Y ÷ (B ÷ AD)	days						
M6 Buying costs/ No. of purchases	T ÷ Z	£ per order						
M7 Purchases/ No. of purchases	B ÷ Z	£ per order						

Subsidiary ratios for the buyer

Code letter	Item	Month or quarter to (date)					
A	Budgeted purchases						
B	Purchases						
C	Price variance						
D	Value of goods returned and claims agreed						
E	Value of orders outstanding						
F	Value of orders overdue						
G	No. of working days in period						

Ratio		Formula for calculation of ratio	Unit of measurement	Month or quarter to (date)					
N1	Price variance/ Budgeted purchases	C x 100 ÷ A	%						
N2	Suppliers' lead time								
	Value of orders outstanding/Average daily value of purchases	E ÷ (B ÷ G)	Days						
N3	Suppliers' reliability								
	Value of orders overdue/Average daily value of purchases	F ÷ (B ÷ G)	Days						
N4	Quality								
	Value of goods returned and claims agreed/Purchases	D x 100 ÷ B	%						

Financial stability of supplier

Code letter	Item	Supplier					
		A	B	C			
A	Quick assets						
B	Other current assets						
C	Current assets (A + B)						
D	Current liabilities						
E	Equity capital						
F	Sales						
G	Fixed costs						
H	All other costs including tax						
K	Sub total (G + H)						
L	Net profit after tax (F-K)						
M	Purchases from each supplier						
N	Total purchases						

Ratio	Formula for calculation of ratio	Unit of measurement	Supplier					
			A	B				
N5 Current assets/ Current liabilities	C ÷ D	Times						
N6 Quick assets/ Current liabilities	A ÷ D	Times						
N7 Net profit after tax/Equity capital	L x 100 ÷ E	%						
N8 Fixed costs/ Sales	G x 100 ÷ F	%						
N9 Purchases from each supplier/ Total purchases	M x 100 ÷ N	%						

NB It is assumed that the figures for each supplier relate to a year. If this assumption is not correct then ratio N7 should be adjusted to put it on an annual basis.

Chapter 8

Ratios for financial management

The financial management of a company is generally concerned with:

1   Minimising the amount of tax the company pays
2   Raising long and short-term finance
3   Maintaining liquidity
4   Supervising investments
5   Relations between the company and the stock exchange (if the company is quoted)
6   Supervising accounting and data processing activities.

The ratios that should be used to monitor and control these aspects of the company's business are described in this chapter.

8.1 Minimising the Rate of Tax

The subject of taxation is very complicated. Moreover it is a field where information is rendered obsolete at a very rapid rate by changes in legislation. It is proposed therefore to deal with this subject only very briefly in this book. Financial management will attempt to minimise the ratio of

O1 $$\frac{\text{Taxation}}{\text{Net profit before tax}}$$

Among the things which affect the size of this ratio are: the company's status (a close company or not); it location (is it in a development area); current tax legislation; and the source of its profits (are they from overseas and have they been remitted). In pinpointing areas where action may be taken to reduce this ratio it may be useful to

subdivide it according to:

1   The method of calculating the tax (income tax, corporation tax, capital gains tax and so on)
2   The geographical source of income being taxed
3   The subsidiary or division earning the income.

Detailed advice on how to improve ratio O1 should be obtainable from the firm's auditors or a consultant specialising in taxation.

8.2 Raising Finance

The object of raising part of a company's funds from sources other than its ordinary shareholders is to increase the rate of return on their capital. This process is known as gearing (or leverage in America). The underlying idea is very simple. A firm borrows money on which it pays x per cent interest. It invests this money in assets from which it earns y per cent. Provided that y per cent is greater than x per cent the difference is pure gain to the equity shareholder or owner of a business.

Obviously there are risks attached to such a policy. If the rate of interest paid rises and/or the rate of profit earned falls so that the former becomes greater than the latter, the difference is pure loss to the equity shareholder.

Another feature of gearing which may be considered to be a disadvantage by some people is that gearing magnifies any change in the profitability of a firm's assets so that the return on equity capital fluctuates more widely than the change in the return on assets. The following example illustrates this point:

Year	1	2
Balance Sheet	£	£
Equity capital	500	500
Loan capital	500	500
Total capital	1000	1000
and total assets		
Profit and loss account		
Profit from use of assets	150	100
Interest on loan capital	25	25
Net profit	125	75
Ratios		
Profit/Assets	15%	10%
Interest/Loan capital	5%	5%
Net profit/Equity capital	25%	15%

A drop in the profit on assets ratio of 33½ per cent [(15 per cent − 10 per cent) ÷ 15 per cent] has caused a drop in the return on equity capital of 40 per cent [(25 per cent − 15 per cent) ÷ 25 per cent]. Two points should however be noted:

1   In both years the return to the equity shareholder is greater than it would have been if the firm had not financed part of its assets with loan capital

2   If the profit from the use of the assets in year 3 rises to the year 1 level of £150 a 50 per cent [(15 per cent − 10 per cent) ÷ 10 per cent] increase in underlying profitability will lead to a 66⅔ per cent [(25 per cent − 15 per cent) ÷ 15 per cent] increase in the return on equity capital.

Another advantage of gearing is that while profits and asset values tend to rise in a period of inflation the liability to repay the loan capital is fixed in money terms, which means that in real terms it is a decreasing liability. Anyone buying a house on a mortgage is benefiting from this aspect of gearing.

The true cost to a company of any interest payment is the nominal rate

(a)   less the effect of corporation tax (provided it is an allowable deduction— debenture interest is but a preference dividend is not)

(b)   less the effect of inflation

(c)   plus the effect of any issue expenses.

For example

A company has a 7% debenture; issue expenses were 3%; corporation tax is 40%; inflation is 4% pa.

In order to pay 7% on the nominal amount of the debentures it is necessary to earn 7% x 100 ÷ 97 = 7.21% on the £97 actually obtained by the company after deducting the issue expenses from each £100 subscribed by the debenture holders. Debenture interest is an allowable deduction for corporation tax so the cost to the company is therefore

$$7.21\% \times (100 - 40) = 4.32\% \text{ in } \textit{money} \text{ terms}$$

With inflation at 4% the cost to the company is

$$(104.32 \div 1.04) - 100\% = 0.30\% \text{ in } \textit{real} \text{ terms}$$

NB. This rate of interest should be compared with the return on a project only after deducting both corporation tax and the effect of inflation on costs and income. As issue expenses, inflation and corporation tax effect different sources of finance in different degrees it is important to use the real cost of finance in capital budgeting decisions although for the sake of simplicity this is not done in this book.

It is worth while to monitor four main ratios in connection with gearing. They can all be plotted on the same graph. The four ratios and their relationship are shown in Diagram 8-1. The relationship expressed in this and the next two diagrams were developed by the Centre for Interfirm Comparison and are used in certain of its schemes.

The algebraic relationship between the ratios in Diagram 8-1 is as follows:

$$P1 = P2 + (P2 - P3) \times P4$$

Financial management's aim in raising finance is to maximise the difference between ratio P2 and ratio P3 over the likely range of ratio P3 in the medium term. It is because ratio P3 is likely to fluctuate in the short term (say up to three years) that the success of a firm's financial policy is best measured over the medium term (say three to six years).

To calculate ratios P1 to P4 use data assembly and ratio calculation sheet 8-1 at the end of this chapter.

Subsidiary ratios which should also be examined fall into two groups: ratios showing the constituent parts of the borrowed capital total and the rate of interest paid to each source of borrowed capital—*make-up ratios*—and the ratios which lenders and potential lenders look at when assessing a company's financial strength—*constraint ratios*, so called because they measure the factors which act as constraints to the amount a firm can borrow.

Examining the ratios in the first sub-group shows which sources of finance have the most expensive rate of interest and which the cheapest. Management's task is to decrease the former and increase the latter—at least proportionately.

The second sub-group of ratios indicates which sources of finance are relatively untapped and from which, to increase the company's gearing, it should increase its borrowing.

The action outlined in the previous two paragraphs is, of course, subject to the

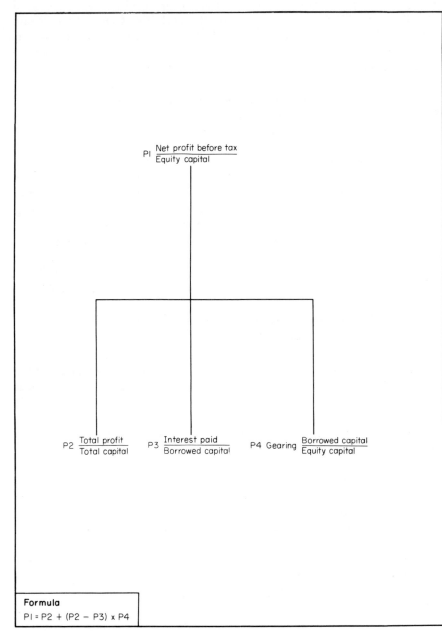

$$P1 \quad \frac{\text{Net profit before tax}}{\text{Equity capital}}$$

$$P2 \quad \frac{\text{Total profit}}{\text{Total capital}} \qquad P3 \quad \frac{\text{Interest paid}}{\text{Borrowed capital}} \qquad P4 \quad \text{Gearing} \quad \frac{\text{Borrowed capital}}{\text{Equity capital}}$$

Formula

$P1 = P2 + (P2 - P3) \times P4$

Diagram 8-1   Gearing and return on equity.
With acknowledgements to the Centre for Interfirm Comparison.

constraint factors which, as already mentioned, potential lenders look at. These factors will be examined in a later part of this chapter.

Any action in the field of gearing needs to be considered in the context of long term movements in the rate of interest. What might appear to be a high rate of interest at the time of borrowing may be low in relation to the average rate of interest over the life of the loan. Or, of course, vice versa.

The flexibility of repayment and indeed of rates of interest is another important consideration. A debenture commits the company to paying interest for a fixed number of years but it does not have to be repaid until the end of its life (usually measured in decades). A bank overdraft does not commit a company to any particular length of time for paying interest and it can be repaid when and if it suits the company, but it will have to be repaid when the bank (or the government through the bank) wants it, which may not be at all convenient for the company. Moreover the rate of interest charged will fluctuate.

At this point it is worth examining the sources, other than the ordinary shareholder, from which a firm can raise finance. They include the following (a note has been added of the relevant interest payment):

1   Preference shares (preference dividend)
2   Debentures ⎫
3   Loans ⎬ (debenture, loan and overdraft interest)
4   Overdrafts ⎭
5   Trade and expense creditors (cash discounts lost)
6   Corporation and/or income tax provisions ⎫
7   Income tax reserves and deferred taxation ⎬ (nil)
8   Investment grants ⎭
9   Hire purchase ⎫ (the interest element as opposed to the
10   Leasing ⎬ repayment element in the charge)
11   Debt factoring (the interest element as opposed to the ledger keeping and debt collection element in the charge)
12   Bill discounting (bill discount)

Traditional measures of gearing include only the first two items in borrowed capital. This restriction may stem from the fact that prior to the Companies Act 1967, information as to the amount of interest paid which had to be disclosed was limited to these two items. I prefer to include all of the items in the above list.* If any reader feels that this is going too far, or finds that there are difficulties in getting the necessary information, the items which are not to be included in borrowed capital and interest

*The arguments for this and a suggested accounting treatment for leased assets are set out in 'Towards a new measure and use of gearing'. C.A. Westwick, *Accounting & Business Research,* No. 1 Winter 1970, pp 18 to 29.

paid must be subtracted from assets, and profits before interest, respectively (see data assembly sheet at end of chapter).

Let us now look at the two groups of ratios already mentioned—the make-up ratios and the constraint ratios.

Make-up ratios

This group can be divided into two sub-groups. In the first, the interest paid on each constituent part of borrowed capital is related to the relevant average amount borrowed to give the rate of interest paid on each part of borrowed capital. For example:

$$\frac{\text{Debenture interest}}{\text{Debentures}} \text{ (per cent)}$$

$$\frac{\text{Interest on overdraft}}{\text{Average overdraft}} \text{ (per cent).}$$

To calculate ratios P5-1 to P5-12 use data assembly and ratio calculation sheet 8-2 at the end of this chapter.

In the second sub-group, each constituent of borrowed capital is related to the total amount of borrowed capital to show the proportion raised from each source. For example:

$$\frac{\text{Debentures}}{\text{Total borrowed capital}} \text{ (per cent)}$$

$$\frac{\text{Average overdraft}}{\text{Total borrowed capital}} \text{ (per cent).}$$

To calculate ratios P6-1 to P6-12 use data assembly and ratio calculation sheet 8-3 at the end of this chapter.

Constraint factors

First, there are the cover ratios:

1 Interest cover

P7 $$\frac{\text{Total profit}}{\text{Interest paid}}$$

shows how vulnerable the lender's interest receipts are to a drop in the borrower's profit.

2 Asset cover

P8 $$\frac{\text{Total assets}}{\text{Borrowed capital}}$$

is an indication of the safety of the lender's capital.

It is said that lenders require these two ratios to be not less than three times, but there are no doubt many exceptions to this rule of thumb in practice. Interest cover is considered the more important of the two. As Professor Paish says, a passenger is normally more interested in the speed of a ship than in the number of lifeboats.

When a company has a number of classes of loan, preference and ordinary capital, each of which has a particular place in the queue for interest or dividends the priority percentage method can be used for measuring the cover of each payment. For example, 'Five per cent debentures 0-3, preference shares 4-20, ordinary dividend 21-40, reserves 41-100' where each figure is a percentage of last year's profit after tax but before debenture interest and preference dividends.

A major constraint on borrowing is the need to maintain the company's liquidity position. The ratios to measure this are described in the next section.

8.3 Maintaining Liquidity

Liquidity ratios should be used not only by financial management to help maintain the firm's liquidity but by the firm's marketing and purchasing management as well. The former need to make sure that the company is selling to firms which are likely to be liquid enough to pay for their purchases. The latter wants to avoid the disruption to the company's inward flow of materials and parts which would result from a supplier going into liquidation.

1 The current ratio

P9 $$\frac{\text{Current assets}}{\text{Current liabilities}}$$

is one test of liquidity—it looks at the assets available to pay liabilities falling due soon.

2 The quick ratio

P10 $$\frac{\text{Quick assets}}{\text{Current liabilities}}$$

is another, more stringent, test of liquidity in that it concentrates on those assets which can be quickly turned into cash—debtors, marketable securities and cash itself; stock is excluded.

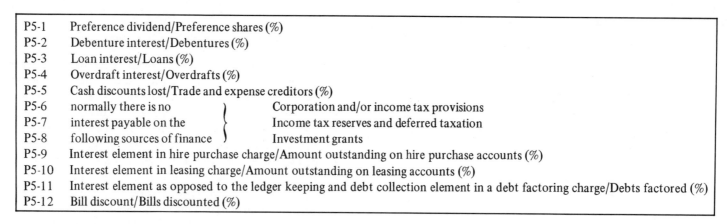

P5-1   Preference dividend/Preference shares (%)
P5-2   Debenture interest/Debentures (%)
P5-3   Loan interest/Loans (%)
P5-4   Overdraft interest/Overdrafts (%)
P5-5   Cash discounts lost/Trade and expense creditors (%)
P5-6   normally there is no   Corporation and/or income tax provisions
P5-7   interest payable on the   }   Income tax reserves and deferred taxation
P5-8   following sources of finance   Investment grants
P5-9   Interest element in hire purchase charge/Amount outstanding on hire purchase accounts (%)
P5-10   Interest element in leasing charge/Amount outstanding on leasing accounts (%)
P5-11   Interest element as opposed to the ledger keeping and debt collection element in a debt factoring charge/Debts factored (%)
P5-12   Bill discount/Bills discounted (%)

Diagram 8-2   Make-up of interest paid. With acknowledgements to the Centre for Interfirm Comparison.

P6-1   Preference shares/Total borrowed capital (%)
P6-2   Debentures/Total borrowed capital (%)
P6-3   Loans/Total borrowed capital (%)
P6-4   Overdrafts/Total borrowed capital (%)
P6-5   Trade and expense creditors/Total borrowed capital (%)
P6-6   Corporation and/or income tax provisions/Total borrowed capital (%)
P6-7   Income tax reserves and deferred taxation/Total borrowed capital (%)
P6-8   Investment grants/Total borrowed capital (%)
P6-9   Amount outstanding on hire purchase accounts/Total borrowed capital (%)
P6-10   Amount outstanding on leasing accounts/Total borrowed capital (%)
P6-11   Debts factored/Total borrowed capital (%)
P6-12   Bills discounted/Total borrowed capital (%)

Diagram 8-3   Make-up of borrowed capital. With acknowledgements to the Centre for Interfirm Comparison.

The conventional standards for these two ratios are 2 to 1 and 1 to 1 respectively (but see below). These two ratios are what might be called first-line tests of liquidity. The interpretation which a lender puts on them will depend on the following second-line factors:

1. How quickly the borrower is turning his stock over (stock/average daily cost of sales). A fast stock turnover will excuse a lower ratio of current assets to current liabilities.
2. How quickly the borrower is getting his debts in (debtors/average daily sales). A fast debt collection will explain a low current asset/current liability ratio.
3. How much credit the borrower is taking (creditors/average daily purchases). Above average credit taken will tend to depress the ratio of current assets/current liabilities.
4. How vulnerable the borrower's profits are to a drop in turnover (fixed costs/total costs). The higher this ratio, the higher the firm's ratio of current assets to current liabilities needs to be to weather any depression.
5. The extent of long-term liabilities maturing in the near future.* If there are any, the current asset/current liability ratio needs to be built up in advance.
6. Proposals for capital expenditure in the future.* If there are any this will run down the current asset/current liability ratio, unless there are
7. Proposals to raise new finance soon (information on this may be found in the firm's annual report, the financial press, or in the firm's Extel or Moodies card).

A new liquidity ratio has been introduced recently in response to the effects of inflation on companies' liquidity. It is

$$\frac{\text{Stock} + \text{debtors} - \text{creditors}}{\text{Long-term capital}}$$

The numerator of this ratio consists of those assets (stock and debtors) which will grow in money terms as a result of inflation less the only source of finance (trade credit) which will automatically compensate for this growth. The higher this ratio is the greater will be the pressure on the company to raise new finance or to increase its dividend cover (that is, retain a higher proportion of profits) in times of inflation.

One last ratio the lender will look at is the fixed capital ratio (long term borrowed capital plus equity capital, in relation to fixed assets) to see that the assets which must remain if the business is to carry on, are financed by capital which is committed for an

---

* Information on these items must be disclosed as a result of the Companies Acts.

equally long period of time. The prudent lender prefers this ratio to be not less than unity.

All the constraint factor ratios are summarised in Diagram 8-4.

To calculate ratios P7 to P15 use data assembly and ratio calculation sheet 8-4 at the end of this chapter.

8.4 Supervision of the Firm's Investments

The investor measures the success of his investment over any period of time by the ratio of his income after taxation to the cost of the original investment (or to its value at the beginning of the period being measured). This is ratio Q1 in Diagram 8-5. I have included in 'income' both the dividend that he has received and the capital gain over the period as this seems common sense. Some accountants may disagree with this, but so as not to bore the general reader I have included the arguments for and against this approach in an appendix to this chapter.

The size of ratio Q1 is determined by four factors (measured by ratios Q2 to Q5):

1. The size of the dividend (the ratio of the gross dividend to his original investment) – ratio Q2.
2. The capital gain (the ratio of the increase of the value of his shareholding to its original cost, that is, I am including all capital gains whether or not they have been 'realised'–ratio Q3.
3. The rate of tax on the dividend – ratio Q4.
4. The rate of tax on the capital gain – ratio Q5.

The size of a company's dividend is affected by a combination of its profitability and its directors' policy on distribution of profit (both of these subjects are dealt with later in this chapter).

The magnitude of the investor's capital gain (ratio Q3) and indeed whether it is positive or negative–is determined by changes in the view of the Stock Exchange of what is the discounted present value of the future dividends of the company. This view will be a compound of:

1. Rates of interest both present and expected
2. An assessment of the rate of growth of the company in general and of its dividends in particular
3. An assessment of the degree of risk to which the company is subjected either directly or indirectly via the industry and/or country in which it operates.

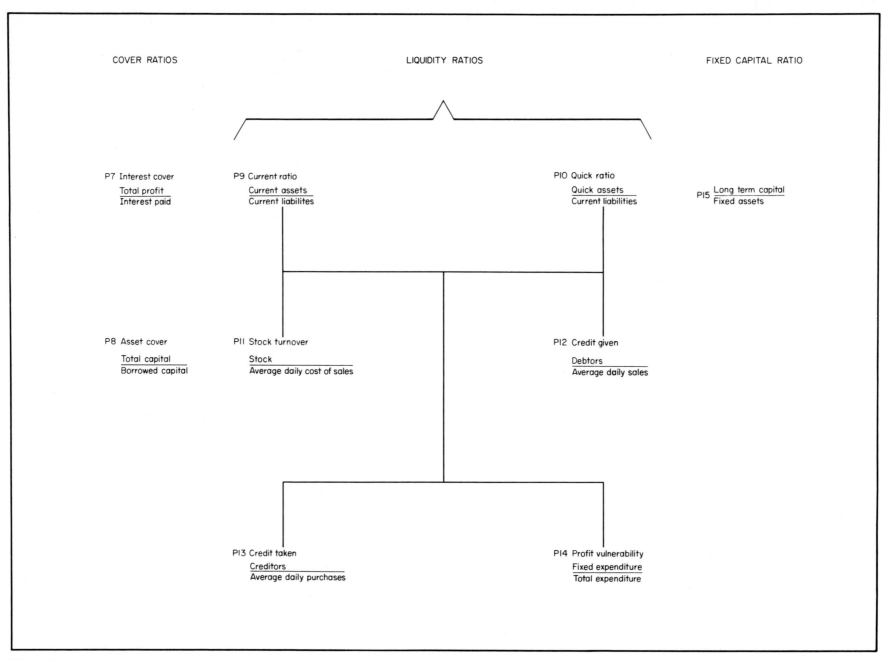

COVER RATIOS | LIQUIDITY RATIOS | FIXED CAPITAL RATIO

P7 Interest cover

$$\frac{\text{Total profit}}{\text{Interest paid}}$$

P9 Current ratio

$$\frac{\text{Current assets}}{\text{Current liabilites}}$$

PIO Quick ratio

$$\frac{\text{Quick assets}}{\text{Current liabilities}}$$

PI5 $\frac{\text{Long term capital}}{\text{Fixed assets}}$

P8 Asset cover

$$\frac{\text{Total capital}}{\text{Borrowed capital}}$$

PII Stock turnover

$$\frac{\text{Stock}}{\text{Average daily cost of sales}}$$

PI2 Credit given

$$\frac{\text{Debtors}}{\text{Average daily sales}}$$

PI3 Credit taken

$$\frac{\text{Creditors}}{\text{Average daily purchases}}$$

PI4 Profit vulnerability

$$\frac{\text{Fixed expenditure}}{\text{Total expenditure}}$$

Diagram 8-4   Constraint factors

164

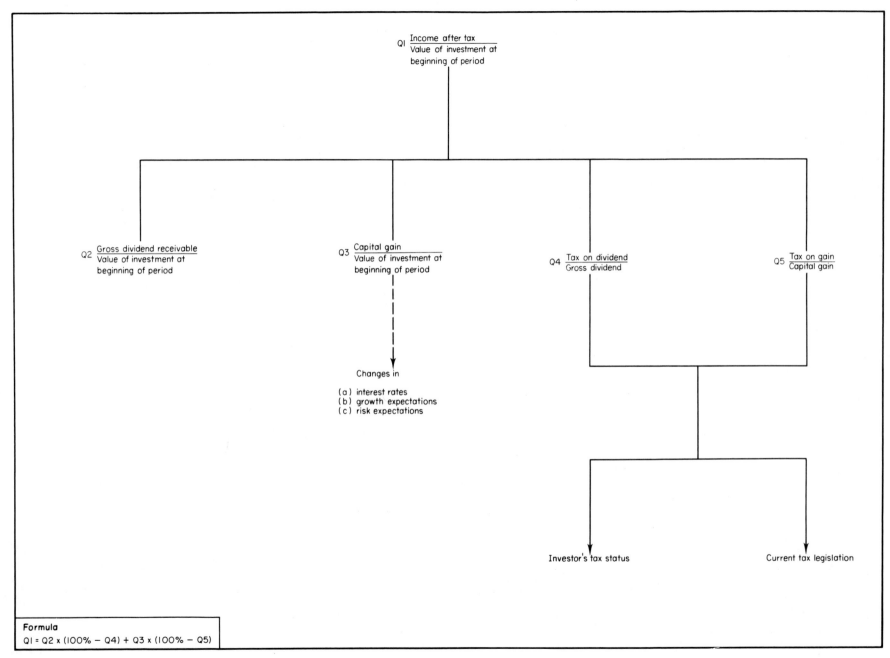

Q1 $\dfrac{\text{Income after tax}}{\text{Value of investment at beginning of period}}$

Q2 $\dfrac{\text{Gross dividend receivable}}{\text{Value of investment at beginning of period}}$

Q3 $\dfrac{\text{Capital gain}}{\text{Value of investment at beginning of period}}$

Q4 $\dfrac{\text{Tax on dividend}}{\text{Gross dividend}}$

Q5 $\dfrac{\text{Tax on gain}}{\text{Capital gain}}$

Changes in

(a) interest rates
(b) growth expectations
(c) risk expectations

Investor's tax status

Current tax legislation

Formula
Q1 = Q2 x (100% − Q4) + Q3 x (100% − Q5)

Diagram 8-5   Investor ratios

The magnitude of the investor's capital gain (ratio Q3) tends to increase if

1   Rates of interest (factor 1) decrease
2   The rate of the company's growth (factor 2) increases
3   The amount of risk to which the company is subjected (factor 3) decreases.

An investment analyst, when assessing the likely size of a company's dividends in the future (factor 2 above), will probably go through the following analytical steps:

1   What is the likely pattern of demand for the products of the industry (or industries) in which the company operates? This will depend on the following factors among others:
    (a)   the point that the analyst believes to have been reached in the 'trade cycle' or 'stop-go' process and his expectations regarding the likely pattern of development of this cycle
    (b)   the nature of the industry—in particular whether it is producing consumption goods such as bread, consumer durables such as cars, or capital goods such as machine tools
    (c)   the quantity of stocks in any pipeline between the industry and the ultimate consumer
    (d)   any abnormal factors affecting the industry, such as likely fall off in boom demand after introduction of new products; exceptional crops of basic raw material; foreign competition/demand for product; tariff changes; etc.
2   What is the likely share of the industry's sales which this company will get? This will depend on the following factors among others:
    (a)   its share in the past
    (b)   the success of any efforts by it or its competitors to change that share
    (c)   special factors (new products, production processes, selling or delivery methods, etc.)
3   Given the company's likely sales from step 2 what are its profits likely to be? This will depend on the following factors among others:
    (a)   the size of stocks that it is carrying or, for capital goods industries, the length of its order book, (that is, how much of these sales will need to be/can be met from current production capacity)
    (b)   the proportion of its costs which are fixed (that is, which are not likely to change significantly with the anticipated change in volume)
    (c)   any changes in price for the company's product (from the affects of competition or the lack of it)
    (d)   any changes in the prices of the company's inputs (such as materials and labour) from the effects of competition (or lack of it) unionism, inflation, etc.
4   Given the profit (from step 3) what are the earnings for the ordinary shareholder going to be? This will depend on
    (a)   prior charges (such as debenture interest and preference dividends)
    (b)   tax.
5   Given the earnings what is the dividend likely to be? This will depend on
    (a)   the payout ratio or dividend cover (see p167) maintained in the past
    (b)   management's estimate of the permanence of any change in earnings (any short-lived change is less likely to affect the dividends—the cover ratio will be allowed to change instead)
    (c)   whether the earnings are going up or down—directors are more reluctant to cut a dividend (provided it is not 'uncovered') than to increase one
    (d)   the amount of cash available. Part or all of the profit may have already been invested in assets or used to repay liabilities or may be needed for new investment (either for replacement of assets or for expansion) and may not therefore be available for dividend
    (e)   tactical reasons. Management may wish to influence the company's share price if it is making a bid for another company, repelling a bid or contemplating a rights issue.

The magnitude of ratio Q3 is affected by the consensus of views arrived at by reasoning similar to the above. The rate of tax paid on dividends and payable on capital gains (ratios Q4 and Q5) will depend on the combination of the investor's tax status (company or individual, surtax payer or entitled to age relief) and current tax legislation.

As an example, assume that X, a standard rate taxpayer, bought 100 shares at £1.25 each in Y Limited. During the year he receives a dividend of 5 per cent and at the end of the year the shares are worth £1.50 each. He pays income tax at 38.75 per cent and capital gains tax at half this rate.

Gross dividend (100 at 5 per cent)	£5.00
Less income tax at 38.75 per cent	£1.94
Net dividend	£3.06
Capital gain—unrealised (100 × £0.25)	£25.00
Less provision for long-term capital gains tax [at 19.375 per cent (half standard rate)]	£4.84
Net gain	£20.16
Total income after tax	£23.22

Q1

$$\frac{\text{Income after tax}}{\text{Value of investment at beginning of period}}$$

£23.22 ÷ £125.00 = 18.6%

Q2

$$\frac{\text{Gross dividend receivable}}{\text{Original value of investment}}$$

£5.00 ÷ £125.00 = 4.0%

Q3

$$\frac{\text{Capital gain}}{\text{Original value of investment}}$$

£25.00 ÷ £125.00 = 20.0%

Q4

$$\frac{\text{Tax on dividend}}{\text{Gross dividend}}$$

£1.94 ÷ £5.00 = 38.8%

Q5

$$\frac{\text{Tax on gain}}{\text{Capital gain}}$$

£4.84 ÷ £25.00 = 19.4%

To calculate ratios Q1 to Q5 use data assembly and ratio calculation sheet 8-5 at the end of this chapter.

8.5 The Company and the Stock Exchange

When considering the purchase or sale of an investment of the company financial management will find it useful to be familiar with the ratios used by stockbrokers, investment analysts, and the financial press. Other occasions when such familiarity will be of use include: the raising of new equity capital; the making of a take-over bid for another company where part or all of the consideration is shares in the bidding company; the receipt of such a bid from another company; a merger.

The ratios have been put into a logical framework in order to bring out their inter-relationship. Financial commentators do not appear to use such a framework of analysis in a formal manner. It is possible that they might find their analysis eased by the following approach.

The first ratio in Diagram 8-6 is the dividend yield of the company. That is the most recent annual dividend per ordinary share divided by the present price of the share. The *dividend yield* is *not* the same as the *rate of dividend declared* by the company. The latter is the total gross dividend as a percentage of the nominal value of the

ordinary shares. For example, if a company has a share capital of 1000 £1 shares and declares a dividend of 10 per cent it will be paying out 10 per cent of £1000, that is £100 or 10p per share.

The dividend yield is the gross (before personal tax) rate of return an investor would receive if:

1   The dividend rate is unchanged, and
2   He paid the current market price of the share.

For example, if the price of the above shares was £2, the dividend yield would be:

$$\frac{10p \times 100}{£2} = 5\%$$

It is only when the market price equals the nominal value of the share that the dividend *yield* and the dividend *rate* are equal.

The dividend rate has little meaning. The dividend yield is the actual current rate of return being earned by the shareholder on the investment. The size of ratio R1 depends on:

1   The earnings yield (profit after corporation tax, minorities and preference dividend but before ordinary dividend per share divided by the present price of the share)—ratio R2
2   The dividend cover (profit after corporation tax, minorities and preference dividends divided by the ordinary gross dividend)—ratio R3.

Ratio R1 increases if either ratio R2 increases (generally a satisfactory sign) or ratio R3 decreases (which might be an unhealthy sign, or merely a correction of ultra-conservatism in the past, or an indication that management considers the drop in ratio R2 to be a temporary phenomenon).

In recent years it has become increasingly fashionable, and it is now standard practice, to use the P/E or price/earnings ratio (ratio R2a) as a substitute for, or in addition to, the earnings yield. One is merely the reciprocal of the other. A P/E of 12.5 for example is equivalent to an earnings yield of 8.0 per cent. Thus the concept is one of the share price representing so many times or year's purchase of earnings, rather than the earnings representing a certain percentage return on the cost of the investment.

The advantage of using P/E ratios rather than earnings yields is that they facilitate international comparisons, particularly with American stocks because this is the generally accepted yardstick of share evaluation in the United States. The disadvantage is that the P/E ratio cannot be directly compared with the dividend yield to show the extent to which the dividend is covered. Nor can it be directly compared

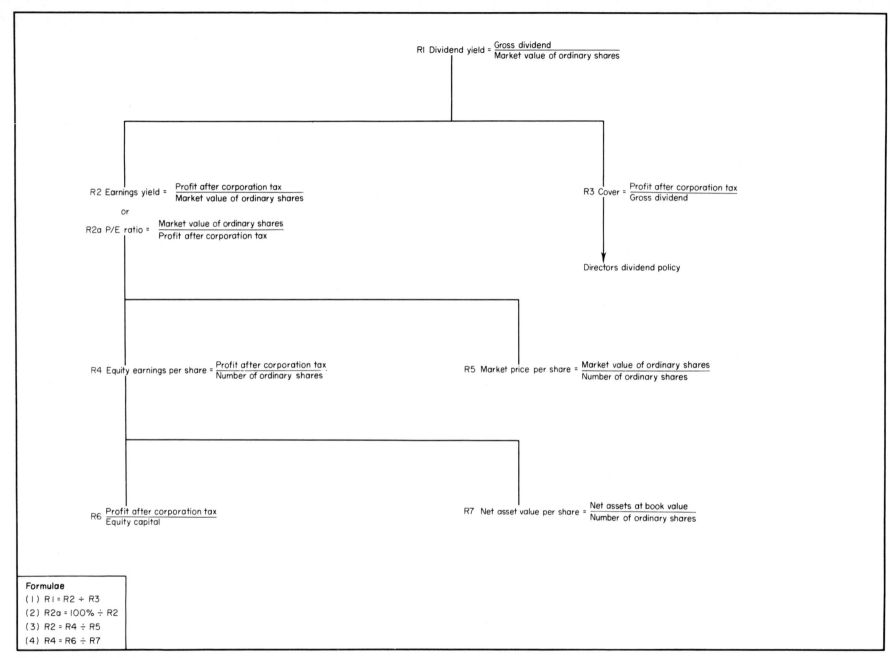

R1 Dividend yield = $\dfrac{\text{Gross dividend}}{\text{Market value of ordinary shares}}$

R2 Earnings yield = $\dfrac{\text{Profit after corporation tax}}{\text{Market value of ordinary shares}}$

or

R2a P/E ratio = $\dfrac{\text{Market value of ordinary shares}}{\text{Profit after corporation tax}}$

R3 Cover = $\dfrac{\text{Profit after corporation tax}}{\text{Gross dividend}}$

Directors dividend policy

R4 Equity earnings per share = $\dfrac{\text{Profit after corporation tax}}{\text{Number of ordinary shares}}$

R5 Market price per share = $\dfrac{\text{Market value of ordinary shares}}{\text{Number of ordinary shares}}$

R6 $\dfrac{\text{Profit after corporation tax}}{\text{Equity capital}}$

R7 Net asset value per share = $\dfrac{\text{Net assets at book value}}{\text{Number of ordinary shares}}$

Formulae

(1) R1 = R2 ÷ R3

(2) R2a = 100% ÷ R2

(3) R2 = R4 ÷ R5

(4) R4 = R6 ÷ R7

Diagram 8-6   Stock Exchange Ratios

with the returns available on fixed interest or other investments.

P/E ratios are published in a number of papers, including the Financial Times and The Times. As standards of comparison they require to be used with caution however as different papers (and different stockbrokers) calculate the Earnings part of the ratio in different ways. The main areas of difference are:

1. The treatment of corporation tax (the alternatives are: to use the figure in the accounts; to substitute a 'normal' charge where the figure in the accounts is sub- or super-normal)
2. The treatment of extraordinary items in the profit and loss account
3. The treatment of convertible loan stock (some brokers calculate the P/E ratio by dividing the price per share by the earnings per share and in calculating the latter in appropriate circumstances increase earnings by the amount of interest which will be saved when the loan stock is converted to ordinary shares and increase the number of ordinary shares by the number of new ones).

The subject is discussed at length in the Accounting Standard on Earnings per share published by the Council of the Institute of Chartered Accountants in England and Wales (M3 April 1972).

It is to be hoped that the increased comparability which this standard will provide from 31 December 1972 will lead to most of the differences disappearing.

The size of a company's earnings yield (ratio R2) is determined by:

1. The equity earnings per share (ratio R4) and
2. The market price per share (ratio R5).

We have already described the factors affecting the market price of a share (ratio R5) in our discussion of ratio Q3 above (see p 163 and 166). Equity earnings per share (ratio R4) are affected by the size of two ratios:

1. The net profit on the equity capital of the company (ratio R6)
2. The net asset value per share (the book value of the ordinary capital and reserves divided by the number of ordinary shares)—ratio R7.

Ratio R7 (net asset value per share) provides a necessary mathematical link between equity earnings per share (ratio R4, which is ratio R6 ÷ ratio R7) and net profit on equity capital (ratio R6). Some investment analysts and financial journalists endow it with a significance, particularly in relation to the market price per share (ratio R5). My own view is that any difference between market price and asset value per share is a reflection of the different approach of the stock exchange and of the company accountant. The stock exchange bases its valuations on what it can perceive in the future; the accountant bases his valuation on what has been spent in the past. Or, to express the difference more elaborately, the former is, broadly speaking, always estimating a discounted present value for a hypothetical stream of future (growing or contracting) receipts. The latter is accumulating, in accordance with generally accepted conventions, a depreciated sum of past expenditures.

The size of the asset value per share (ratio R7) does provide to some extent a lower limit for the market price (ratio R5). How far market price will fall below asset value per share in adverse circumstances depends partly on the marketability of the firm's assets and partly on takeover hopes. If the assets are very specific in their use, asset value per share provides negligible protection to the market price.

To some extent the ratio of R5 to R7 (that is of the market price to the net asset value) is a measure of the market's opinion of the management of the company. The more of a company's assets that are human as opposed to physical, the more likely are ratios R5 and R7 to diverge. Such companies are catered for in the last part of Chapter 11. A leading firm of London stockbrokers has a rule of thumb that says they need to have strong reasons for recommending a share standing at, say, more than three times its asset value. Similarly they hesitate in recommending a sale of shares whose price is, say, less than half the asset value.

In using the ratio of asset values per share it is necessary to consider the following questions:

1. Are the asset values realistic? Is property undervalued (because of, for example, the effects of inflation)? Could stock realise its book value in conditions of a forced sale?
2. How marketable are the assets? Property, quoted investments and, of course, cash are usually highly marketable; stock, plant and machinery, debtors are often much less marketable.
3. What is the company's gearing (see p 158)? In a highly geared company a small drop in asset value could wipe the ordinary shareholders' stake out of existence. Conversely a small rise in value could make a big jump in equity assets.

An investment analyst's reactions to the size of a company's profit on equity capital ratio (ratio R6) would be as follows:

1. If profit on equity capital is high for the industry, can the company maintain it? Is it high because of good management or because of lack of competition? If the profit on equity capital is likely to drop, when will the crunch come? Have the management sufficient foresight, ability and resources to bring out a new winner as the old one fades before competition or change in demand?

2   If profit on equity capital is low for the industry what recovery potential
         has the company, or is it doomed to go to the wall?

Some of the main factors which affect a company's net profit after tax are shown in
Diagram 8-7. These have been described earlier in this chapter.

     As an example of the application of ratios R1 to R7, assume that firm Y has
1 800 000 £1 ordinary shares, the market price of which is £1.50. It declared a
dividend of 5 per cent on profits after tax of £200 000. Its net assets were £2 200 000.

R1   Dividend yield $=$ $\dfrac{\text{Gross dividend}}{\text{Market value of ordinary shares}}$

                         $=$ $\dfrac{\text{£1 800 000} \times 5\%}{1\ 800\ 000 \times \text{£1.50}}$ $= 3.3\%$

R2   Earnings yield $=$ $\dfrac{\text{Profit after corporation tax}}{\text{Market value of ordinary shares}}$

                         $=$ $\dfrac{\text{£200 000}}{1\ 800\ 000 \times \text{£1.50}}$ $= 7.4\%$

R2a   P/E ratio $=$ $\dfrac{\text{£2 700 000}}{200\ 000}$ $= 13.5$

R3   Cover $=$ $\dfrac{\text{Profit after corporation tax}}{\text{Gross dividend}}$

                         $=$ $\dfrac{\text{£200 000}}{\text{£90 000}}$ $= 2.2$ times

R4   Equity earnings per share $=$ $\dfrac{\text{Profit after corporation tax}}{\text{Number of ordinary shares}}$

                         $=$ $\dfrac{\text{£200 000}}{1\ 800\ 000}$ $= \text{£0.111}$

R5   Market price per share (given) $= \text{£1.50}$

R6   Return on equity capital $=$ $\dfrac{\text{Profit after corporation tax}}{\text{Equity capital}}$

                         $=$ $\dfrac{\text{£200 000}}{\text{£2 200 000}}$ $= 9.1\%$

R7   Net asset value per share $=$ $\dfrac{\text{£2 000 000}}{1\ 800\ 000}$ $= \text{£1.22}$

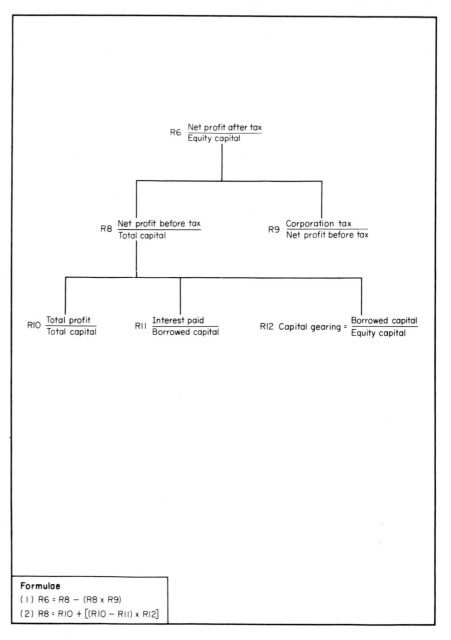

Diagram 8-7   Overall company ratios

To calculate ratios R1 to R7 use data assembly and ratio calculation sheet 8.6 at the end of this chapter.

To calculate ratios R8 to R12 use data assembly and ratio calculation sheet 8-7 at the end of this chapter.

8.6 Supervision of Data Processing

In supervising the firm's accounting and data processing functions financial management is concerned with how much of the firm's income is being spent on these functions. They will seek, within the constraints imposed upon them by other aspects of the company's policy, to minimise the ratio

$$\text{S1} \qquad \frac{\text{Data processing costs}}{\text{Sales}}$$

Data processing costs will include the salaries and wages of, and National Insurance and pension contributions for the relevant staff, depreciation and/or hire charges of the machinery, and may include an appropriate part of the rent, rates, heat, light, cleaning and so on of the offices used.

The costs of data processing are caused not so much by the value of sales but by the volume of transactions. Transactions are the sum of all the items entering the system, such as all purchases, payments, sales, receipts, transfers, and so on. So financial management monitors two other ratios:

$$\text{S2} \qquad \frac{\text{Data processing costs}}{\text{Transactions}}$$

$$\text{S3} \qquad \frac{\text{Transactions}}{\text{Sales}}$$

It may be possible to reduce the first by using different methods of processing, by increasing mechanisation and employing cheaper, less skilled staff. To cut down the number of transactions in relation to the value of sales calls for the co-operation of other departments in increasing the value of orders placed or received on any one occasion, by decreasing the frequency of payments (by changing from weekly to monthly payment for employees), and so on.

To calculate ratios S1 to S3 use data assembly and ratio calculation sheet 8-8 at the end of this chapter.

The data processing department will also be producing reports. Ideally, one would have a ratio of

$$\text{S4} \qquad \frac{\text{Value (to management) of reports}}{\text{Cost of producing them}}$$

However, it is likely to be difficult to persuade management to put a monetary value on the reports they ask for and/or get. It might be a salutary exercise for all concerned if the exercise was tried though! As an alternative it would be possible to attach a note of the cost of producing a report to the document itself.

Another exercise which it would be worth carrying out periodically—particularly if the number of reports required tended, as it nearly always does, to grow—is as follows. Ask the users of reports to rank them in order of their usefulness. This ranking can be built up by means of the paired comparison technique. Each user is asked to compare each report he receives with each other report and to decide whether:

1   Report A is more useful than B (A is awarded 2 points)
2   Report B is more useful than A (B is awarded 2 points)
3   Reports A and B are of equal value—this 'decision' or lack of decision is to be discouraged (A and B are awarded 1 point each).

The data processing department assesses the marginal cost of producing the report (that is, the cost that would be saved by the data processing and other departments if the report were not produced). The points awarded to the report and its marginal cost are then graphed as in Diagram 8-8. The area of the graph can be subdivided into three bands as shown.

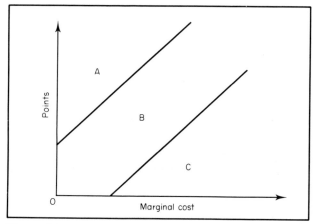

Diagram 8-8   Value and cost of reports

Band A. High-value low-cost reports. Almost certainly should be continued.

Band B. Value more or less in line with cost (that is, either high-value high-cost, or low-value low-cost, or medium-value medium-cost). The production of these reports should be given a mild degree of questioning.

Band C. Low-value high-cost reports. The case for dropping these is high. Arguments for retaining them must be strong.

Appendix 8.1

A Note on Capital Gains

Should capital gains be included in an investor's income as well as the dividend(s) he has received? Obviously there are differences between dividends and capital gains:

1   A dividend is received in cash, whereas a capital gain is an increase in the value of the share on the market. The company will not ask for the dividend back, but a change in market sentiment may quickly reduce a capital gain.

2   Dividends and capital gains are taxed at different rates and in different ways. It is because of this that capital gains are more attractive for a surtax payer than dividends.

3   Trustee and executorship law distinguishes firmly between the treatment of items deemed to be income and capital.

Against these differences need to be set such considerations as the following:

1   Dividends can be reinvested, with the result that they are no longer cash but are part of the value of the share. They then begin to look very similar to capital gains. Most building societies and unit trusts have provisions for the automatic investment of dividends. Some unit trusts have accumulator units where all income is automatically reinvested.

2   Capital gains can be realised in whole or in part. They then begin to look similar to dividends. At least one property bond has a plan for the automatic withdrawal of capital gains.

3   Some accountants appear to be worried that the capital gain has not been realised.

Yet, as one author has pointed out, it would be impossible to distinguish between *A* who holds shares in company *X* on which there is an unrealised capital gain, and *B* who also holds shares in company *X* but who has realised his capital gain and used the proceeds to reinvest in company *X*. Except, of course, that *B* has had to pay dealing expenses and has turned his liability to capital gains tax from a contingent to an actual one.

I wonder whether accountants would have the same reservations about combining dividends and capital gains if the latter were 'losses'. I suspect that they would be happier to reduce dividend income by unrealised capital losses to show a net figure of disposable income.

When evaluating the performance of an investment, and particularly when comparing one investment with another, I consider that a more meaningful result is obtained by adding together the gross dividend(s) and the capital gain and subtracting from this sum the income tax, surtax and capital gains tax either paid or payable. Readers who disagree with this can simplify Diagram 8-5 by the omission of ratios Q3 and Q5 and by changing the numerator of ratio Q1 to 'Net dividend'.

Gearing and return on equity

Code letter	Item	Month or quarter to (date)					
A	Total profit						
B	Interest paid						
C	Net profit before tax (A − B)						
D	Average borrowed capital						
E	Average equity capital						
F	Average total capital (D + E)						
G	Number of calendar days in period						

Gearing and return on equity

Ratio	Formula for calculation of ratio	Unit of measurement	Month or quarter to (date)					
P1 Net profit before tax/ Equity capital	C x 100 ÷ E x 365 ÷ G	% pa						
P2 Total profit/ Total capital	A x 100 ÷ F x 365 ÷ G	% pa						
P3 Interest paid/ Borrowed capital	B x 100 ÷ D x 365 ÷ G	% pa						
P4 *Gearing* Borrowed capital/ Equity capital	D ÷ E	times						

Make-up of interest paid and borrowed capital

Code letter	Item	Month or quarter to (date)					
A	Preference dividend						
B	Debenture interest						
C	Loan interest						
D	Overdraft interest						
E	Cash discounts lost						
F	Interest element in hire purchase charge						
G	Interest element in leasing charge						
H	Interest element in debt factoring charge						
K	Bill discount						
L	Interest paid (A+B+C+D+E+F+G+H+K)						
M	Average preference shares						
N	Average debentures						
P	Average loans						
Q	Average overdrafts						
R	Average trade and expense creditors						
S	Average corporation and/or income tax provisions						
T	Average income tax reserves and deferred taxation						
W	Average investment grants						
Y	Average amount outstanding on hire purchase accounts						
Z	Average amount outstanding on leasing accounts						
AA	Average debts factored						
AB	Average bills discounted						
AC	Average total borrowed capital (M+N+P+Q+R+S+T+W+Y+Z+AA+AB)						
AD	Number of calendar days in period						

Make-up of interest paid

Ratio		Formula for calculation of ratio	Unit of measurement	Month or quarter to (date)					
P5-1	Preference dividend/ Preference shares	$A \times 100 \div M$ $\times 365 \div AD$	% pa						
P5-2	Debenture interest/ Debentures	$B \times 100 \div N$ $\times 365 \div AD$	% pa						
P5-3	Loan interest/ Loans	$C \times 100 \div P$ $\times 365 \div AD$	% pa						
P5-4	Overdraft interest/ Overdrafts	$D \times 100 \div Q$ $\times 365 \div AD$	% pa						
P5-5	Cash discounts lost/Trade and expense creditors	$E \times 100 \div R$ $\times 365 \div AD$	% pa						
P5-9	Interest element in hire purchase charge/ Amount outstanding on hire purchase accounts	$F \times 100 \div Y$ $\times 365 \div AD$	% pa						
P5-10	Interest element in leasing charge/Amount outstanding on leasing accounts	$G \times 100 \div Z$ $\times 365 \div AD$	% pa						
P5-11	Interest element in debt factoring charge/Debts factored	$H \times 100 \div AA$ $\times 365 \div AD$	% pa						
P5-12	Bill discount/ Bills discounted	$K \times 100 \div AB$ $\times 365 \div AD$	% pa						

Make-up of borrowed capital

Ratio		Formula for calculation of ratio	Unit of measurement	Month or quarter to (date)						
P6-1	Preference shares/ Total borrowed capital	M x 100 ÷ AC	%							
P6-2	Debentures/Total borrowed capital	N x 100 ÷ AC	%							
P6-3	Loans/Total borrowed capital	P x 100 ÷ AC	%							
P6-4	Overdrafts/Total borrowed capital	Q x 100 ÷ AC	%							
P6-5	Trade and expense creditors/Total borrowed capital	R x 100 ÷ AC	%							
P6-6	Corporation &/or income tax provisions/ Total borrowed capital	S x 100 ÷ AC	%							
P6-7	Income tax reserves & deferred taxation/Total borrowed capital	T x 100 ÷ AC	%							
P6-8	Investment grants/ Total borrowed capital	W x 100 ÷ AC	%							
P6-9	Amount outstanding on hire purchase accounts/Total borrowed capital	Y x 100 ÷ AC	%							
P6-10	Amount outstanding on leasing accounts/ Total borrowed capital	Z x 100 ÷ AC	%							
P6-11	Debts factored/ Total borrowed capital	AA x 100 ÷ AC	%							
P6-12	Bills discounted/ Total borrowed capital	AB x 100 ÷ AC	%							

Data assembly sheet 8-4

Constraint factors

Code letter	Item	Month or quarter to (date)					
A	Average debtors						
B	Average other quick assets						
C	Average quick assets (A+B)						
D	Average stock						
E	Average other current assets						
F	Average current assets (C+D+E)						
G	Average creditors						
H	Average other current liabilities						
K	Average current liabilities (G+H)						
L	Average borrowed capital						
M	Average long term capital						
N	Average total capital						
P	Purchases						
Q	Cost of sales						
R	Fixed expenditure						
S	Total expenditure						
T	Interest paid						
W	Total profit						
Y	Sales						
Z	Fixed assets						
AA	No of working days in period						
AB	No of calendar days in period						

Constraint factors

Ratio	Formula for calculation of ratio	Unit of measurement	Month or quarter to (date)					
P7 *Interest cover* Total profit/ Interest paid	W ÷ T	times						
P8 *Asset cover* Total capital/ Borrowed capital	N ÷ L	times						
P9 *Current ratio* Current assets/ Current liabilities	F ÷ K	times						
P10 *Quick ratio* Quick assets/ Current liabilities	C ÷ K	times						
P11 *Stock turnover* Stock/ Average daily cost of sales	D ÷ (Q ÷ AA)	days						
P12 *Credit given* Debtors/ Average daily sales	A ÷ (Y ÷ AB)	days						
P13 *Credit taken* Creditors/ Average daily purchases	G ÷ (P ÷ AB)	days						
P14 *Profit vulnerability* Fixed expenditure/ Total expenditure	R x 100 ÷ S	%						
P15 *Fixed Capital Ratio* Long term capital/ Fixed assets	M ÷ Z	times						

Investor ratios

Code letter	Item	Year to (date)					
A	Value of investment at beginning of period						
B	Value of investment at end of period						
C	Capital gain (B—A)						
D	Gross dividend receivable						
E	Sub total (C+D)						
F	Tax on dividend						
G	Tax on gain						
H	Sub total (F+G)						
K	Income after tax (E—H)						

NB As dividends usually relate to a year it is probably not worthwhile calculating these ratios for a period less than a year. They may however be calculated more frequently than annually.

Ratio		Formula for calculation of ratio	Unit of measurement	Year to (date)					
Q1	Income after tax/Value of investment at beginning of period	K x 100 ÷ A	% pa						
Q2	Gross dividend receivable/Value of investment at beginning of period	D x 100 ÷ A	% pa						
Q3	Capital gain/ Value of invest- ment at beginning of period	C x 100 ÷ A	% pa						
Q4	Tax on dividend/ Gross dividend	F x 100 ÷ D	%						
Q5	Tax on gain/ Capital gain	G x 100 ÷ C	%						

Data assembly sheet 8-6

Stock exchange ratios

Code letter	Item	Year to (date)					
A	Profit after corporation tax						
B	Gross dividend						
C	Number of ordinary shares						
D	Net assets at book value						
E	Market value of ordinary shares						
F	Equity capital						

NB As dividends usually relate to a year it is probably not worthwhile calculating these ratios for a period less than a year. They may however be calculated more frequently than annually.

Stock exchange ratios

Ratio	Formula for calculation of ratio	Unit of measurement	Year to (date)					
R1 *Dividend Yield* Gross dividend/ Market value of ordinary shares	B x 100 ÷ E	% pa						
R2 *Earnings Yield* Profit after corporation tax/ Market value of ordinary shares	A x 100 ÷ E	% pa						
R2(a) *P/E Ratio* Market value of ordinary shares/ Profit after corporation tax	E ÷ A	times						
R3 *Cover* Profit after corporation tax/ Gross dividend	A ÷ B	times						
R4 *Equity earnings per share* Profit after corporation tax/Number of ordinary shares	A ÷ C	£'s per share pa						
R5 *Market price per share* Market value of ordinary shares/ Number of ordinary shares	E ÷ C	£'s per share						
R6 Profit after corporation tax/ Equity capital	A x 100 ÷ F	% pa						
R7 *Net asset value per share* Net assets at book value/ Number of ordinary shares	D ÷ C	£'s per share						

Overall company ratios

Code letter	Item	Month or quarter to (date)					
A	Total profit						
B	Interest paid						
C	Net profit before tax (A—B)						
D	Corporation tax						
E	Net profit after tax (C—D)						
F	Average equity capital						
G	Average borrowed capital						
H	Average total capital (F+G)						
K	No of calendar days in period						

Overall company ratios

Ratio	Formula for calculation of ratio	Unit of measurement	Month or quarter to (date)					
R6 Net profit after tax/ Equity capital	E x 100 ÷ F x 365 ÷ K	% pa						
R8 Net profit before tax/ Total capital	C x 100 ÷ H x 365 ÷ K	% pa						
R9 Corporation tax/ Net profit before tax	D x 100 ÷ C	%						
R10 Total profit/ Total capital	A x 100 ÷ H x 365 ÷ K	% pa						
R11 Interest paid/ Borrowed capital	B x 100 ÷ G x 365 ÷ K	% pa						
R12 *Capital gearing* Borrowed capital/ Equity capital	G ÷ F	times						

Data assembly sheet 8-8

Data processing

Code letter	Item	Month or quarter to (date)					
A	Data processing costs						
B	Sales						
C	Transactions						

Data processing

Ratio	Formula for calculation of ratio	Unit of measurement	Month or quarter to (date)					
S1 Data processing costs/Sales	A x 100 ÷ B	%						
S2 Data processing costs/ Transactions	A ÷ C	£ per transaction						
S3 Transactions per £100 of sales	C x 100 ÷ B	Numbers						

Chapter 9

Ratios for production management

In Chapter 1 it was stated that it is desirable to provide each manager with a single key ratio which measures the degree of his success. Such a ratio will relate the results achieved by production management to the resources available.

The result that production management is striving for is to reduce production costs; not to reduce them in isolation, however, but *in relation to* the sales value of what is being produced. A useful ratio is therefore

$$\frac{\text{Production costs}}{\text{Sales value of production}}$$

This ratio cannot be used as the *key* production ratio because it does not take into account the resources—the assets—used to achieve it. These production assets are: raw materials stock, work in progress, finished goods stock, factory premises, and the plant, machinery and factory vehicles such as fork lift trucks. Instead of using this ratio, therefore, it is possible to measure the same relationship by using the figure of production contribution, that is sales value of production *minus* production costs. Then the key production ratio becomes:

T1 $\qquad \dfrac{\text{Production contribution}}{\text{Production assets}}$

The subsidiary ratios that production management uses to indicate the causes of a change in the key ratio depend on whether it is possible to obtain a reliable and meaningful measure of maximum output or not. If such a measure is not obtainable, the ratios described next are used; if one is obtainable the ratios described in Section 9.2 are applicable.

9.1 No Measure of Maximum Output Obtainable*

The key ratio can be improved by action:

1   To reduce costs in relation to output, provided that either no increase in asset investment is called for, or the reduction in costs outweighs the increased investment.

2   To reduce asset investment in relation to output provided that such a reduction does not impair the ratio of costs to output.

From this it will· be seen that the first two subsidiary ratios for production management are

T2 $\qquad \dfrac{\text{Production costs}}{\text{Sales value of production}}$

T3 $\qquad \dfrac{\text{Sales value of production}}{\text{Production assets}}$

It is useful to proceed one stage farther in the analysis of both ratios T2 and T3. Subsidiary to T2 will be the main constituents of production costs measured by their appropriate ratios, such as

T4 $\qquad \dfrac{\text{Direct materials cost}}{\text{Sales value of production}}$

---

*The analysis contained in the following section, and particularly ratios T2 to T15, follows closely that devised and extensively used by the Centre for Interfirm Comparison. The concept behind the use of ratio T1 as a key ratio for the production function, and the integration of subsequent ratios beneath it, takes the practical development of the subject a stage further.

$$T5 \qquad \frac{\text{Direct labour cost}}{\text{Sales value of production}}$$

$$T6 \qquad \frac{\text{Production overheads}}{\text{Sales value of production}}$$

Any slowing down of the turnover of production assets (ratio T3) will have been caused by one or more of the following events. Any improvement in the turnover of production assets will have to come from action in one or more of the following fields: *Raw materials stock turnover* is slowing down, indicated by

$$T7 \qquad \frac{\text{Raw materials stock}}{\text{Average daily purchases}} \qquad rising$$

Shopfloor time is lengthening, or work in progress is building up, indicated by

$$T8 \qquad \frac{\text{Work in progress}}{\text{Average daily value of issues to production and products completed}} \qquad rising$$

Finished stock is building up, indicated by

$$T9 \qquad \frac{\text{Finished goods stock}}{\text{Average daily value of production completed}} \qquad rising$$

Utilisation of premises is dropping, indicated by

$$T10 \qquad \frac{\text{Value of factory premises}}{\text{Sales value of production}} \qquad rising$$

or by

$$T13 \qquad \frac{\text{Sales value of production}}{\text{Area of factory premises}} \qquad falling$$

Value of premises is rising, indicated by

$$T12 \qquad \frac{\text{Value of factory premises}}{\text{Area of factory premises}} \qquad rising$$

Utilisation of plant, machinery and factory vehicles is dropping, indicated by

$$T11 \qquad \frac{\text{Value of plant}}{\text{Sales value of production}} \qquad rising$$

Average age of plant is falling, as a result of old plant being replaced by new, indicated by

$$T14 \qquad \frac{\text{Plant, etc., at depreciated value}}{\text{Plant, etc., at undepreciated value}} \qquad rising$$

Changes in the sizes of ratios T10 and T11 have to be interpreted with care. There is nearly always a lag between an investment being made in a fixed asset, such as premises or plant, and the benefit of higher throughput or lower costs being obtained. This means that during such a period of lag, ratios T10 and T11 will deteriorate, although there is no real cause for alarm.

This situation can be dealt with by omitting the cost of new fixed assets from the numerators of ratios T10 and T11 until the assets are fully 'on stream'. The danger of such a course of action is that it removes from the system one of the devices that will constantly remind production management of the importance of getting the asset into profitable use. A compromise would be to have two figures for ratio T11, one including and the other excluding the value of unproductive fixed assets.

If the value of the fixed assets included in the numerators of ratios T10 and T11 is taken to be cost less depreciation, these two ratios will tend to decrease as the asset gets older. Such a change would be misleading if it was thought to indicate an improvement. This situation can be dealt with by using both the depreciated and the undepreciated values of these assets for these two ratios while still using the depreciated value for ratio T1.

This may seem inconsistent but it is not so. The depreciated value must be used for ratio T1 because as the asset gets older the profit from its use declines, either because its running costs have increased or the price that can be got for its output has declined. It is only reasonable to relate this declining profit to the decreasing value of the asset when measuring the efficiency with which it is being used. The total value of the output from the asset is likely to decline much less markedly, if at all, and for this reason it is better to relate the volume of output to an undepreciated value of the asset as is done in ratio T15. Volume of output is related to the depreciated value of the asset in ratio T11 in order to provide a link between ratio T15 and ratios T3 and T1. The average age of the assets is measured by ratio T14 in terms of the percentage of useful life remaining. (See also the discussion of this subject in Appendix 1.1.)

Over the course of the life of most fixed assets an appreciable degree of inflation will almost certainly take place. As output will be measured in terms of these inflated pounds, ratios T10 and T11 will decrease as a result of inflation as well as a result of real improvements in output. The best method of dealing with this problem is to use replacement values in place of the original cost.

Replacement values are useful for insurance purposes as well. They may be obtained from a study of the literature of machinery manufacturers and estate agents or by using suitable price indices. Such indices may be purchased from the Economist Intelligence Unit.

The ratios for production management to use when no measure of maximum output is obtainable are summarised in Diagram 9-1.

To calculate ratios T1 to T15 use data assembly and ratio calculation sheet 9-1 at the end of this chapter.

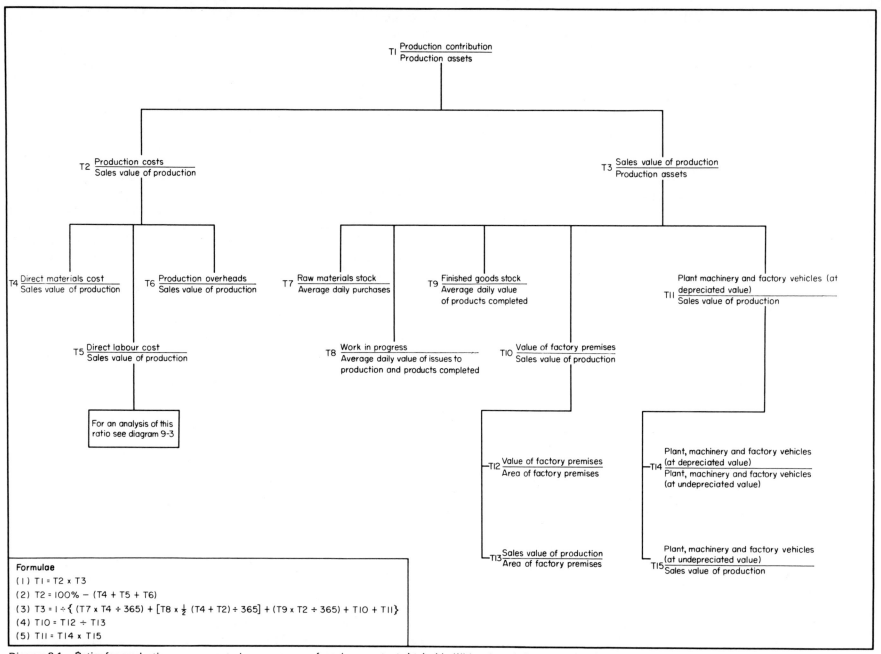

$$T1 \quad \frac{\text{Production contribution}}{\text{Production assets}}$$

$$T2 \quad \frac{\text{Production costs}}{\text{Sales value of production}}$$

$$T3 \quad \frac{\text{Sales value of production}}{\text{Production assets}}$$

$$T4 \quad \frac{\text{Direct materials cost}}{\text{Sales value of production}}$$

$$T6 \quad \frac{\text{Production overheads}}{\text{Sales value of production}}$$

$$T7 \quad \frac{\text{Raw materials stock}}{\text{Average daily purchases}}$$

$$T9 \quad \frac{\text{Finished goods stock}}{\text{Average daily value of products completed}}$$

$$T11 \quad \frac{\text{Plant machinery and factory vehicles (at depreciated value)}}{\text{Sales value of production}}$$

$$T5 \quad \frac{\text{Direct labour cost}}{\text{Sales value of production}}$$

$$T8 \quad \frac{\text{Work in progress}}{\text{Average daily value of issues to production and products completed}}$$

$$T10 \quad \frac{\text{Value of factory premises}}{\text{Sales value of production}}$$

For an analysis of this ratio see diagram 9-3

$$T12 \quad \frac{\text{Value of factory premises}}{\text{Area of factory premises}}$$

$$T13 \quad \frac{\text{Sales value of production}}{\text{Area of factory premises}}$$

$$T14 \quad \frac{\text{Plant, machinery and factory vehicles (at depreciated value)}}{\text{Plant, machinery and factory vehicles (at undepreciated value)}}$$

$$T15 \quad \frac{\text{Plant, machinery and factory vehicles (at undepreciated value)}}{\text{Sales value of production}}$$

Formulae

(1) $T1 = T2 \times T3$

(2) $T2 = 100\% - (T4 + T5 + T6)$

(3) $T3 = 1 \div \{ (T7 \times T4 \div 365) + [T8 \times \frac{1}{2} (T4 + T2) \div 365] + (T9 \times T2 \div 365) + T10 + T11 \}$

(4) $T10 = T12 \div T13$

(5) $T11 = T14 \times T15$

Diagram 9-1   Ratios for production management when no measure of maximum output obtainable. With acknowledgements to the Centre for Interfirm Comparison.

192

9.2 Measure of Maximum Output Obtainable

If a measure of maximum output is obtainable production management has a more sophisticated analytical tool. Performance will still be measured by the ratio of

$$T1 \qquad \frac{\text{Production contribution}}{\text{Production assets}}$$

but the factors influencing it are divided into five instead of the two used in the previous section (production costs/sales value of production and sales value of production/production assets). The five factors are the relationships between

1. Variable production costs and actual output—ratio U2
2. Variable production assets and actual output—ratio U3
3. Fixed production costs and maximum output—ratio U5
4. Fixed production assets and maximum output—ratio U6
5. Capacity utilisation (actual output as a percentage of maximum output)—ratio U4.

Variable production costs are those that tend to vary directly with the volume of output, such as the value of materials used.

Variable production assets are those whose level is likely to change as the volume of production changes, such as stocks of raw materials.

Fixed production costs are those wich do not change with changes in output. An example would be the rent of a factory.

Fixed production assets are those whose value does not fluctuate with changes in sales volume, such as the value of plant.

Both fixed production costs and assets are associated with a certain level of potential output. They are incurred or exist whether that potential is realised or not. They are the consequence of being *in* business rather than of *doing* business. They increase only if there is a substantial change in the capacity of the organisation to handle a volume of business.

The disadvantage of the method of analysis outlined in the previous section is that a change in only one factor causes a number of ratios to change. This is an uneconomical use of ratios. It is like having two speedometers in a car. If the volume of output increases but all other aspects of the firm's efficiency remain unchanged then under the method of analysis described in the previous section the following ratios change

$$T2 \qquad \frac{\text{Production costs}}{\text{Sales value of production}}$$

$$T3 \qquad \frac{\text{Sales value of production}}{\text{Production assets}}$$

$$T6 \qquad \frac{\text{Production overheads}}{\text{Sales value of production}}$$

$$T10 \qquad \frac{\text{Value of factory premises}}{\text{Sales value of production}}$$

$$T11 \qquad \frac{\text{Value of plant}}{\text{Sales value of production}}$$

Under the second method of analysis, the only ratio that changes is

$$U4 \qquad \frac{\text{Actual output}}{\text{Maximum output}}$$

The third tier of ratios is virtually the same as for the less sophisticated method of analysis. The whole set for use by production management where a measure of maximum output is obtainable is summarised in Diagram 9-2.

To calculate ratios U1 to U18 use data assembly and ratio calculation sheet 9-2 at the end of this chapter.

9.3 Shopfloor Ratios

Labour intensive shops

In Diagram 9-1 and 9-2 we suggested that the production manager would look at, among other ratios, the ratio of direct labour cost to sales value of production (ratio T5 or U8). The factors affecting this ratio are, in most manufacturing businesses, so important that we are devoting the whole of this section to them.

In this section we have attempted to use British Standard terminology wherever possible. The references in brackets after some words are to BS 3138: 1969 *Glossary of Terms used in Work Study*, the relevant parts of which have been reproduced in Appendix 1 to this chapter.

Ratio V1 in Diagram 9-3 is the same as ratio T5 in Diagram 9-1 and ratio U8 in Diagram 9-2. In some circumstances (as where light assembly work of expensive components is undertaken) it would be better to use value added in place of sales value of production. Value added being defined as sales value of production *less* direct materials cost.

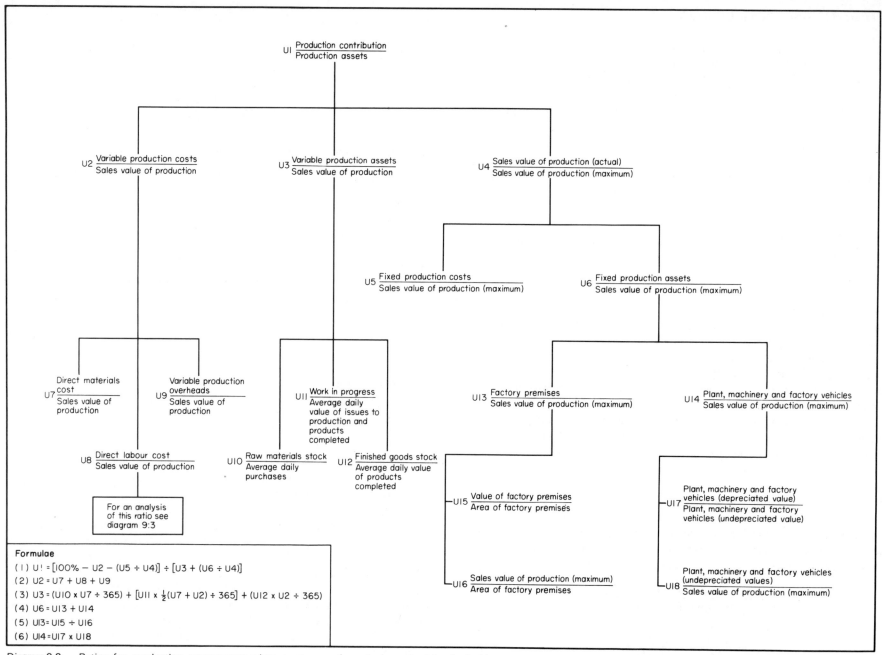

Diagram 9-2   Ratios for production management when a measure of maximum output is obtainable

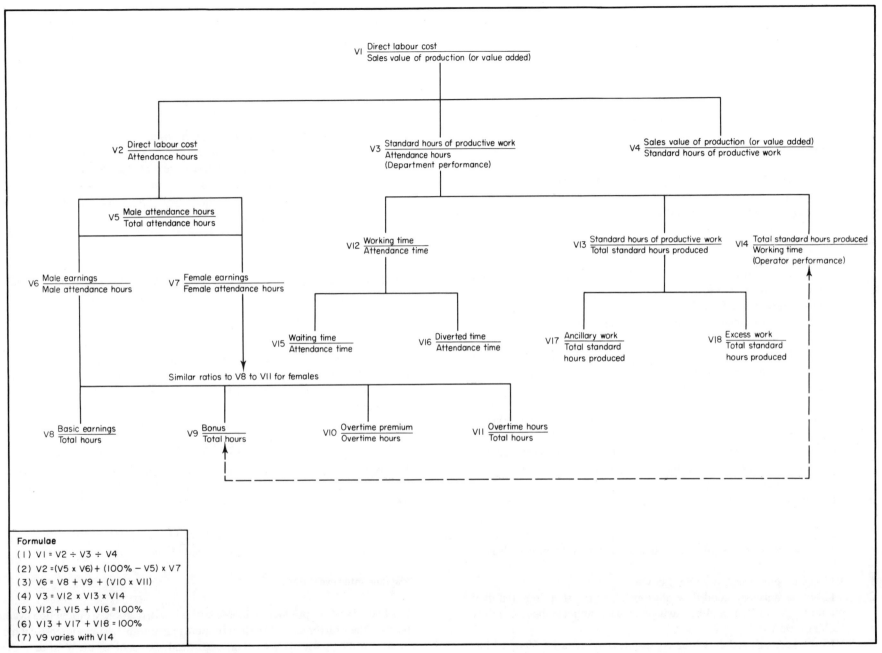

V1 $\dfrac{\text{Direct labour cost}}{\text{Sales value of production (or value added)}}$

V2 $\dfrac{\text{Direct labour cost}}{\text{Attendance hours}}$

V3 $\dfrac{\text{Standard hours of productive work}}{\text{Attendance hours}}$ (Department performance)

V4 $\dfrac{\text{Sales value of production (or value added)}}{\text{Standard hours of productive work}}$

V5 $\dfrac{\text{Male attendance hours}}{\text{Total attendance hours}}$

V12 $\dfrac{\text{Working time}}{\text{Attendance time}}$

V13 $\dfrac{\text{Standard hours of productive work}}{\text{Total standard hours produced}}$

V14 $\dfrac{\text{Total standard hours produced}}{\text{Working time}}$ (Operator performance)

V6 $\dfrac{\text{Male earnings}}{\text{Male attendance hours}}$

V7 $\dfrac{\text{Female earnings}}{\text{Female attendance hours}}$

V15 $\dfrac{\text{Waiting time}}{\text{Attendance time}}$

V16 $\dfrac{\text{Diverted time}}{\text{Attendance time}}$

V17 $\dfrac{\text{Ancillary work}}{\text{Total standard hours produced}}$

V18 $\dfrac{\text{Excess work}}{\text{Total standard hours produced}}$

Similar ratios to V8 to V11 for females

V8 $\dfrac{\text{Basic earnings}}{\text{Total hours}}$

V9 $\dfrac{\text{Bonus}}{\text{Total hours}}$

V10 $\dfrac{\text{Overtime premium}}{\text{Overtime hours}}$

V11 $\dfrac{\text{Overtime hours}}{\text{Total hours}}$

Formulae

(1) V1 = V2 ÷ V3 ÷ V4

(2) V2 = (V5 × V6) + (100% − V5) × V7

(3) V6 = V8 + V9 + (V10 × V11)

(4) V3 = V12 × V13 × V14

(5) V12 + V15 + V16 = 100%

(6) V13 + V17 + V18 = 100%

(7) V9 varies with V14

Diagram 9-3   Shopfloor ratios (labour intensive)

The size of ratio V1 is the resultant of three forces:

1 Average earnings per clock hour (ratio V2)
2 The output of standard hours (35008) in relation to attendance time (A1004)—ratio V3. (Note: This is approximately equal to Department Performance—A1023).
3 The sales value of the work produced in a standard hour (ratio V4).

The size of a firm's average earnings per clock hour (ratio V2) will depend on:

1 The proportion of hours worked by men to those worked by women (on the assumption that differences in pay will continue)—ratio V5, and
2 The average earnings of each sex (ratios V6 and V7).

An employee's average earnings is determined by:

1 The basic rate (ratio V8)
2 The bonus earned (ratio V9)
3 The overtime premium (ratio V10)
4 The proportion of overtime worked (ratio V11).

The amount of bonus (ratio V9) depends on the type of incentive scheme and the average operator performance (A1022)—see ratio V14 below.
 Ratio V3—the Department Performance—depends on:

1 The proportion of attendance time that is working time (A1006) as opposed to waiting (33017) or diverted time (A1005)—ratio V12.
2 The proportion of standard hours produced by the employees that are of saleable work or productive work (A1012) as opposed to excess work (A1014) or ancillary work (A1013)—ratio V13.
3 The average operator performance (A1022)—ratio V14.

Obviously production management will keep all of the above ratios under review—most particularly those that they can most directly influence, such as:

1 V11—by keeping overtime working down
2 V12—by organising a good flow of work on to the shopfloor and thus minimising ratio V15, and by having adequate indirect labour and thus curbing ratio V16
3 V13—by keeping batches as long as possible (but see ratios T9 or U12 in Diagrams 9-1 and 9-2) indicated by a low ratio V17, and by making sure

that the workers use the correct methods and have the right materials, machines and tools available, indicated by a low ratio V18
4 V14—by encouragement, good employee relations, good training and a properly designed incentive scheme.

Some ratios are to some extent outside production management's control such as:

1 V4—largely the sales department's responsibility but can be improved by value analysis which is sometimes a production responsibility, and by method improvement, an industrial engineering responsibility
2 V5—largely determined by local supply and the personnel department, but the production engineer could devise different methods which would require cheaper (female) labour
3 V8 and V10 are the result of local supply and demand and national agreements.

To calculate ratios V1 to V18 use data assembly and ratio calculation sheet 9.3 at the end of this chapter.

Indirect workers

There are two ways of dealing with this increasingly important group of workers who work within the factory but who are not classified as direct, such as storemen, maintenance workers, setters and foremen. The first is to add to the hours of these people the diverted time of the directs and to monitor the total indirect time by the ratio

$$V19 \quad \frac{\text{Total indirect hours}}{\text{Direct hours (direct attendance hours less diverted time)}}$$

The second is to use the cost of both direct and indirect workers as the numerator of ratios V1 and V2 and the total attendance time of these two groups as the denominator of ratios V2 and V3 and so on down the set of V ratios. Ratio V16 will then become

$$\frac{\text{Total indirect hours}}{\text{Attendance time}}$$

Machine-intensive shops

In situations where production labour cost is low in relation to production overheads, because the firm (or individual shop) is more machine than labour intensive it may not be worthwhile to use the V set of ratios. Instead one could use the W ratios of Diagram 9-4. Not surprisingly it will be seen that they have similarities to the V ratios.

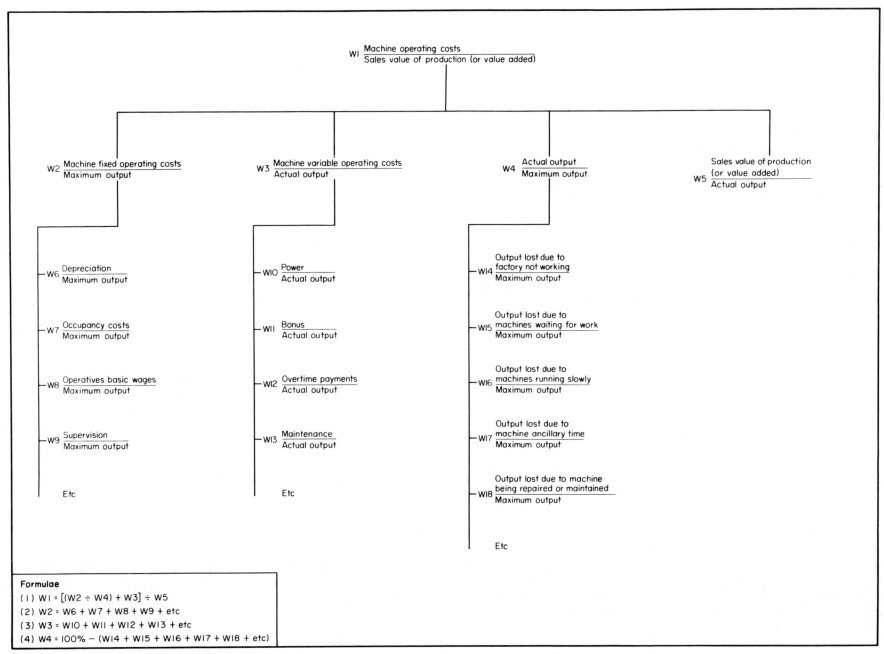

W1 $\dfrac{\text{Machine operating costs}}{\text{Sales value of production (or value added)}}$

W2 $\dfrac{\text{Machine fixed operating costs}}{\text{Maximum output}}$

W3 $\dfrac{\text{Machine variable operating costs}}{\text{Actual output}}$

W4 $\dfrac{\text{Actual output}}{\text{Maximum output}}$

W5 $\dfrac{\text{Sales value of production (or value added)}}{\text{Actual output}}$

W6 $\dfrac{\text{Depreciation}}{\text{Maximum output}}$

W7 $\dfrac{\text{Occupancy costs}}{\text{Maximum output}}$

W8 $\dfrac{\text{Operatives basic wages}}{\text{Maximum output}}$

W9 $\dfrac{\text{Supervision}}{\text{Maximum output}}$

Etc

W10 $\dfrac{\text{Power}}{\text{Actual output}}$

W11 $\dfrac{\text{Bonus}}{\text{Actual output}}$

W12 $\dfrac{\text{Overtime payments}}{\text{Actual output}}$

W13 $\dfrac{\text{Maintenance}}{\text{Actual output}}$

Etc

W14 $\dfrac{\text{Output lost due to factory not working}}{\text{Maximum output}}$

W15 $\dfrac{\text{Output lost due to machines waiting for work}}{\text{Maximum output}}$

W16 $\dfrac{\text{Output lost due to machines running slowly}}{\text{Maximum output}}$

W17 $\dfrac{\text{Output lost due to machine ancillary time}}{\text{Maximum output}}$

W18 $\dfrac{\text{Output lost due to machine being repaired or maintained}}{\text{Maximum output}}$

Etc

Formulae

(1) W1 = [(W2 ÷ W4) + W3] ÷ W5

(2) W2 = W6 + W7 + W8 + W9 + etc

(3) W3 = W10 + W11 + W12 + W13 + etc

(4) W4 = 100% − (W14 + W15 + W16 + W17 + W18 + etc)

Diagram 9-4   Shopfloor ratios (machine intensive)

The production manager's key ratio for a machine intensive shop is the machine operating costs in relation to sales value of production (or to value added)—ratio W1 in Diagram 9-4. Ratio W1 is affected by four main forces:

1   The costs of providing the shop's *capacity to produce.* These costs, described as machine fixed operating costs, do not vary significantly with the volume of actual production. They are related however to the maximum output the machinery is capable of if run twenty-four hours a day, 365 days a year (ratio W2). This output could be measured in standard hours, or gallons, or square yards, or whatever is suitable.
2   The costs of producing the shop's *actual output*—the machines' variable operating costs (ratio W3).
3   The proportion of the maximum output that is actually achieved (ratio W4).
4   The sales value of the actual output (ratio W5).

The machines' fixed operating costs will include:

1   Occupancy costs—the cost of the factory space (rent, rates, heating, lighting, cleaning, insurance)
2   The operatives' basic wages—the payment for being there as opposed to for producing output
3   The wages of supervisors, chargehands, foremen, inspectors and other people whose pay does not vary with volume of output
4   Depreciation, in so far as this is a function of time (when it would more correctly be described as obsolescence). To the extent that depreciation is a function of use it should be included under variable costs. In most cases, in practice, it is treated however as a fixed cost.

The magnitude of these costs is largely determined by the type of machinery used and the organisation of the shop. The size of ratio W2 cannot easily be changed in the short term. This emphasises the importance of careful purchase, layout and pre-production planning.

The machines' variable operating costs will include: power; operatives' bonuses and overtime payments; maintenance; etc. Ratio W3 can be improved by attention to the design of the product, by study of the method of production, by the practice of preventive maintenance, by good production planning and a fair incentive scheme.

Ratio W4 can be improved by action on all or some of the following fronts:

1   Longer or more shifts (ratio W14)
2   Reduction of idle time due to lack of work (ratio W15)

3   Good maintenance (ratio W16)
4   Good set-up procedures (ratio W17)
5   Long batches (ratio W17)
6   Timely maintenance (ratio W18).

Ratio W5 is very similar to ratio V4 (see page 196). Improvements to this can be obtained by:

1   A better price
2   Value analysis
3   Method improvements.

To calculate ratios W1 to W18 use data assembly and ratio calculation sheet 9-4 at the end of this chapter.

9.4 Economic Batch Quantity (EBQ)

In order to improve its key ratio (production contribution/production assets) production management will want to optimise the level of the stocks which are its responsibility:

1   Raw materials stock (responsible jointly with the buyer)
2   Work in progress
3   Finished goods stock (responsible jointly with sales management).

The technique for determining the optimum level of raw material stocks (economic order quantity) was briefly outlined in the chapter for the buyer (see page 146); an analogous technique (economic batch quantity) is used by production management to determine the optimum level of finished goods stock.

The basis of economic batch quantity (EBQ) theory is that production costs are made up of three elements:

1   Variable production costs (which vary only with the quantity made—materials, labour, power)
2   Ancillary production costs (which vary only with the number of batches made—costs of setting up, cleaning and changing over machines from one item to the next)
3   Carrying costs (which vary with the quantity stored and the time left in store—rent of the store, insurance, wastage and so on).

If these three costs are graphed, the result will be similar to Diagram 9-5, which shows that total production costs per unit are at a minimum of £OA when the size of the batch is OB units. This is the economic batch quantity (EBQ). It is characteristic of such curves that cost rises more steeply for batches smaller than the EBQ and less steeply for batches larger than the EBQ, indicating that it is desirable to prevent batches from being smaller than the EBQ, but that it is less important if they are slightly larger than the EBQ. However each production department must construct its own graphs for its own products and circumstances and draw its own conclusions as to appropriate action.

hen the smaller will be the amount of capital tied up in work in progress.

Diagram 9-6 illustrates the relationship between

1   The various stock turnover ratios that the production manager will monitor.
2   The flows of materials through the factory.
3   The absolute quantities of stock.

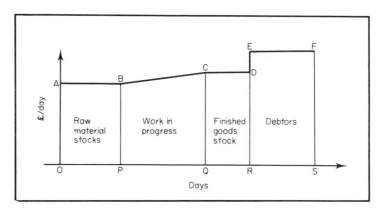

Diagram 9-6   Stock turnover ratios, flow of materials and time in stock

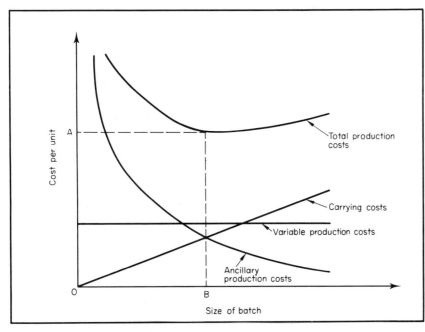

Diagram 9-5   Economic batch quantity

The magnitude of (ratios T8 or U11)

$$\frac{\text{Work in progress}}{\text{Average daily value of issues to production and products completed}}$$

depends entirely on the length of time taken to complete a product. The better is production control, so that delays between production processes are minimised, and the better is production engineering, so that actual manufacturing time is minimised,

In Diagram 9-6, the vertical axis measures the average value per day; the horizontal axis the average number of days. On both axes the days are 'real' days. The diagram is simplified to the extent of assuming that stock levels are not rising or falling.

OA equals the average daily value of raw materials purchased, and PB equals the average daily value of raw material issued to production. OP equals the average number of days raw materials stays in stock. The area OABP therefore equals the average value of raw material stock.

PQ equals the average number of days required to make a product (shop-floor time) and QC equals the average daily value of completed products. The area PBCQ represents the average value of work in progress.

QR equals the average number of days finished goods stay in stock; RD equals the average daily value of sales (at cost). The area QCDR therefore equals the average value of finished goods stock.

RS equals the average number of days' credit taken by customers, and RE equals the average daily value of sales (selling price); SF equals the average daily value of cash received from debtors. The area REFS therefore equals the averages value of debtors.

The current assets utilisation ratios which are measured in terms of pounds per £1000 are the areas OABP, PBCQ, QCDR, and REFS divided by sales (RE $\times$ 365) divided by 1000. The ratios which are measured in terms of days are the lengths OP, PQ, QR, and RS.

The fact that the vertical heights increase as one moves from left to right in the diagram emphasises that a day at a later stage in the production/sales process ties up more capital than one at an earlier stage.

Appendix 9.1
Extract from *Glossary of Terms used in Work Study,*
British Standards Institution (BS 3138: 1969)

Note: Copies of the complete standard may be obtained from British Standards Institution, Sales Department, 101 Pentonville Road, London N1 9ND.

35008 **standard unit of work,** i.e. **standard hour, standard minute**	A unit of work consists partly of work and partly of *relaxation*, the proportion of *relaxation* to work varying with the nature of the *job*. In current practice the unit has a value such that 100, 80, 60 or 1 are produced in one hour when *unrestricted work* is carried out at *standard performance,* i.e. at 100 *British Standard scale*. (It is recommended that the basis with 1 or 60 units per hour be adopted in future and that these units be termed standard hours (SHs) or standard minutes (SMs) respectively.)
A1002 **overtime**	That part of *attendance time* which is spent by a worker at the place or places of employment in excess of or outside the normal *working day* or *week*.
A1004 **attendance time** CLOCK HOURS/MINUTES	The total time spent by a worker at the place or places of employment, whether working or available for work, for which payment is made.
A1005 **diverted time** LOST TIME	That part of *attendance time* when a worker is engaged on other than productive or ancillary work, e.g. committee work, accidents, etc.
A1006 **working time**	Time taken to do the work including authorised relaxation.
A1012 **productive work**	Work which alters the physical or chemical nature of the product or advances the process as a necessary contribution to its completion.
A1013 **ancillary work**	Service or any other work related to a process which it is not appropriate to classify as productive.
A1014 **excess work**	Extra work occasioned by departures from the specified method or materials for which control standards have been established.
A1022 **operator performance** TRUE PERFORMANCE	An indication of the effectiveness of a worker or group of workers whilst on *measured* or *estimated work*.

Ratio of: total *standard times* for all *measured* and *estimated work*
to: time on *measured* and *estimated work* (excluding *diverted* and *waiting time*).
$\Big\}$ x 100

A1023 **department performance**　An indication of the effectiveness of a department or section.

Ratio of: total *standard times* for *measured* and *estimated work*
to: time on *measured* and *estimated work* plus any *waiting* or *diverted time* for which the department is responsible.
$\Big\}$ x 100

Alternatively:

Ratio of: total *standard times* for *measured* and *estimated work* plus *uncontrolled work* at assessed performance.
to: total *attendance time* excluding time on *allocated work,* if any, and *waiting* or *diverted time* for which the department is not responsible.
$\Big\}$ x 100

Ratios for the production director when no measure of maximum output obtainable

Code letter	Item	Month or quarter to (date)					
A	Raw materials stock at beginning of period						
B	Purchases						
C	Sub total (A + B)						
D	Raw materials stock at end of period						
E	Raw materials issued to production=direct materials cost (C − D)						
F	Direct labour cost						
G	Production overheads						
H	Production costs (E + F + G)						
K	Work in progress at beginning of period						
L	Sub total (H + K)						
M	Work in progress at end of period						
N	Production cost of goods made (L−M)						
P	Finished goods stock at beginning of period						
Q	Sub total (N + P)						
R	Finished goods stock at end of period						
S	Production costs of goods sold (Q − R)						

Data assembly sheet 9-1: *continued*

Ratios for the production director when no measure of maximum output obtainable

Code letter	Item	Month or quarter to (date)					
T	Sales						
W	Sales value of production (N x T ÷ S)						
Y	Production contribution (W − H)						
Z	Value of factory premises						
AA	Plant machinery and factory vehicles (at undepreciated value)						
AB	Plant machinery and factory vehicles (at depreciated value)						
AC	Production assets (1/2[A+D+K+M+P+R] +Z+AB)						
AD	Area of factory premises						
AE	No. of working days in period						
AF	No. of working days in year						

Ratios for the production director when no measure of maximum output is obtainable

Ratio	Formula for calculation of ratio	Unit of measurement	Month or quarter to (date)					
T1 Production contribution/ Production assets	Y x 100 ÷ AC x AF ÷ AE	% pa						
T2 Production costs/ Sales value of production	H x 100 ÷ W	%						
T3 Sales value of production/ Production assets	W ÷ AC x AF ÷ AE	times per year						
T4 Direct materials cost/Sales value of production	E x 100 ÷ W	%						
T5 Direct labour cost/Sales value of production	F x 100 ÷ W	%						
T6 Production overheads/ Sales value of production	G x 100 ÷ W	%						
T7 Raw materials stock/ Average daily purchases	½ (A + D) ÷ (B ÷ AE)	days						
T8 Work in progress/ Average daily value of issues to production and products completed	½(K + M) ÷ ½ [(B + N) ÷ AE]	days						
T9 Finished goods stock/Average daily value of products completed	½ (P + R) ÷ (N ÷ AE)	days						

Ratios for the production director when no measure of maximum output is obtainable

Ratio		Formula for calculation of ratio	Unit of measurement	Month or quarter to (date)					
T10	Value of factory premises/Sales value of production	$Z \times 1000 \div (W \times AF \div AE)$	‰ pa						
T11	Plant machinery and factory vehicles (at depreciated value)/Sales value of production	$AB \times 1000 \div (W \times AF \div AE)$	‰ pa						
T12	Value of factory premises/ Area of factory premises	$Z \div AD$	£ per sq. ft.						
T13	Sales value of production/ Area of factory premises	$W \times AF \div AE \div AD$	£'s per year per sq. ft.						
T14	Plant machinery and factory vehicles: depreciated value/ Undepreciated value	$AB \times 100 \div AA$	%						
T15	Plant machinery and factory vehicles (at undepreciated value)/Sales value of production	$AA \times 1000 \div (W \times AF \div AE)$	‰ pa						

Data assembly sheet 9-2

Ratios for the production director—When a measure of maximum output is obtainable

Code letter	Item	Month or quarter to (date)					
A	Raw materials stock at beginning of period						
B	Purchases						
C	Sub total (A + B)						
D	Raw materials stock at end of period						
E	Raw materials issued to production = direct materials cost (C−D)						
F	Direct labour cost						
G	Variable production overheads						
H	Variable production costs (E+F+G)						
K	Fixed production costs						
L	Total production costs (H + K)						
M	Work in progress at beginning of period						
N	Sub total (L + M)						
P	Work in progress at end of period						
Q	Production cost of goods made (N−P)						
R	Finished goods stock at beginning of period						
S	Sub total (Q+R)						
T	Finished goods stock at end of period						
U	Production cost of goods sold (S + T)						

Ratios for the production director—When a measure of maximum output is obtainable

Code letter	Item	Month or quarter to (date)					
V	Sales						
W	Sales value of production (actual) ($Q \times V \div U$)						
Y	Sales value of production (maximum)						
Z	Production contribution ($W-L$)						
AA	Average value of factory premises						
AB	Average value of plant , machinery and factory vehicles (depreciated value)						
AC	Fixed production assets ($AA+AB$)						
AD	Variable production assets ½($A+D+L+N+Q+S$)						
AE	Production assets ($AC+AD$)						
AF	Area of factory premises						
AG	Plant machinery and factory vehicles (undepreciated value)						
AH	No. of working days in period						
AK	No. of working days in year						

Ratios for the production director—When a measure of maximum output is obtainable

Ratio	Formula for calculation of ratio	Unit of measurement	Month or quarter to (date)					
U1 Production contribution/ Production assets	Z x 100 ÷ AE x AK ÷ AH	% pa						
U2 Variable production costs/Sales value of production	H x 100 ÷ W	%						
U3 Variable production assets/Sales value of production	AD x 1000 ÷ (W x AK ÷ AH)	‰ pa						
U4 Sales value of production (actual)/ Sales value of production (maximum)	W x 100 ÷ Y	%						
U5 Fixed production costs/ Sales value of production (maximum)	K x 100 ÷ Y	%						
U6 Fixed production assets/ Sales value of production (maximum)	AC x 1000 ÷ (Y x AK ÷ AH)	‰ pa						
U7 Direct materials cost/Sales value of production	E x 100 ÷ W	%						
U8 Direct labour cost/Sales value of production	F x 100 ÷ W	%						
U9 Variable production overheads/Sales value of production	G x 100 ÷ W	%						
U10 Raw materials stock/ Average daily purchases	½(A+D) ÷ (B ÷ AH)	days						

Ratios for the production director—When a measure of maximum output is obtainable

Ratio		Formula for calculation of ratio	Unit of measurement	Month or quarter to (date)						
U11	Work in progress/ Average daily value of issues to production and products completed	½ (M+P) ÷ [(B+Q) ÷ (AH x 2)]	days							
U12	Finished goods stock/Average daily value of products completed	½(R+T) ÷ (Q ÷ AH)	days							
U13	Factory premises/ Sales value of production (maximum)	AA x 1000 ÷ (Y x AK ÷ AH)	‰ pa							
U14	Plant, machinery and factory vehicles/ Sales value production (maximum)	AB x 1000 ÷ (Y x AK ÷ AH)	‰ pa							
U15	Value of factory premises/Area of factory premises	AA ÷ AF	£ per sq. ft.							
U16	Sales of value of production (maximum)/ Area of factory premises	Y x AK ÷ AH ÷ AF	£'s pa per sq. ft.							
U17	Plant, machinery and factory vehicles: depreciated/ Undepreciated value	AB x 100 ÷ AG	%							
U18	Plant, machinery and factory vehicles (undepreciated value)/ Sales value of production (maximum)	AG x 1000 ÷ (Y x AK ÷ AH)	‰ pa							

Data assembly sheet 9-3

Shopfloor ratios (labour intensive)

Code letter	Item	Month or quarter to (date)					
A	Male basic earnings						
B	Male bonus						
C	Male overtime premium						
D	Male earnings (A + B + C)						
E	Female basic earnings						
F	Female bonus						
G	Female overtime premium						
H	Female earnings (E + F + G)						
K	Direct labour cost (D + H)						
L	Male basic hours						
M	Male overtime hours						
N	Male attendance hours (L + M)						
P	Female basic hours						
Q	Female overtime hours						
R	Female attendance hours (P + Q)						
S	Attendance time (N + R)						
T	Waiting time						
W	Diverted time						
Y	Working time (S − T − W)						

Shopfloor ratios (labour intensive)

Code letter	Item	Month or quarter to (date)					
Z	Ancillary work						
AA	Excess work						
AB	Standard hours of productive work						
AC	Total standard hours produced						
AD	Sales value of production (or value added)						

Shopfloor ratios (labour intensive)

Ratio	Formula for calculation of ratio	Unit of measurement	Month or quarter to (date)					
V1 Direct labour cost/sales value of production (or value added)	K x 100 ÷ AD	%						
V2 Direct labour cost/ Attendance hours	K ÷ S	£ per hr						
V3 Standard hours of productive work/ Attendance hours (Department performance)	AB x 100 ÷ S	%						
V4 Sales value of production (or value added)/ Standard hours of productive work	AD ÷ AB	£ per st. hr						
V5 Male attendance hours/ Total attendance hours	N x 100 ÷ S	%						
V6 Male earnings/ Male attendance hours	D ÷ N	£ per hr						
V7 Female earnings/ Female attendance hours	H ÷ R	£ per hr						
V8 Basic earnings/ Total hours	A ÷ N	£ per hr						
V9 Bonus/ Total hours	B ÷ N	£ per hr						
V10 Overtime premium/ Overtime hours	C ÷ M	£ per hr						

Ratio		Formula for calculation of ratio	Unit of measurement	Month or quarter to (date)						
V11	Overtime hours/ Total hours	M x 100 ÷ N	%							
V12	Working time/ Attendance time	Y x 100 ÷ S	%							
V13	Standard hours of productive work/ Total standard hours produced	AB x 100 ÷ AC	%							
V14	Total standard hours produced/ Working time (operator performance)	AC x 100 ÷ Y	%							
V15	Waiting time/ Attendance time	T x 100 ÷ S	%							
V16	Diverted time/ Attendance time	W x 100 ÷ S	%							
V17	Ancillary work/ Total standard hours produced	Z x 100 ÷ AC	%							
V18	Excess work/ Total standard hours produced	AA x 100 ÷ AC	%							

Shopfloor ratios (machine intensive)

Code letter	Item	Month or quarter to (date)					
A	Depreciation						
B	Occupancy costs						
C	Operatives' basic wages						
D	Supervision						
E	Other machine fixed operating costs						
F	Machine fixed operating costs (A+B+C+D+E)						
G	Power						
H	Bonus						
K	Overtime payments						
L	Maintenance						
M	Other machine variable operating costs						
N	Machine variable operating costs (G+H+K+L+M)						
P	Machine operating costs (F+N)						
Q	Actual output						
R	Output lost due to factory not working						
S	Output lost due to machines waiting for work						
T	Output lost due to machines running slowly						
U	Output lost due to machine ancillary time						
V	Output lost due to machine being repaired or maintained						
W	Output lost due to other causes						
Y	Maximum output (Q+R+S+T+U+V+W)						
Z	Sales value of production (or value added)						

Shopfloor ratios (machine intensive)

Ratio	Formula for calculation of ratio	Unit of measurement	Month or quarter to (date)					
W1 Machine operating costs/ Sales value of production (or value added)	P x 100 ÷ Z	%						
W2 Machine fixed operating costs/ Maximum output	F ÷ Y	£ per unit of output						
W3 Machine variable operating costs/ Actual output	N ÷ Q	£ per unit of output						
W4 Actual output/ Maximum output	Q x 100 ÷ Y	%						
W5 Sales value of production (or value added) / Actual output	Z ÷ Q	£ per unit of output						
W6 Depreciation/ Maximum output	A ÷ Y	£ per unit of output						
W7 Occupancy costs/ Maximum output	B ÷ Y	£ per unit of output						
W8 Operatives basic wages/ Maximum output	C ÷ Y	£ per unit of output						
W9 Supervision/ Maximum output	D ÷ Y	£ per unit of output						
W10 Power/Actual output	G ÷ Q	£ per unit of output						
W11 Bonus/Actual output	H ÷ Q	£ per unit of output						
W12 Overtime payments/ Actual output	K ÷ Q	£ per unit of output						
W13 Maintenance/ Actual output	L ÷ Q	£ per unit of output						
W14 Output lost due to factory not working/ Maximim output	R x 100 ÷ Y	%						

Ratio		Formula for calculation of ratio	Unit of measurement	Month or quarter to (date)					
W15	Output lost due to machines waiting for work/Maximum output	S x 100 ÷ Y	%						
W16	Output lost due to machines running slowly/ Maximum output	T x 100 ÷ Y	%						
W17	Output lost due to machine ancillary time/ Maximum output	U x 100 ÷ Y	%						
W18	Output lost due to machine being repaired or maintained/ Maximum output	V x 100 ÷ Y	%						

Chapter 10

Ratios for personnel management

What ratios should the personnel department look at? Obviously this depends on what the department is responsible for. Let us assume that its responsibilities are recruiting, training and industrial relations. In Chapter 1 it was stated that it is desirable to provide each manager with a single key ratio which measures the degree of his success. In the case of the personnel department such a ratio would probably relate the costs of the department plus the costs of poor personnel policies (this total will for convenience be called personnel costs) to the size of the total work force. Personnel costs would include:

1   Recruitment and replacement
2   Training and retraining
3   Other personnel department costs
4   Wage increases in excess of national agreement
5   Production lost through poor industrial relations.

This last cost may be hard to quantify accurately but it should include at least the value of profit lost (not the value of sales lost) as a result of strikes, go slows, workings to rule, and so on.

The size of the work force would be an average over the relevant period, part time workers being counted as an appropriate fraction. The personnel department's key ratio would then be

$$X1 \qquad \frac{\text{Personnel costs}}{\text{Average number of employees}}$$

The department would attempt to minimise this ratio over the medium term. To do this it would be necessary to balance the costs of items 1, 2, 3 and 4 above against the costs which would result from not spending enough on them (item 5).

The main subsidiary ratios which the department could use are shown in Diagram

218

10-1. They are discussed under the three headings of recruitment, training and industrial relations.

To calculate ratios X1 to X4 use data assembly and ratio calculation sheet 10.1 at the end of this chapter.

10.1   Recruitment

The costs of recruiting are fairly easily identified. They include the time of the firm's own staff, the cost of advertisements, agency fees, and candidates' expenses. The best measure of the benefits of recruiting is the number of recruits which the firm retains for a worthwhile period (say more than one year). So the ratio which would be used to monitor this aspect of the personnel department's work would be:

$$X2 \qquad \frac{\text{Recruiting costs}}{\text{Recruits retained}} \qquad \text{(see Diagram 10-2)}$$

Action that would lead to a reduction in this ratio would include:

1   Cutting the costs per recruit interviewed (ratio X5) (or increasing the cost in order to achieve 2 and 3 below)
2   Being more selective of interviewees so that a higher proportion can be offered a job (ratio X6)
3   Being more careful to whom jobs are offered so that a higher proportion accept the job (ratio X7) and, having accepted, stay for a worthwhile period (the length of this period will obviously vary from job to job)—ratio X8

If the size of the personnel department's work warranted it, these ratios could be calculated separately for males and for females and for different types of jobs.

To calculate ratios X2 and X5 to X8 use data assembly and ratio calculation sheet 10-2 at the end of this chapter.

10.2 Training

Probably the best ratio to monitor the performance of the training department is

X3 $\dfrac{\text{Training costs}}{\text{Average number of employees}}$

This ratio can be improved by:

1   Curbing the costs of training per trainee day (ratio X9), either by action on the cost side or by increasing the numbers trained for the same cost.
2   Reducing the number of days needed to train new recruits by improved teaching methods (ratio X10).
3   Keeping the number of recruits at a reasonable level in relation to the total number of employees (ratio X11). Too few recruits may imply stagnation; too many, either poor selection or too high a turnover of employees (or, of course, both).

To calculate ratios X3 and X9 to X11 use data assembly and ratio calculation sheet 10-3 at the end of this chapter.

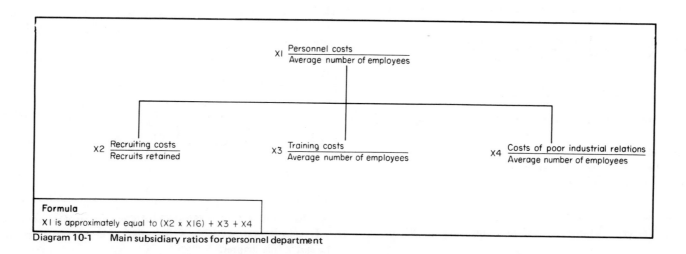

Diagram 10-1   Main subsidiary ratios for personnel department

10.3 Industrial Relations

Under the heading of industrial relations (IR) the personnel department could look at a number of ratios. It has already been suggested that

$$X4 \quad \frac{\text{Costs of poor IR}}{\text{Average number of employees}}$$

should be monitored. In addition the two components of X4 can be shown separately:

$$X12 \quad \frac{\text{Cost of wage increases in excess of national agreements}}{\text{Average number of employees}}$$

$$X13 \quad \frac{\text{Cost of production lost through poor IR}}{\text{Average number of employees}}$$

particularly as there may well need to be 'horse trading' between X12 and X13 in order to minimise X4 and X1 because bad industrial relations will affect recruiting and training costs and performance as well.

If X4, X12 and X13 are not used, the following crude measure of the state of IR could be used

$$X14 \quad \frac{\text{Number of man-days lost through strikes, etc.}}{\text{Number of man-days worked}}$$

It has been suggested that absenteeism is a more sensitive measure of the state of IR, and a rise in its level may give early warning of larger trouble looming, so it would be useful to monitor

$$X15 \quad \frac{\text{Number of man-days lost through absenteeism}}{\text{Number of man-days worked}}$$

Staff turnover or employee wastage, as measured by

$$X16 \quad \frac{\text{Number of leavers}}{\text{Average number of employees}}$$

is another crude measure of the IR climate in a firm. P.J. Samuel* has suggested two better ones:

X17 The employee stability index

$$\frac{\text{Number of employees with 12 months service now}}{\text{Total employed a year ago}}$$

and

---

*P.J. Samuel, *Labour Turnover? Towards a Solution*—Institute of Personnel Management, 1969.

X18 The skill conservation index

$$\frac{\text{Number of employees with over 12 months service now}}{\text{Total employed now}}$$

A modification of Samuel's own example will illustrate the difference between these three indices. The data are as follows:

1. Company *A* loses during the year every person employed at the beginning of the year. As he leaves, each is replaced by someone who remains until the following year.
2. Company *B* loses in the course of a year half the people it employed at the beginning of that year. Their replacements also leave before the end of a year and have to be replaced.
3. Company *C* loses four people at the beginning of the year. Their jobs are filled by a succession of people, each of whom stays only a fortnight.

In addition, all three companies expand their work force by fifty people from 100 to 150, that is, the average number of employees during the year is 125. Table 10-1 shows the effect on ratios X16, X17 and X18.

Clearly there is a link between X8 (recruits staying/recruits accepting) and X11 (trainees/total employees) on the one hand and X17 and X18 (employee stability and skill conservation) on the other. Poor recruiting will lead to high training costs, low stability and poor skill conservation. It is as well therefore, that in most firms all these activities are the responsibility of a single department.

Ratio	Company	A	B	C
X16	Employee wastage	$\frac{100}{125} = 80\%$	$\frac{50+50}{125} = 80\%$	$\frac{4 \times 25}{125} = 80\%$
X17	Employee stability	$\frac{0}{100} = 0\%$	$\frac{50}{100} = 50\%$	$\frac{96}{100} = 96\%$
X18	Skill conservation	$\frac{0}{150} = 0\%$	$\frac{50}{150} = 33\%$	$\frac{96}{150} = 64\%$

Table 10-1 Effect on ratios X16 to X18 of different rates of labour turnover

To calculate ratios X12 to X18 use data assembly and ratio calculation sheet 10-4 at the end of this chapter.

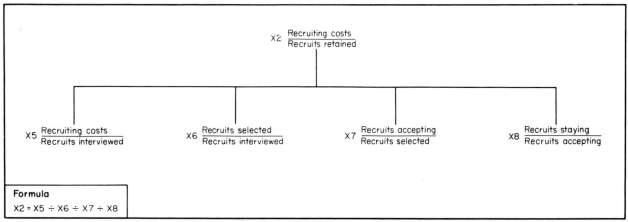

Diagram 10-2   Recruiting ratios

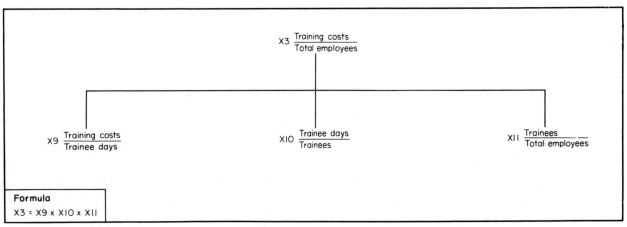

Diagram 10-3   Training ratios

Data assembly sheet 10-1
Main subsidiary ratios for personnel department

Code letter	Item	Month or quarter to (date)					
A	Recruiting costs						
B	Training costs						
C	Costs of poor Industrial Relations						
D	Other personnel department costs						
E	Personnel costs (A+B+C+D)						
F	Recruits retained						
G	Average number of employees						
H	No. of working days in period						
K	No. of working days in year						

Main subsidiary ratios for personnel department

Ratio	Formula for calculation of ratio	Unit of Measurement	Month or quarter to (date)					
X1 Personnel costs/ Average number of employees	E ÷ G x K ÷ H	£ per head per year						
X2 Recruiting costs/ Recruits retained	A ÷ F x K ÷ H	£ per head per year						
X3 Training costs/ Average number of employees	B ÷ G x K ÷ H	£ per head per year						
X4 Costs of poor Industrial Relations/ Average number of employees	C ÷ G x K ÷ H	£ per head per year						

Recruiting ratios

Code letter	Item	12 months or 4 quarters to (date)					
A	Recruits interviewed						
B	Recruits selected						
C	Recruits accepting						
D	Recruits staying (or retained)						
E	Recruiting costs						

NB As the process of interviewing, selection and acceptance may well take longer than a month (or even a quarter for more senior staff) and as it will not be known if a recruit is going to stay for a worthwhile period until the end of that period, it would not be sensible to calculate ratios based on items measured in the same month. One can either follow separate batches of candidates for a year (or whatever is the length of the 'worthwhile' period) and use each column of the work sheets for a separate batch, or calculate a moving annual average. The work sheets have been headed up for the second method but the first method is perhaps the more scientific.

Recruiting ratios

Ratio		Formula for calculation of ratio	Unit of measurement	12 months or 4 quarters to (date)					
X2	Recruiting costs/ Recruits retained	E ÷ D	£'s per head						
X5	Recruiting costs/ Recruits interviewed	E ÷ A	£'s per head						
X6	Recruits selected/ Recruits interviewed	B x 100 ÷ A	%						
X7	Recruits accepting/ Recruits selected	C x 100 ÷ B	%						
X8	Recruits staying/ Recruits accepting	D x 100 ÷ C	%						

Training ratios

Code letter	Item	Month or quarter to (date)					
A	Training costs						
B	Trainees						
C	Trainee days						
D	Total employees						
E	Number of calendar days in period						

Training ratios

Ratio	Formula for calculation of ratio	Unit of measurement	Month or quarter to (date)					
X3 Training costs/ Total employees	A ÷ D x 365 ÷ E	£'s per head per annum						
X9 Training costs/ Trainee days	A ÷ C	£'s per man day						
X10 Trainee days/ Trainees	C ÷ B	Days per man						
X11 Trainees/ Total employees	B x 100 ÷ D	%						

Data assembly sheet 10-4

Industrial relations ratios

Code letter	Item	Month or quarter to (date)					
A	Cost of wage increases in excess of national agreements						
B	Cost of production lost through poor IR						
C	Number of man-days lost through strikes						
D	Number of man-days lost through absenteeism						
E	Number of man-days worked						
F	Number of leavers						
G	Number of employees with 12 months service now						
H	Number of employees with over 12 months service now						
K	Total employed a year ago						
L	Total employed now						
M	Average number of employees						
N	Number of working days in period						
P	Number of working days in year						

Industrial relations ratios

Ratio		Formula for calculation of ratio	Unit of measurement	Month or quarter to (date)					
X12	Cost of wage increases in excess of national agreements/ Average number of employees	$A \div M \times P \div N$	£'s per head pa						
X13	Cost of production lost through poor IR/Average number of employees	$B \div M$	£'s per head						
X14	Number of man-days lost through strikes, etc./ Number of man-days worked	$C \times 100 \div E$	%						
X15	Number of man-days lost through absenteeism/ Number of man-days worked	$D \times 100 \div E$	%						
	Staff turnover								
X16	Number of leavers/ Average number of employees	$F \times 100 \div M$ $\times P \div N$	% pa						
	Employee stability index								
X17	Number of employees with 12 months service now/ Total employed a year ago	$G \times 100 \div K$	%						
	Skill conservation index								
X18	Number of employees with over 12 months service now/ Total employed now	$H \times 100 \div L$	%						

Chapter 11

Operating ratios for non-manufacturing organisations

Many of the ratios in this book are of general applicability, but a considerable number have related specifically to manufacturing concerns. The contents of this chapter are intended to redress this imbalance to some extent. There are separate sections for the merchant, the retailer, the professional firm and hotels. The sets of ratios proposed for the first three categories of operation are based in part on schemes developed by the Centre for Interfirm Comparison.

11.1 Ratios for a Merchanting Organisation

A merchanting concern measures its operating success in the same way as a manufacturer, that is by the ratio of

$$Y1 \qquad \frac{\text{Operating profit}}{\text{Operating assets}}$$

The subsidiary ratios it uses are similar to those used by a manufacturing company but with a number of important differences (see Diagram 11-1). A merchant's ratio of operating profit to operating assets is affected, in the same way as a manufacturer's ratio, by:

1 The profitability of his sales (operating profit/sales—ratio Y2)
2 His turnover of assets (sales/operating assets—ratio Y3)

It is at this stage of the analysis that a difference occurs. A merchanting (as opposed to a manufacturing) concern may prefer to analyse the factors affecting its profit margin on sales (ratio Y2) between those affecting its gross margin (ratio Y4) and its overheads (ratio Y5). Gross margin (ratio Y4) is affected by:

1 Product mix (this calls for a number of switching ratios—such as

hardwood sales/total sales and softwood sales/total sales for a timber business, or food sales/total sales and clothing sales/total sales for a department store—ratios Y6, Y7
2 Buying price for each part of the product mix—ratio Y10
3 Selling price of each part of the product mix—ratio Y11.

Overheads can be analysed between such factors as rent and rates, wages and so on. A merchant's turnover of assets is affected by

1 Stock turnover (ratio Y14)
2 Speed of debt collection (ratio Y15)
3 Utilisation of premises (ratio Y16).

To calculate ratios Y1 to Y18 use data assembly and ratio calculation sheet 11-1 at the end of this chapter.

The set of ratios in Diagram 11-1 is open to the criticism that a change in just one factor—the level of sales—will affect more than one ratio, which is an uneconomical use of ratios. For example, ratios Y2 (operating profit/sales) and Y3 (sales/operating assets) will probably both change if the level of sales rises or falls.

An improved set depends on the ability to arrive at a figure for 'maximum sales' achievable with the present set-up. The present set-up is not a very precise concept but most managers will have a feel for the meaning in their own businesses. It is usually related to the limitations imposed by the existing premises. If maximum sales can be defined with reasonable accuracy, the set of ratios in Diagram 11-2 can be used by a merchant.

Gross profit and current assets are most likely to vary with the level of actual sales, so they are related (in ratios Z2 and 3) to actual sales. Overheads and the value of

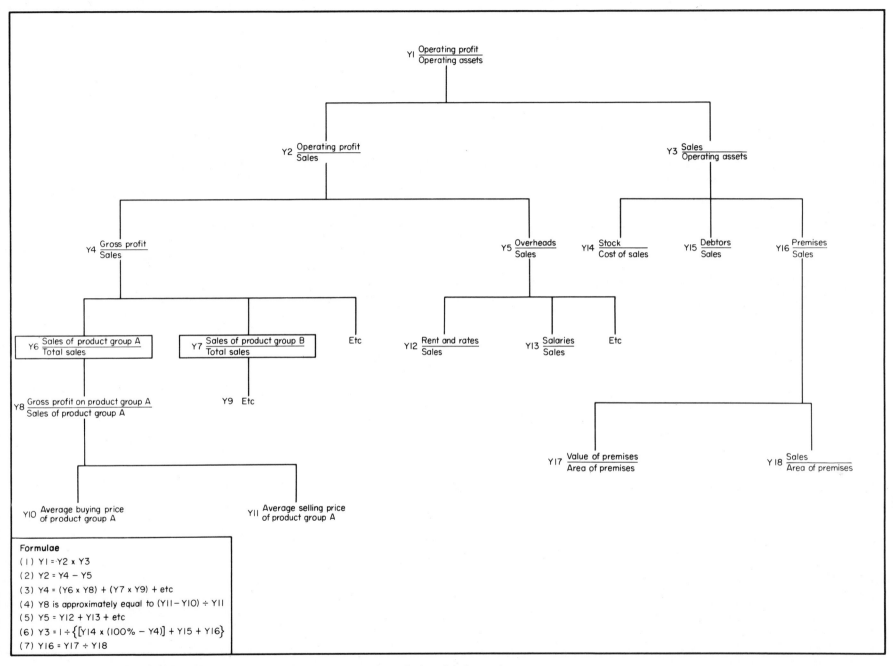

Diagram 11-1   Ratios for a merchanting business. With acknowledgements to the Centre for Interfirm Comparisons

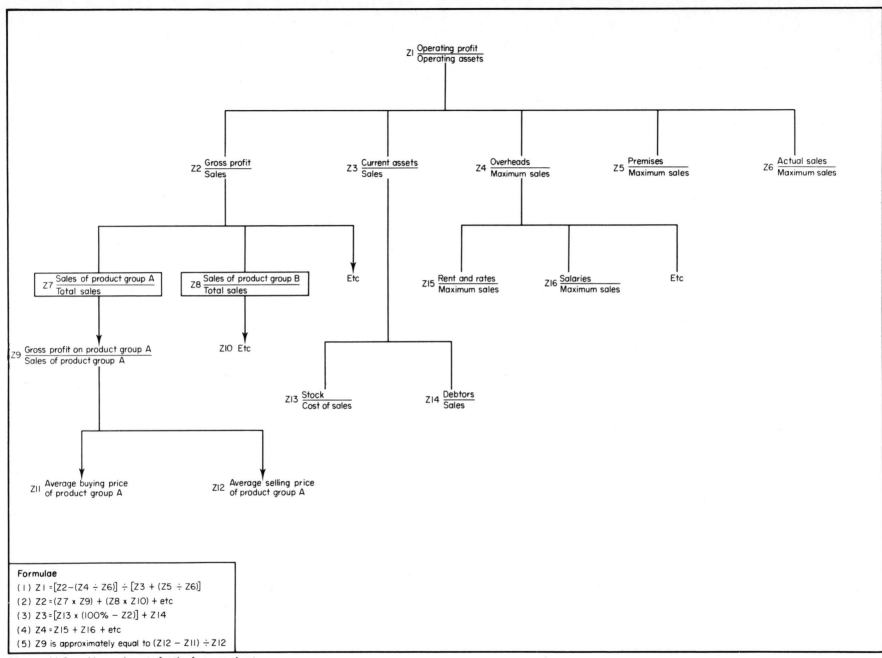

Formulae

(1) $Z1 = [Z2 - (Z4 \div Z6)] \div [Z3 + (Z5 \div Z6)]$

(2) $Z2 = (Z7 \times Z9) + (Z8 \times Z10) + etc$

(3) $Z3 = [Z13 \times (100\% - Z2)] + Z14$

(4) $Z4 = Z15 + Z16 + etc$

(5) $Z9$ is approximately equal to $(Z12 - Z11) \div Z12$

Diagram 11-2   Alternative set of ratios for a merchant

232

premises are related to the size of the 'present set-up' and so are related (in ratios Z4 and 5) to maximum sales.

With this set of ratios a change in the level of sales should affect only ratio Z6 (actual sales/maximum sales). Ratios Z2 to Z5 should be unchanged.

To calculate ratios Z1 to Z16 use data assembly and ratio calculation sheet 11-2 at the end of this chapter.

11.2 Ratios for a Retailing Organisation

Although the ratios that a merchanting organisation could use (Diagrams 11-1 and 11-2) could also be used by a retailer. This part of the chapter, however, describes a set of ratios specifically for retailers.

A retailer's return on assets (ratio AA1 Diagram 11-3) depends on his profit margin on sales (AA2) and his turnover of assets (AA3). This profit margin on sales (AA2) is in turn dependent on his gross profit (AA4), his salary bill (AA5), and his other overheads (ratio AA6). He can improve his gross profit (AA4) by aiming at a higher mark up or target gross profit (AA7) and avoiding as much as possible subsequent mark downs (AA8) and shortages or stock losses (AA9).

To improve ratio AA5, a retailer needs to keep the average salary paid under review (AA10) but here he will be as much the subject of market forces as he is his own master. He can, however increase the number of transactions per employee (AA11) and the average value of each sale (AA12).

Stock and premises are the retailer's main assets. Ratios AA3 and AA3a (for an explanation of the need for ratio AA3a see Appendix 1.1) can be improved by an increase in stock turnover (AA13 and AA15) or premises utilisation (AA14). The value of the premises is fixed but AA14 can be improved by increasing the amount of selling floor or shelf space (AA16) (by putting in more shelves or by cutting down storage as opposed to selling space) and the sales per square or shelf foot (ratio AA17).

To calculate ratios AA1 to AA17 use data assembly and ratio calculation sheet 11-3 at the end of this chapter.

11.3 Ratios for Professional Firms

In some cases return on capital is not a suitable measure of the success with which a business is being run. Either the firm has no capital in a meaningful sense or the capital it has is not a proper measure of the resources it is using. Usually firms are partnerships of professional men (such as stockbrokers, management consultants, estate agents, consulting engineers, chartered accountants). The assets of such firms are their staff, so one could put a value on them related to their salaries but this idea does not appeal to the author as much as the following.

Most professional firms are still partnerships and from the partners' point of view a good measure of the firm's success is the profit per partner (ratio AB1 in Diagram 11-4). Profit will be after deducting such a salary as the partner would command on the open market (a nice piece of judgement that, but it can be done).

Ratio AB1 will grow:

1   If the ratio of expenses (including the partners' salaries) to revenue (ratio AB2) can be curbed,
2   If the revenue per partner (ratio AB3) can be increased.

A professional firm's staff can be divided into those responsible for:

1   Getting the business (partners and senior staff usually)
2   Doing the professional work
3   Administering the firm.

If one is going to tackle ratio AB2 it is worth looking, therefore, at the following ratios:

1   Business getting staff salaries/revenue (ratio AB4)
2   'Doing' staff salaries/revenue (ratio AB5)
3   Administrative staff salaries/revenue (ratio AB6)
4   All costs other than salaries/revenue (ratio AB7).

Ratio AB4 can be decreased by:

1   Persuading (and helping if necessary) the business getting staff to sell more (ratio AB9).
2   Employing less expensive staff on business getting if the present staff are 'over qualified' (ratio AB8).
3   Slowing down the increases given to business getting staff if their remuneration has got out of line with the market (ratio AB8).
4   Introducing a bonus scheme whereby increases in ratio AB9 are rewarded by bonuses which increase AB8 less than proportionately.

Ratio AB4 is also influenced by whether the order book is rising or falling (ratio AB10). Similar arguments apply to ratios AB5 and AB6—see ratios AB11 and AB12, and AB13, AB14 and AB15.

To calculate ratios AB1 to AB15 use data assembly and ratio calculation sheet 11-4 at the end of this chapter.

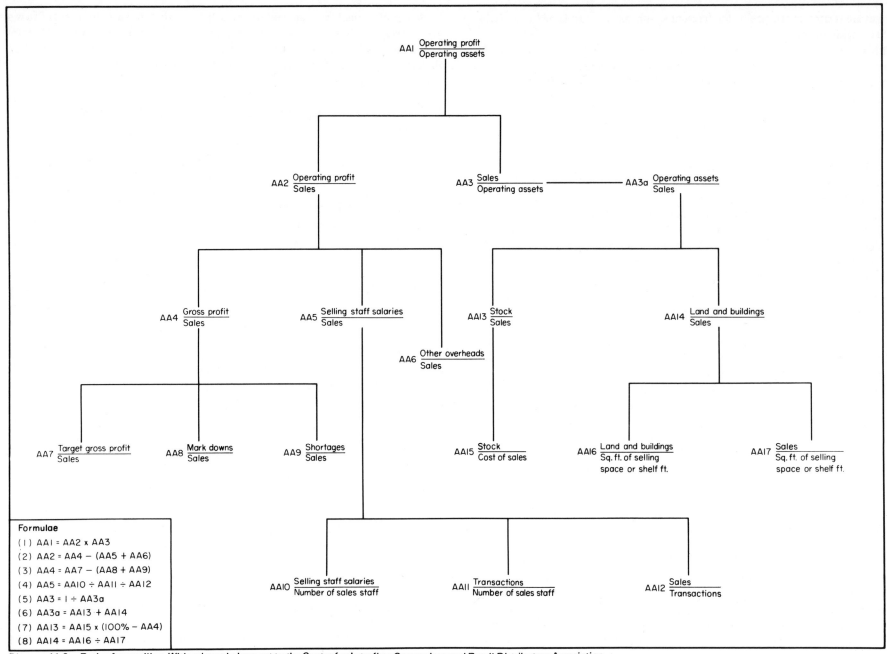

Diagram 11-3 Ratios for retailing. With acknowledgement to the Centre for Interfirm Comparison and Retail Distributors Association.

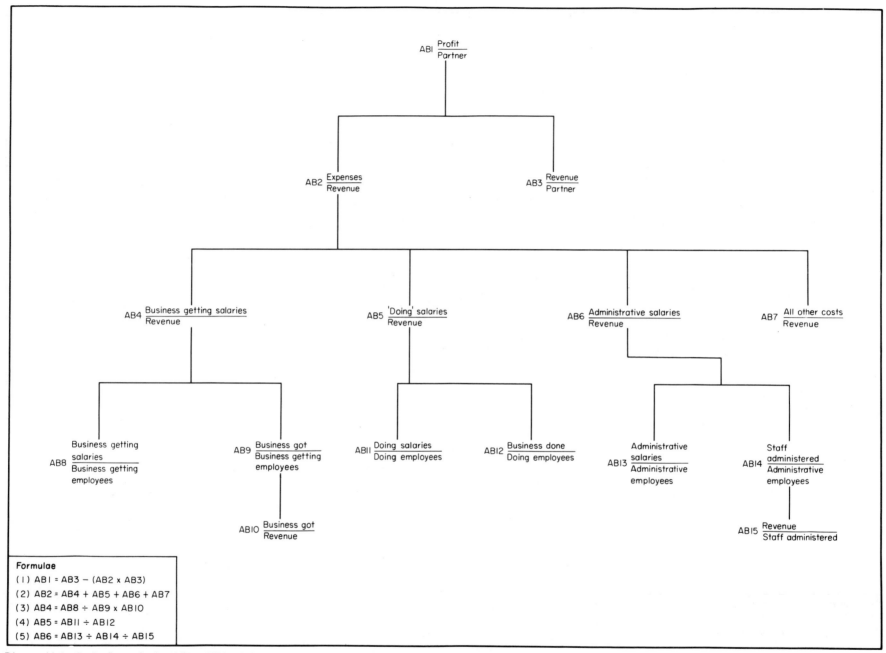

Diagram 11-4   Ratios for professional firms. With acknowledgements to the Centre for Interfirm Comparison.

235

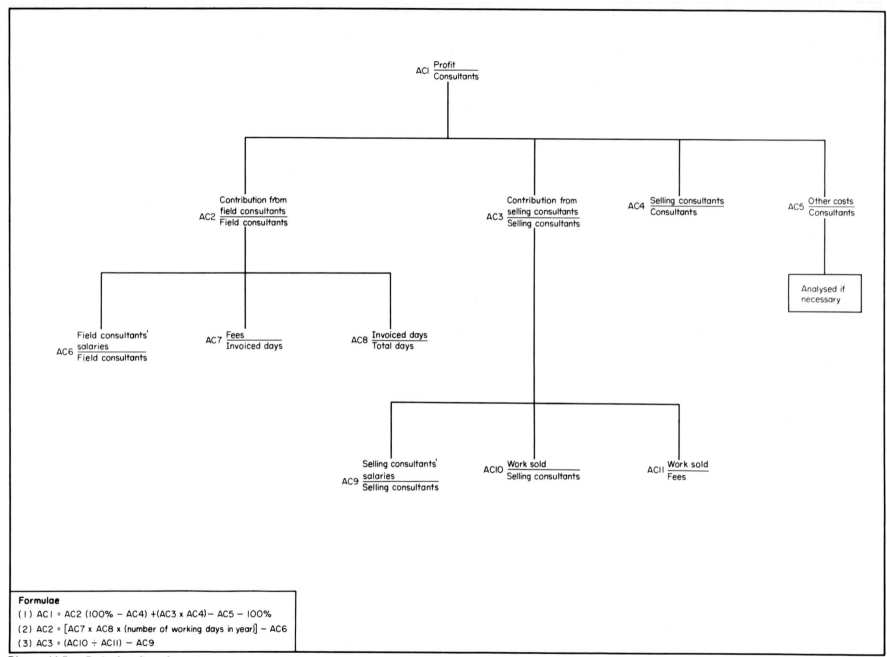

AC1 $\dfrac{\text{Profit}}{\text{Consultants}}$

AC2 $\dfrac{\text{Contribution from field consultants}}{\text{Field consultants}}$

AC3 $\dfrac{\text{Contribution from selling consultants}}{\text{Selling consultants}}$

AC4 $\dfrac{\text{Selling consultants}}{\text{Consultants}}$

AC5 $\dfrac{\text{Other costs}}{\text{Consultants}}$

Analysed if necessary

AC6 $\dfrac{\text{Field consultants' salaries}}{\text{Field consultants}}$

AC7 $\dfrac{\text{Fees}}{\text{Invoiced days}}$

AC8 $\dfrac{\text{Invoiced days}}{\text{Total days}}$

AC9 $\dfrac{\text{Selling consultants' salaries}}{\text{Selling consultants}}$

AC10 $\dfrac{\text{Work sold}}{\text{Selling consultants}}$

AC11 $\dfrac{\text{Work sold}}{\text{Fees}}$

Formulae

(1) AC1 = AC2 (100% − AC4) +(AC3 x AC4) − AC5 − 100%

(2) AC2 = [AC7 x AC8 x (number of working days in year)] − AC6

(3) AC3 = (AC10 ÷ AC11) − AC9

Diagram 11-5   Ratios for a firm of consultants

An alternative set of ratios for a professional firm is given in Diagram 11-5. It was designed with management consultants in mind but it could be used by firms in other professions.

In this set the key ratio is

AC1   Profit per consultant

Consultants include staff in the field doing the job and staff, however entitled, selling jobs. It does not include administrative and 'back up' staff such as librarians. This key ratio can be improved by:

1. Improving the contribution from the consultants in the field (ratio AC2)—'contribution' is revenue from clients less the field consultants' salaries.
2. Improving the contribution from the consultants selling jobs to clients (ratio AC3)—'contribution' is revenue from clients less the selling consultants' salaries.
3. Optimising the balance between selling consultants and field consultants (ratio AC4).
4. Minimising the overhead burden of 'other costs' (including the salaries of administrative and back up staff) without unduly diminishing the services provided to the field and sales staff by these costs (ratio AC5).

Improving the contribution of field staff (ratio AC2) depends on:

1. Optimising the salaries they receive (ratio AC6)—paying enough to attract and retain suitably qualified staff.
2. Suitable charging for jobs—indicated by the ratio of fee revenue per invoiced day (ratio AC7).
3. Maximising the utilisation of field staff on paying jobs measured by the ratio of invoiced days to total days (ratio AC8)

The sales staff's contribution can be improved by:

1. Optimising their salaries (ratio AC9) in a similar way to field staff salaries.
2. Maximising the amount of sales obtained from clients per sales consultant (ratio AC10).

If a firm of consultants is expanding (or contracting), work sold will be greater (or smaller) than fees earned. Whichever of these situations is occuring will be shown by ratio AC11 (work sold/fees) being greater or less than 100 per cent.

To calculate ratios AC1 to AC11 use data assembly and ratio calculation sheet 11.5 at the end of this chapter.

11.4 Ratios for Hotels

The Hotels and Catering EDC's *A Standard System of Hotel Accounting* (HMSO, 1969) recommends the use of the following ratios:

AF1 $\dfrac{\text{Gross profit}}{\text{Sales}}$ (per cent)

AF2 $\dfrac{\text{Net Profit}}{\text{Sales}}$ (per cent)

AF3 $\dfrac{\text{Current assets}}{\text{Current liabilities}}$ (times)

AF4 $\dfrac{\text{Current assets (less stock)}}{\text{Current liabilities}}$ (times)

AF5 $\dfrac{\text{Stocks}}{\text{Cost of sales}}$ (days stock)

AF6 $\dfrac{\text{Debtors}}{\text{Credit sales}}$ (days credit)

AF7 $\dfrac{\text{Hotel net operating profit}}{\text{Capital employed in hotel operation}}$ (per cent)

AF8 $\dfrac{\text{Rooms occupied}}{\text{Rooms in hotel}}$ (per cent)   (Room occupancy)

AF9 $\dfrac{\text{Number of guests}}{\text{Guest capacity}}$ (per cent)   (Bed occupancy)

AF10 $\dfrac{\text{Room sales}}{\text{Rooms occupied}}$ (£/room)

AF11 $\dfrac{\text{Room sales}}{\text{Number of guests}}$ (£/room)

AF12 $\dfrac{\text{Meals served}}{\text{Restaurant seating capacity}}$ (per cent)

AF13 $\dfrac{\text{Restaurant sales}}{\text{Meals served}}$ (£/meal)

Further details of these ratios and the underlying accounting system will be found in the book quoted. Ratios 1 to 7 should be familiar to readers of this book. Ratios 8, 9 and 12 are measures of capacity utilisation. Ratios 10, 11 and 13 are measures of average prices obtained.

The ratios listed by the EDC are obviously valuable to hotel management. It is suggested however that it would be more useful:

1 To have a key ratio to monitor overall managerial performance
2 To provide an integrated set of ratios to explain differences between the key ratio and the standard selected by management
3 To highlight the contribution to profit, and the amount of capital used in earning that profit, from each of the major departments within the hotel.

A set of ratios which is designed to meet the above objectives is shown in Diagram 11-6.

The hotel manager will measure his success by the size of ratio

AG1 $\qquad \dfrac{\text{Operating profit}}{\text{Operating assets}}$

by comparison with his chosen standard.

In order to improve his key ratio (ratio AG1) he can either:

1 Improve the contribution ratios of any or all of the three main divisions of his hotel—the rooms, the restaurants and the bars—(ratios AG6, AG7 and AG8)

and/or

2 Reduce the size of his overheads (ratio AG9) or the proportion of his assets not used in any of the three main income earning divisions (ratio AG5)

and/or

3 Increase the proportion of his assets invested in the more profitable parts and reduce the proportion invested in the less profitable parts.

The hotel manager will probably be able to do 3 only in the medium to long term. Moreover he will be constrained by the need to attract customers by offering a wide range of facilities each at a competitive price.

The contribution from rooms ratio (ratio AG6) may be improved by either:

1 Raising the price per room or per guest (ratio AG10 or AG10a) and/or
2 Reducing the room variable costs (linen, cleaning, etc). per occupied room (ratio AG11) and/or
3 Increasing the room occupancy (ratios AG12 or AG12a) and/or
4 Reducing the investment per room (again medium to long term only).

Hotel managers will realise that it may be possible to increase the room occupancy rate (ratio AG12) by *reducing* the price (ratio AG10) or even by increasing the amount of assets or service (ratios AG13 or AG11). The art of good hotel management is to balance all four ratios AG10 to AG13 over the whole year in order to maximise ratio AG6.

Similar arguments apply to the restaurant—the price of the meal (ratio AG14) must be balanced with the costs of preparing and serving it (ratio AG15) and the expense of the restaurant and kitchens in relation to the former's seating capacity (ratio AG17) in order to get a good capacity utilisation (ratio AG16) so as to maximise the contribution ratio AG7.

In the bar it is not possible to measure capacity meaningfully. The ratios to use are:

1 The gross profit on the drinks (ratio AG18),
2 The proportion of the price paid out in wages (ratio AG19),
3 The stock turnover (ratio AG20), and
4 The investment in other bar assets in relation to sales (ratio AG21).

It is suggested that the length of credit taken by the hotel's customers should be kept under surveillance by means of ratio AG22.

It may be neccessary to analyse the utilisation of other non-allocated assets and the overheads in addition.

The set of ratios in Diagram 11-6 is primarily for the day-to-day management of the hotel. In addition the hotel management will also need to use some or all of the ratios described in Chapter 8 to plan and monitor its financial affairs.

To calculate ratios AG1 to AG22 use data assembly and ratio calculation sheet 11-6 at the end of this chapter.

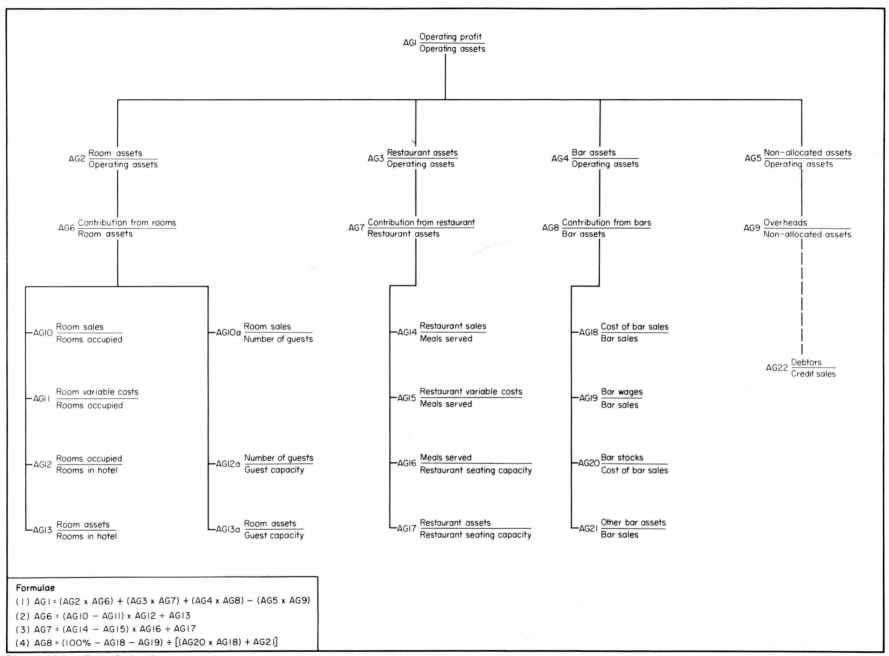

Diagram 11-6   Ratios for hotels

239

The Evolution of a Set of Ratios for Firms in the Accountancy Profession

In Chapter 1 it was stated that 'selecting ratios is an exercise which must be done by each firm and manager individually'. This appendix contains an illustration of this process in practice.

A board was set up by the Institute of Chartered Accountants in England and Wales' Technical Committee to advise on the implementation of an Interfirm Comparison for accounting firms in public practice. The author is secretary to this advisory board. Two suggestions as to the ratios which might be included in the comparison were placed before the board. One suggestion was of the set of ratios shown in Diagram 11-4; another suggestion was of the list of ratios shown in Diagram 11-7 extracted from an article entitled 'Assessing the efficiency of an Accounting Firm' by M.H. Cabourn-Smith, *Accountancy* December 1970. The board agreed with the principles (from Chapter 1) of:

1   A key ratio
2   Logical 'cause-and-effect' linkage.

It also agreed that the ratios should be easily calculated even by firms with less sophisticated management accounting systems.

The board's final choice is shown in Diagram 11-8. The following points are of interest:

1   Whereas ratio AE1 profit/number of partners, is *the* key ratio, ratios AE2 profit/fees; AE18 debtors and work in progress at selling price/fees; AE21 partners' average remuneration; AE22 growth (fees this year/fees last year); and AE23 staff turnover (number of staff leaving during the year/average number of staff during the year) are considered to be of almost equal importance.

2   Because of the number of key, or important ratios, not all ratios are wholly or partly logically linked (20 out of 23 are). There are, in fact, two sub-sets of ratios (AE1 to AE17 and AE18 to AE20) which are internally linked but are not logically connected to each other.

3   Only six of the ratios in Diagram 11-8 are in either Diagram 11-4 or 11-7 (ratios AE1, 2, 3, 5, 18 and 19). However, many of them will be found either elsewhere in this book or can be derived from ratios in diagram 11-4 or 11-7. The thinking behind their choice is wholly consistent with the principles set out in this book

The board's choice makes an excellent example of a workable compromise being better than the sum of its parts.

To calculate ratios AE1 to AE23 use data assembly and ratio calculation sheet 11-7 at the end of this chapter.

AD1	Productive staff cost to fees
AD2	Accomodation cost to fees
AD3	Administration expenses to fees
AD4	Profit to fees
AD5	Work in progress to fees
AD6	Debtors plus work in progress at cost to fees
AD7	Capital employed to fees
AD8	Profit to capital employed
AD9	Fees divided by total number of partners and productive staff
AD10	Average size of fee

Diagram 11-7   List of ratios for assessing the efficiency of an accounting firm (first version)

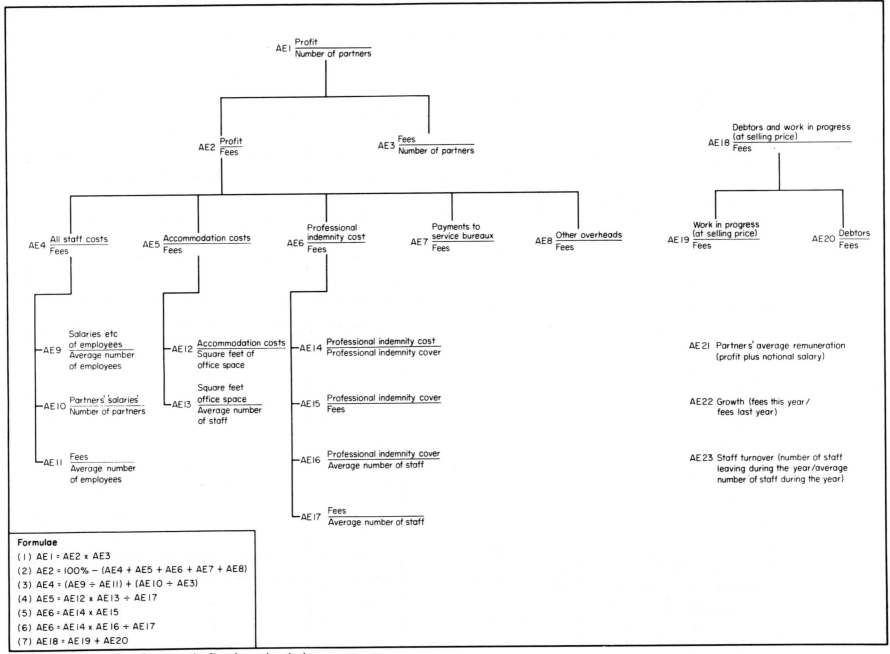

Formulae

(1) AE1 = AE2 x AE3

(2) AE2 = 100% − (AE4 + AE5 + AE6 + AE7 + AE8)

(3) AE4 = (AE9 ÷ AE11) + (AE10 ÷ AE3)

(4) AE5 = AE12 x AE13 ÷ AE17

(5) AE6 = AE14 x AE15

(6) AE6 = AE14 x AE16 ÷ AE17

(7) AE18 = AE19 + AE20

Diagram 11-8   Set of ratios for accounting firms (second version)

241

Ratios for a merchanting business

Code letter	Item	Product group A (1)	B (2)	C (3)	Total (4)
Part 1					
A	Quantity bought				
B	Quantity sold				
C	Purchases				
D	Stock at beginning of period				
E	Sub total (C + D)				
F	Stock at end of period				
G	Cost of sales (E − F)				
H	Sales				
K	Gross profit (H − G)				

Code letter	Item	Month or quarter to (date)					
Part 2							
L	Rent and rates						
M	Salaries						
N	Other overheads						
P	Total overheads (L + M + N)						
Q	Gross profit (equals K4 above)						
R	Operating profit (Q − P)						
S	Stock (equals ½(D4 + F4 above)						
T	Average value of debtors						
U	Premises						
V	Operating assets (S + T + U)						
W	No. of working days in period						
Y	No. of working days in year						
Z	No. of calendar days in period						
AA	Area of premises						

Ratios for a merchanting business

Ratio	Formula for calculation of ratio	Unit of measurement	Month or quarter to (date)					
Y1 Operating profit/ Operating assets	R x 100 ÷ V x Y ÷ W	% pa						
Y2 Operating profit/ Sales	R x 100 ÷ H4	%						
Y3 Sales/ Operating assets	H4 ÷ V x Y ÷ W	Times per year						
Y4 Gross profit/Sales	Q x 100 ÷ H4	%						
Y5 Overheads/Sales	P x 100 ÷ H4	%						
Y6 Sales of product group A/ Total sales	H1 x 100 ÷ H4	%						
Y7 Sales of product group B/ Total sales	H2 x 100 ÷ H4	%						
Y8 Gross profit on product group A/ Sales of product group A	K1 x 100 ÷ H1	%						
Y9 Gross profit on product group B/ Sales of product group B	K2 x 100 ÷ H2	%						
Y10 Average buying price of product group A	C1 ÷ A1	£'s per unit						
Y11 Average selling price of product group A	H1 ÷ B1	£'s per unit						
Y12 Rent and rates/ Sales	L x 100 ÷ H4	%						
Y13 Salaries/Sales	M x 100 ÷ H4	%						
Y14 Stock/Cost of sales	S x W ÷ G4	days						
Y15 Debtors/Sales	T x Z ÷ H4	days						
Y16 Premises/Sales	U x 1000 ÷ (H4 x Y ÷ W)	‰ pa						
Y17 Value of premises/ Area of premises	U ÷ AA	£ per sq.ft.						
Y18 Sales/Area of premises	H4 x Y ÷ W ÷ AA	£ pa per sq.ft.						

Alternative set of ratios for a merchant

Code letter	Item	Product group A (1)	B (2)	C (3)	Total (4)
Part 1					
A	Quantity bought				
B	Quantity sold				
C	Purchases				
D	Stock at beginning of period				
E	Sub total (C + D)				
F	Stock at end of period				
G	Cost of Sales (E − F)				
H	Sales				
K	Gross profit (H − G)				

Code letter	Item	Month or quarter to (date)					
Part 2							
L	Rent and rates						
M	Salaries						
N	Other overheads						
P	Total overheads (L + M + N)						
Q	Gross profit (equals K4 above)						
R	Operating profit (Q − P)						
S	Stock (equals ½(D4 + F4 above))						
T	Average value of debtors						
U	Current assets (S + T)						
V	Premises						
W	Operating assets (U + V)						
Y	Maximum sales						
Z	Number of working days in period						
AA	Number of working days in year						
AB	Number of calendar days in period						

Alternative set of ratios for a merchant

Ratio		Formula for calculation of ratio	Unit of measurement	Month or quarter to (date)					
Z1	Operating profit/ Operating assets	R x 100 ÷ W x AA ÷ Z	% pa						
Z2	Gross profit/ Sales	Q x 100 ÷ H4	%						
Z3	Current assets/ Sales	U x 1000 ÷ (H4 x AA ÷ Z)	‰ pa						
Z4	Overheads/ Maximum sales	P x 100 ÷ Y	%						
Z5	Premises/ Maximum sales	V x 1000 ÷ (Y x AA ÷ Z)	‰ pa						
Z6	Actual sales/ Maximum sales	H4 x 100 ÷ Y	%						
Z7	Sales of product group A/ Total sales	H1 x 100 ÷ H4	%						
Z8	Sales of product group B/ Total sales	H2 x 100 ÷ H4	%						
Z9	Gross profit on product group A/ Sales of product group A	K1 x 100 ÷ H1	%						
Z10	Gross profit on product group B/ Sales of product group B	K2 x 100 ÷ H2	%						
Z11	Average buying price of product group A	C1 ÷ A1	£'s per unit						
Z12	Average selling price of product group A	H1 ÷ B1	£'s per unit						
Z13	Stock/Cost of sales	S x Z ÷ G4	days						
Z14	Debtors/Sales	T x AB ÷ H4	days						
Z15	Rent and rates/ Maximum sales	L x 100 ÷ Y	%						
Z16	Salaries/ Maximum sales	M x 100 ÷ Y	%						

Data assembly sheet 11-3

Ratios for retailing

Code letter	Item	Month or quarter to (date)					
A	Target gross profit						
B	Mark downs						
C	Shortages						
D	Gross Profit (A − B − C)						
E	Selling staff salaries						
F	Other overheads						
G	Operating profit (D − E − F)						
H	Sales						
K	Number of sales staff						
L	Transactions						
M	Stock						
N	Land and buildings						
P	Operating assets (M + N)						
Q	Sq. ft. of selling space or shelf ft.						
R	Number of working days in period						
S	Number of working days in year						

Ratios for retailing

Ratio		Formula for calculation of ratio	Unit of measurement	Month or quarter to (date)					
AA1	Operating profit Operating assets	$G \times 100 \div P \times S \div R$	% pa						
AA2	Operating profit/ Sales	$G \times 100 \div H$	%						
AA3	Sales/ Operating assets	$H \div P \times S \div R$	Times per year						
AA3a	Operating assets/ Sales	$P \times 1000 \div (H \times S \div R)$	‰ pa						
AA4	Gross profit/ Sales	$D \times 100 \div H$	%						
AA5	Selling staff salaries/ Sales	$E \times 100 \div H$	%						
AA6	Other overheads/ Sales	$F \times 100 \div H$	%						
AA7	Target gross profit/ Sales	$A \times 100 \div H$	%						
AA8	Mark downs/ Sales	$B \times 100 \div H$	%						
AA9	Shortages/ Sales	$C \times 100 \div H$	%						
AA10	Selling staff salaries/ Number of sales staff	$E \div K \times S \div R$	£'s per head pa						
AA11	Transactions/ Number of sales staff	$L \div K \times S \div R$	Transactions per head pa						
AA12	Sales/ Transactions	$H \div L$	£'s per transactions						
AA13	Stock/ Sales	$M \times 1000 \div (H \times S \div R)$	‰ pa						
AA14	Land and buildings/ Sales	$N \times 1000 \div (H \times S \div R)$	‰ pa						
AA15	Stock/Cost of sales	$M \div (H - D) \times S \div R$	days						
AA16	Land and buildings/ Sq. ft. of selling space or shelf ft.	$N \div Q$	£ per sq, or shelf ft.						
AA17	Sales/ Sq. ft. or selling space or shelf ft	$H \div Q$	£ per sq, or shelf ft.						

Data assembly sheet 11-4
Ratios for professional firms

Code letter	Item	Month or quarter to (date)					
A	Business getting salaries						
B	'Doing' salaries						
C	Administrative salaries						
D	All other costs						
E	Expenses (A + B + C + D)						
F	Revenue (= business done)						
G	Profit (F − E)						
H	Business getting employees						
K	Doing employees						
L	Staff administered (H + K)						
M	Administrative employees						
N	Total employees						
P	Partners						
Q	Business got						
R	Number of calendar days in period						

Ratio	Formula for calculation of ratio	Unit of measurement	Month or quarter to (date)					
AB1 Profit/ Partner	G ÷ P x 365 ÷ R	£'s per head pa						
AB2 Expenses/ Revenue	E x 100 ÷ F	%						
AB3 Revenue/ Partner	F ÷ P x 365 ÷ R	£'s per head pa						
AB4 Business getting salaries/ Revenue	A x 100 ÷ F	%						
AB5 'Doing' salaries/ Revenue	B x 100 ÷ F	%						
AB6 Administrative salaries/ Revenue	C x 100 ÷ F	%						
AB7 All other costs/ Revenue	D x 100 ÷ F	%						
AB8 Business getting salaries/ Business getting employees	A ÷ H x 365 ÷ R	£'s per head pa						
AB9 Business got/ Business getting employees	Q ÷ H x 365 ÷ R	£'s per head pa						
AB10 Business got/ Revenue	Q x 100 ÷ F	%						
AB11 Doing salaries/ Doing employees	B ÷ K x 365 ÷ R	£'s per head pa						
AB12 Business done/ Doing employees	F ÷ K x 365 ÷ R	£'s per head pa						
AB13 Administrative salaries/ Administrative employees	C ÷ M x 365 ÷ R	£'s per head pa						
AB14 Staff administered/ Administrative employees	L ÷ M	Men per head						
AB15 Revenue/ Staff administered	F ÷ L x 365 ÷ R	£'s per head pa						

Data assembly sheet 11-5

Ratios for a firm of consultants

Code letter	Item	Month or quarter to (date)					
A	Fees						
B	Field consultants' salaries						
C	Contribution from field consultants (A − B)						
D	Selling consultants' salaries						
E	Contribution from selling consultants (A − D)						
F	Other costs						
G	Profit (C + E − F − A)						
H	Work sold						
K	Field consultants						
L	Selling consultants						
M	Consultants (K + L)						
N	Invoiced days						
P	Number of calendar days in period						

Ratios for a firm of consultants

Ratio	Formula for calculation of ratio	Unit of measurement	Month or quarter to (date)					
AC1 Profit/ Consultants	$G \div M \times 365 \div P$	£'s per head pa						
AC2 Contribution from field consultants/ Field consultants	$C \div K \times 365 \div P$	£'s per head pa						
AC3 Contribution from selling consultants/ Selling consultants	$E \div L \times 365 \div P$	£'s per head pa						
AC4 Selling consultants/ Consultants	$L \times 100 \div M$	%						
AC5 Other costs/ Consultants	$F \div M \times 365 \div P$	£'s per head pa						
AC6 Field consultants' salaries/ Field consultants	$B \div K \times 365 \div P$	£'s per head pa						
AC7 Fees/Invoiced days	$A \div N$	£'s per day						
AC8 Invoiced days/ Total days	$N \times 100 \div (K \times P)$	%						
AC9 Selling consultants' salaries/ Selling consultants	$D \div L \times 365 \div P$	£'s per head pa						
AC10 Work sold/ Selling consultants	$H \div L \times 365 \div P$	£'s per head pa						
AC11 Work sold/ Fees	$H \times 100 \div A$	%						

251

Ratios for hotels

Code letter	Item	Month or quarter to (date)					
A	Average room assets						
B	Average restaurant assets						
C	Average bar stocks						
D	Average other bar assets						
E	Average bar assets (C + D)						
F	Average debtors						
G	Average other non-allocated assets						
H	Average non-allocated assets (F + G)						
K	Average operating assets (A+B+E+H)						
L	Room Sales						
M	Room variable costs						
N	Contribution from rooms (L − M)						
P	Restaurant sales						
Q	Restaurant variable costs						
R	Contribution from restaurant (P − Q)						
S	Bar sales						
T	Cost of bar sales						
U	Bar wages						
V	Contribution from bars (S − T − U)						
W	Overheads						
Y	Operating profit (N + R + V − W)						
Z	Credit sales						
AA	Rooms in hotel						
AB	Rooms occupied (times no. of days occupied)						
AC	Guest capacity						
AD	No. of guests (times no. of days stayed)						
AE	Restaurant seating capacity						
AF	Meals served						
AG	No. of days in period						

Ratios for hotels

Ratio		Formula for calculation of ratio	Unit of measurement	Month or quarter to (date)					
AG1	Operating profit/ Operating assets	Y x 100 ÷ K x 365 ÷ AG	% pa						
AG2	Room assets/ Operating assets	A x 100 ÷ K	%						
AG3	Restaurant assets/ Operating assets	B x 100 ÷ K	%						
AG4	Bar assets/ Operating assets	E x 100 ÷ K	%						
AG5	Non-allocated assets/ Operating assets	H x 100 ÷ K	%						
AG6	Contribution from rooms/Room assets	N x 100 ÷ A x 365 ÷ AG	% pa						
AG7	Contribution from restaurant/ Restaurant assets	R x 100 ÷ B x 365 ÷ AG	% pa						
AG8	Contribution from bars/ Bar assets	V x 100 ÷ E x 365 ÷ AG	% pa						
AG9	Overheads/ Non-allocated assets	W x 100 ÷ H x 365 ÷ AG	% pa						
AG10	Room sales/ Rooms occupied	L ÷ AB	£ per room per day						
AG10(a)	Room sales/ No. of guests	L ÷ AD	£ per guest per day						
AG11	Room variable costs/ Rooms occupied	M ÷ AB	£ per room per day						

Ratios for hotels

Ratio		Formula for calculation of ratio	Unit of measurement	Month or quarter to (date)					
AG12	Rooms occupied/ Rooms in hotel	AB x 100 ÷ (AA x AG)	%						
AG12(a)	No. of guests/ Guest capacity	AD x 100 ÷ (AC x AG)	%						
AG13	Room assets/ Rooms in hotel	A ÷ AA	£ per room						
AG13(a)	Room assets/ Guest capacity	A ÷ AC	£ per head						
AG14	Restaurant sales/ Meals served	P ÷ AF	£ per meal						
AG15	Restaurant variable costs/ Meals served	Q ÷ AF	£ per meal						
AG16	Meals served/ Restaurant seating capacity	AF x 100 ÷ (AE x AG)	%						
AG17	Restaurant assets/ Restaurant seating capacity	B ÷ AE	£ per seat						
AG18	Cost of bar sales/ Bar sales	T x 100 ÷ S	%						
AG19	Bar wages/ Bar sales	U x 100 ÷ S	%						
AG20	Bar stocks/ Cost of bar sales	C ÷ (T ÷ AG)	days						
AG21	Other bar assets/ Bar sales	D x 1000 ÷ (S x 365 ÷ AG)	%₀₀ pa						
AG22	Debtors/ Credit sales	F ÷ (Z ÷ AG)	days						

NB, It is assumed that the hotel is open throughout the year. If it is not substitute the number of days it is open for 365 in all the above formulae.

Set of ratios for accounting firms (second version)

Code letter	Item	Month or quarter to (date)					
A	Salaries etc. of employees						
B	Partners' salaries						
C	All staff costs (A + B)						
D	Accommodation costs						
E	Professional indemnity cost						
F	Payments to service bureaux						
G	Other overheads						
H	Subtotal (C+D+E+F+G)						
K	Fees						
L	Profit (K−H)						
M	Work in progress (at selling price)						
N	Debtors						
P	Debtors and work in progress (at selling price) (M + N)						
Q	Average number of employees						
R	Average number of partners						
S	Average number of staff (Q+R)						
T	Sq ft of office space						
W	Professional indemnity cover						
Y	Fees last year						
Z	No. of staff leaving during the period						
AA	No. of calendar days in period						

Set of ratios for accounting firms (second version)

Ratio		Formula for calculation of ratio	Unit of measurement	Month or quarter to (date)					
AE1	Profit/ No. of partners	L x 365 ÷ AA ÷ R	£ per head pa						
AE2	Profit/ Fees	L x 100 ÷ K	%						
AE3	Fees/No. of partners	K x 365 ÷ AA ÷ R	£ per head pa						
AE4	All staff costs/ Fees	C x 100 ÷ K	%						
AE5	Accommodation costs/ Fees	D x 100 ÷ K	%						
AE6	Professional indemnity cost/Fees	E x 100 ÷ K	%						
AE7	Payments to service bureaux/ Fees	F x 100 ÷ K	%						
AE8	Other overheads/ Fees	G x 100 ÷ K	%						
AE9	Salaries etc. of employees/ Average no. of employees	A x 365 ÷ AA ÷ Q	£ per head pa						
AE10	Partners' salaries/ No. of partners	B x 365 ÷ AA ÷ R	£ per head pa						
AE11	Fees/ Average no employees	K x 365 ÷ AA ÷ Q	£ per head pa						
AE12	Accommodation costs/ Sq ft of office space	D x 365 ÷ AA ÷ T	£ pa per sq ft						
AE13	Sq ft of office space/ Average no. of staff	T ÷ S	Sq ft per head						

258

Ratio	Formula for calculation of ratio	Unit of measurement	Month or quarter to (date)					
AE14 Professional indemnity cost/ Professional indemnity cover	E x 365 ÷ AA ÷ W x 100	% pa						
AE15 Professional indemnity cover/ Fees	W x100 ÷ (K x365 ÷ AA)	% pa						
AE16 Professional indemnity cover/ Average no. of staff	W ÷ S	£ per head						
AE17 Fees/ Average no. of staff	K x 365 ÷ AA ÷ S	£ per head pa						
AE18 Debtors and work in progress (at selling price)/ Fees	P x 1000 ÷ (K x 365 ÷ AA)	‰ pa						
AE19 Work in progress (at selling price)/ Fees	M x 1000 ÷ (K x 365 ÷ AA)	‰ pa						
AE20 Debtors/Fees	N x 1000 ÷ (K x 365 ÷ AA)	‰ pa						
AE21 Partners' average remuneration (profit plus notional salary)	(L + B) x 365 ÷ AA ÷ R	£ per head pa						
AE22 Growth (fees this year/fees last year)	K x 365 ÷ AA x 100 ÷ Y	% pa						
AE23 Staff turnover (number of staff leaving during the year/Average number of staff during the year)	Z x 365 ÷ AA x 100 ÷ S	% pa						

PART THREE

Chapter 12

Integrated control by ratios

In this final chapter we shall be concentrating on *four* topics. First of all we shall be bringing together the ratios previously discussed in separate chapters to show how they form an integrated whole. Secondly we shall describe how this integrated set of ratios can be used for analysis, that is finding out what is going wrong and what is going right. Next it will be demonstrated how the same integrated set of ratios can be used by management when planning their company's future, remedying the weaknesses and capitalising on the strengths indicated by the analysis. Finally the use of integrated ratios for monitoring and controlling the implementation of these plans is described.

12.1 Integrated Ratios

Previous chapters have dealt with the ratios which individual managers should consider using to help monitor and control their parts of the complete business. Exceptions to this departmental approach are Chapters 4 and 5.

In this chapter we shall be concentrating on an integrated approach to the whole business in the course of which most of the ratios already described will be re-presented. Detailed descriptions of the ratios will not be repeated (back references to earlier chapters will be given); the emphasis will be on the interrelationship of the ratios within the context of the whole environment of the business.

This integrated approach will show the causal links which exist between activities on the shop floor at one end of the chain, and the income of an individual investor in the company at the other end of the chain. Diagram 12-1 shows:

1   The major blocks of ratios which have direct causal links within the company.

2   To whom information is available about each block and the degree of interest he is likely to have about the content of each block.
3   The nature of the indirect influences of the major blocks of ratios from outside the company.

The major blocks of ratios are shown in the second column in Diagram 12-1. The double-headed arrow between them indicates that it is possible to proceed from block to block in either direction. The process of analysis is carried out by moving down the chain. The cause-and-effect linkage tends to move up the chain (changes in lower blocks of ratios are far more likely to affect upper blocks of ratios than vice versa). The planning process, as will be explained in more detail later, tends to move from initiating changes in lower blocks to their effects on higher blocks. However, if these effects are considered to be not satisfactory, questions of the type 'by how much would x have to be altered to achieve y?' would be asked, going down the chain from y in a higher block to x in a lower block.

The rather peculiar shapes in the first column of Diagram 12-1 are the result of.

1   Indicating who has access to information about each block by means of a vertical line alongside the block.
2   Indicating the degree of interest by the class of person by the horizontal width of the shape alongside the block.

For example, the individual shareholder (or, more likely, his advisors—financial analysts, brokers, and so on) has information about himself, the stock market, and each company's financial policy, but no or negligible information about matters in blocks farther down the chain. His degree of interest in the information is likely to diminish as he moves down the chain from himself, via the stock market, to the company's financial policy.

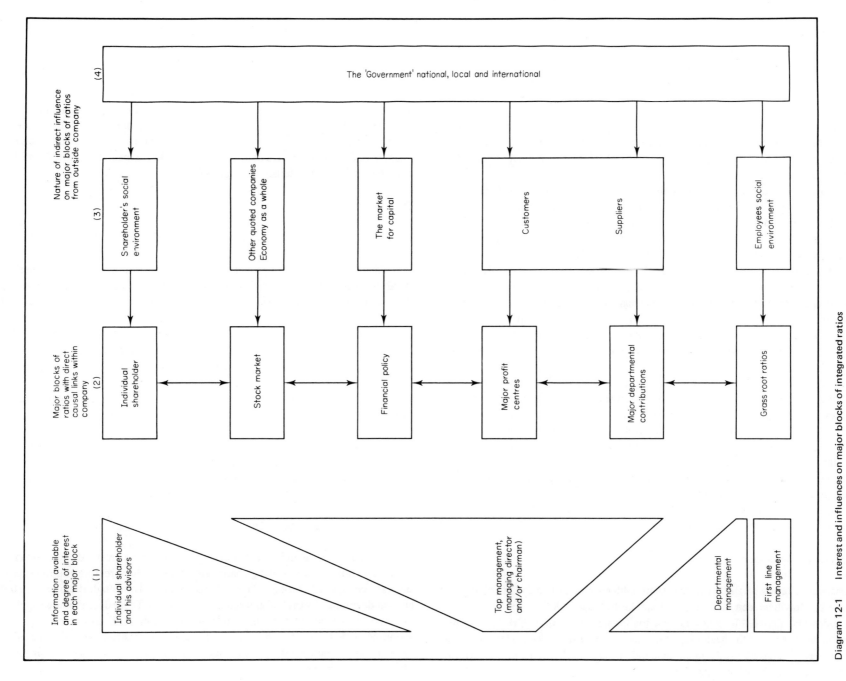

Diagram 12-1   Interest and influences on major blocks of integrated ratios

263

As well as the 'cause-and-effect' links between blocks of ratios within a company, each block is subject to indirect influences from outside the company. These influences are outlined in the third column in diagram 12.1. For example, the ratios which the individual shareholder is primarily interested in are directly affected by the stock market but his attitude to them, and indeed, some of the ratios themselves, are indirectly affected by his social enviroment (by his age, tax status etc.).

An all-pervading indirect influence on the major blocks of ratios is the government—local, national and international (including the Common Market, GATT and so on) and governmental agencies such as NEDO. This influence is represented in column 4 of Diagram 12-1.

All the 'influence' arrows move from right to left; there is of course 'feedback' from the ratios to the types of influence and this could have been shown by arrows from left to right. They were omitted however to avoid unduly cluttering the diagram.

The diagram should not be thought of as describing a static situation. The relationships it describes change continuously over time. The amount of information available to decision takers and its relative interest change. The effects of activities at the 'grass roots' levels move up the chain like electronic impulses along nerve cells. As the effects are perceived by the decision takers plans are made and action taken which in turn affect the 'grass roots'. The whole environment outside the company affects it and the company, in turn, modifies the environment. Government attempts to influence the environment while the people who make up the environment attempt to influence the government.

One should imagine the shapes and blocks in the diagram now expanding, now contracting, while pulses of information move upwards and outwards from column 2 and pulses of decisions and influences move inwards and downwards to column 2. All the parts shown in the diagram form an interrelated whole—what biologists call an ecosystem. A suitable simile for the relationships portrayed in Diagram 12-1 would not be drawn from the world of architecture—it is not a structure like a pyramid or Stonehenge—but from the sciences of living matter—it is much more like a pond on a summer's day or the nervous and muscular systems of an animal.

To continue the biological analogy for one moment longer, each major block of ratios will now be dissected in turn and the main constituents examined.

The individual shareholder

The constituent ratios of the individual shareholder's block of ratios are shown in Diagram 12-2. It will be seen that this is very similar to Diagram 8-5.

The individual shareholder's key ratio is his income in relation to the cost of his investment or its value at the beginning of the period under review (ratio Q1). The size of this ratio is affected by his personal dividend yield (ratio Q2) his capital gain (ratio Q3) and the rates of tax he has to pay (ratios Q4 and Q5).

The government and the shareholder's social environment affect his tax rates (ratios Q4 and Q5). His capital gain (ratio Q3) is the result of changes in the stock market's expectations about a number of factors (listed on diagram) these in turn are influenced by the behaviour of other quoted companies and the economy as a whole.

The direct link with the stock market block of ratios is via ratio Q2 (gross dividend receivable/value of investment at beginning of period) but formula 2 indicates that ratio Q3 (capital gain/value of investment at beginning of period) is also involved. The constituent ratios in the individual shareholder's block are more fully described in Chapter 8. The manner in which the stock market expectations are derived is also described in Chapter 8 starting on page 166.

The stock market

The individual ratios in the stock market block are shown in Diagram 12-3. This is a simplified and modified form of Diagram 8-6.

Dividend yield (ratio R1) provides the link with the individual shareholder's block of ratios (Diagram 12-2). It is a function of the earnings yield or P/E ratio (ratios R2 or R2a) and the dividend cover (ratio R3). It is with dividend cover that outside influences begin to have their effect (see diagram 12.3) but it will be more convenient to discuss them at the same time as those on the market price of the share (ratio R5).

The magnitude of the P/E ratio (ratio R2a) is determined by the equity earnings per share (ratio R4) and the market price of the share (ratio R5). The size of a company's dividend cover (ratio R3) is, in practice, determined by the directors. Their actions are affected by their policy and their expectations concerning the future. These expectations are in turn affected by:

1   The government's actions or promised or threatened actions (dividend restraint, lame ducks, stop-go, and so on).
2   What other companies are doing or are thought likely to be doing (increasing or cutting their dividends, threatening or being victims of takeovers)
3   The actual and expected behaviour of the economy as a whole.

Many of the factors which affect the size of a company's dividend cover also effect its share price but instead of being channelled through the directors and their decisions they are channelled through the stock market, that is through the buy, sell, hold or abstain decisions of all actual and potential investors. These decisions are largely based on expectations; about the company's dividend policy, about other companies, the economy, and the government. In a purely logical world they would be based on the type of analysis described on page 166. In practice, rumour, fear and optimism also play their part—in the short term at any rate.

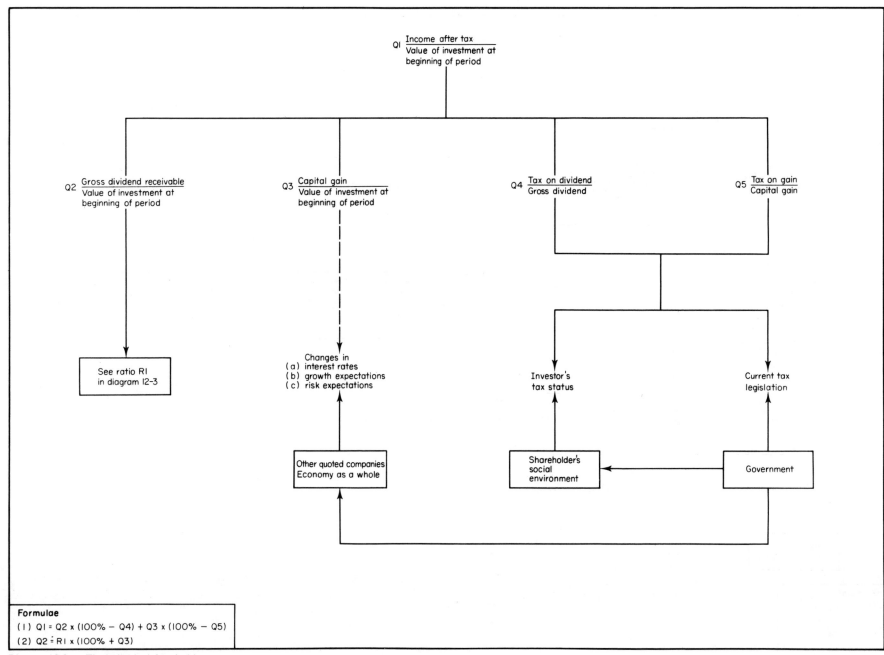

Diagram 12-2   The individual shareholder

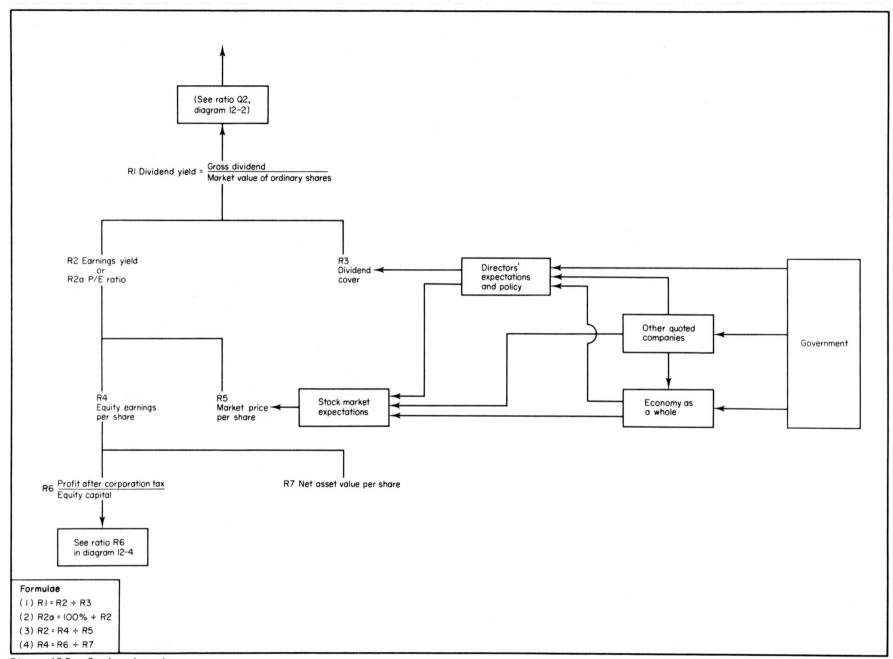

(See ratio Q2,
diagram 12-2)

$$RI\ \text{Dividend yield} = \frac{\text{Gross dividend}}{\text{Market value of ordinary shares}}$$

R2 Earnings yield
or
R2a P/E ratio

R3
Dividend
cover

Directors'
expectations
and policy

Other quoted
companies

Government

R4
Equity earnings
per share

R5
Market price
per share

Stock market
expectations

Economy as
a whole

$$R6\ \frac{\text{Profit after corporation tax}}{\text{Equity capital}}$$

R7 Net asset value per share

See ratio R6
in diagram 12-4

Formulae
(1) RI = R2 ÷ R3
(2) R2a = 100% ÷ R2
(3) R2 = R4 ÷ R5
(4) R4 = R6 ÷ R7

Diagram 12-3   Stock market ratios

The magnitude of a company's equity earnings per share (ratio R4) is determined by its post-tax return on equity capital (ratio R6) and its net asset value per share (ratio R7). Ratio R6 provides the link with the financial policy block of ratios that are described next.

All the stock market ratios are described more fully in Chapter 8 see page 167.

Financial policy

The magnitude of a company's ratio of net profit after tax to equity capital is partly determined by a group of factors which we have labelled for convenience financial policy and partly by its operating success. Financial policy is deal with in this section; operating success in the next three sections.

The individual ratios in the financial policy block are shown in Diagram 12-4. This is an expansion and modification of Diagram 8-7. The ratios which form part of Diagrams 12-4 and 12-5 are similar to ratios employed by the Centre for Interfirm Comparison in certain of its comprehensive schemes.

The size of a company's post-tax return on equity capital (ratio R6) is determined by its pre-tax return on equity capital (ratio R7) and its tax rate (ratio R8). Its tax rate is affected by its tax status, the actions recommended by its tax advisers and the government (see page 158).

Pre-tax return on equity capital (ratio R7) is the result of the total profitability of the business (ratio R9), which will be discussed in the next section, and the rate of interest paid (ratio R10) and the company's capital gearing (ratio R11). These last two are influenced by the 'market for capital' (see Diagram 12-4).

The market for loan capital can be considered as a group of institutions balancing part of the supply of and demand for money. It is influenced by the government's activities directly (bank rate, activities on the gilt edged market, special deposits, HP regulations) and indirectly by its actions taken to stimulate or damp down the economy or parts of it. The supply of money and demand for loan capital is affected by the actions of other companies and the state of economy.

The institutions in the loan capital market must assess the riskiness of the investment (cover ratios are one of the tools for this) and the liquidity of the company. The ratios used are those numbered P7 to P15 and are fully described starting on page 161.

Major profit centres

The magnitude of a company's ratio of total profit to total capital is determined by the activities within its major profit centres. For a small or simple firm there are only two such centres; its principal operations and its minor ones such as investments in securities, subletting of property. The ratios for such a situation are shown in Diagram 12-5.

For a larger firm the ratios of Diagram 12-6 are more appropriate. Diagram 12-6 is similar to Diagram 5-1 and the ratios have been fully described in Chapter 5 starting on page 80.

Major departmental contributions

The three main departments whose contribution goes to make up a company's rate of operating profitability are purchasing, manufacturing and selling. This relationship is illustrated in Diagram 12-7, where the major influences on each department are shown to be suppliers, employees and customers.

Each of the major departments has had a chapter devoted to the ratios suitable to analyse its strengths, weaknesses, and progress. The relevant chapter is indicated in Diagram 12-7. The behaviour of employees, whichever department they work for, is crucial to the success of all companies. It is for this reason that the whole of Chapter 10 (personnel ratios) is devoted to describing suitable ratios for monitoring the behaviour of employees.

Grass root ratios

Fundamentally the success of all companies depends on the soundness of its roots. Without sound roots no business can survive; unfortunately, to continue the analogy, even with sound roots the trunk may be so diseased that the tree is not fruitful.

Grass root ratios are those beyond which it is no longer worthwhile to conduct a formal, numerical, ratio analysis. Thus, they vary with the size and complexity of the company. The larger the company, the deeper it is profitable to delve. The smaller the company, the sooner one reaches an adequate answer.

It is a characteristic of grass root ratios that they tend to be in physical rather than abstract or financial terms—number of calls per representative, for example, rather than percentage return on capital. This is because the basis of all businesses is physical (and mental) work; only at a later stage is this translated into money terms.

Diagram 12-8 shows some of the grass root ratios for the marketing operation and how they link with the key marketing ratio of

$$\frac{\text{Marketing contribution}}{\text{Marketing assets}}$$

The details of the linking ratios and other grass root ratios will be found in Diagrams 6-1, 6-7 and 6-8

Other areas of the business also have grass root ratios but to avoid repetition they are not described here but at the end of the next section on the analytical pathway.

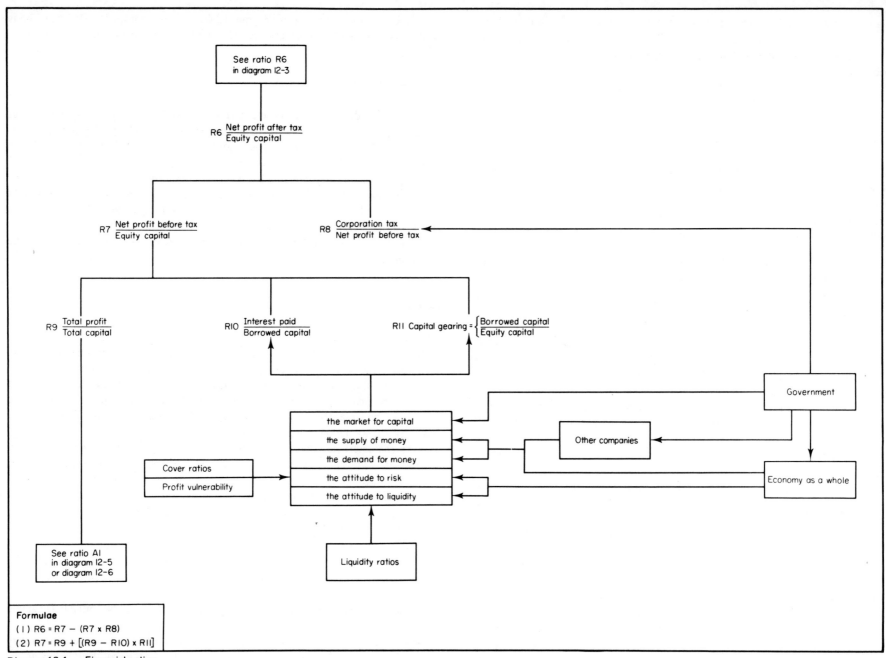

See ratio R6
in diagram 12-3

R6 $\dfrac{\text{Net profit after tax}}{\text{Equity capital}}$

R7 $\dfrac{\text{Net profit before tax}}{\text{Equity capital}}$

R8 $\dfrac{\text{Corporation tax}}{\text{Net profit before tax}}$

R9 $\dfrac{\text{Total profit}}{\text{Total capital}}$

RIO $\dfrac{\text{Interest paid}}{\text{Borrowed capital}}$

RII Capital gearing = $\left\{\dfrac{\text{Borrowed capital}}{\text{Equity capital}}\right.$

the market for capital
the supply of money
the demand for money
the attitude to risk
the attitude to liquidity

Cover ratios

Profit vulnerability

Government

Other companies

Economy as a whole

See ratio AI
in diagram 12-5
or diagram 12-6

Liquidity ratios

Formulae
(I) R6 = R7 − (R7 x R8)
(2) R7 = R9 + [(R9 − RIO) x RII]

Diagram 12-4   Financial policy

268

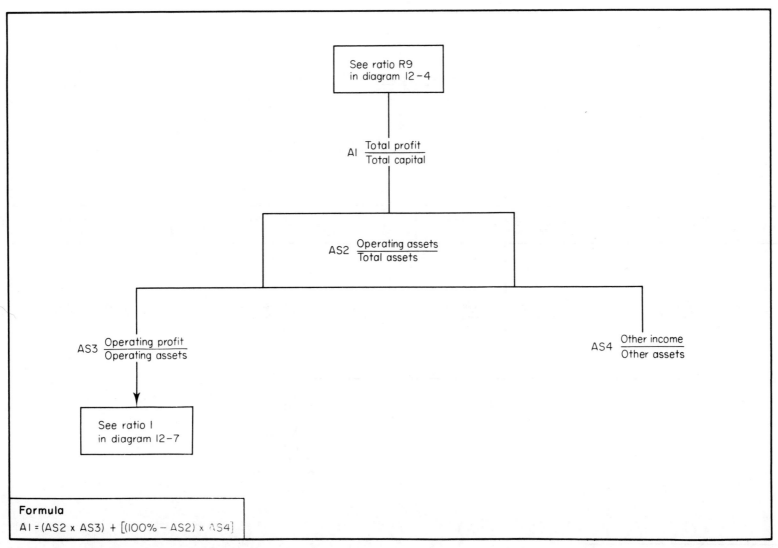

Diagram 12-5   Major profit centres—small company

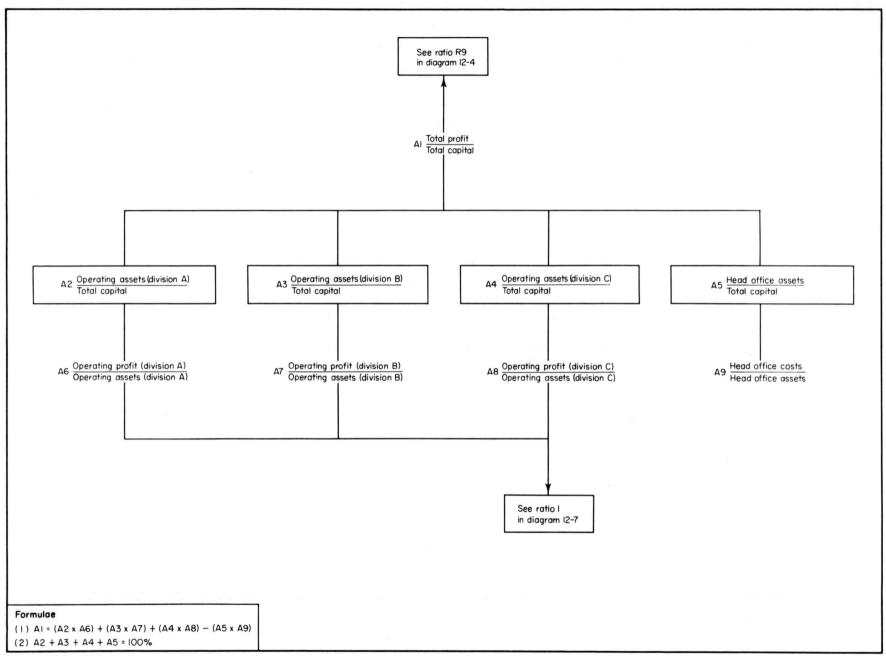

Diagram 12-6   Major profit centres—large company

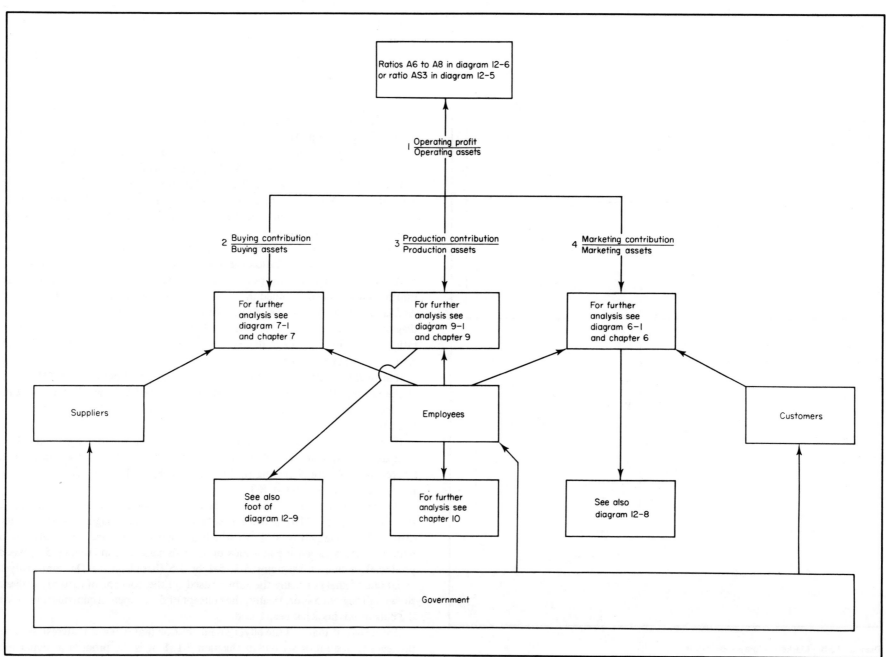

Diagram 12-7   Major departmental contributions

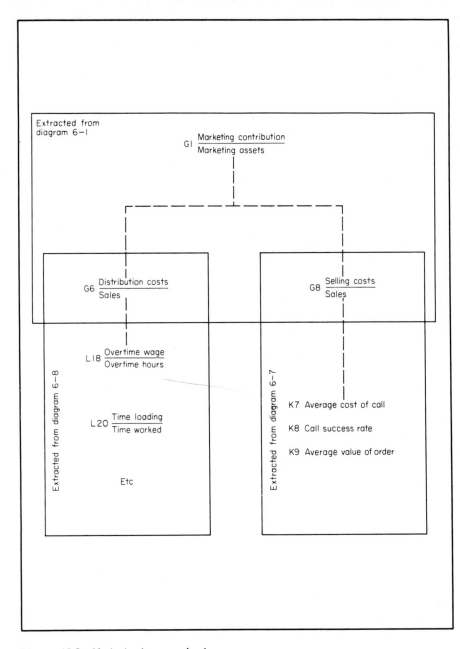

Diagram 12-8   Marketing 'grass root' ratios

12.2 The Analytical Path

Diagram 12-9 illustrates the path an analyst can take when examining the factors which have caused a particular ratio to differ from his standard—whether the standard has been derived from the company's past, the company's budget, or the performance of other companies.

Analysis can commence at any point on the path; it does not have to start right at the top of the diagram. Analysis always proceeds downwards.

Each rectangle in the diagram is a compressed summary of a diagram which has appeared elsewhere in this book. At the top left-hand corner is the diagram number and at the top right is the title. The location of the diagram can be found from the contents table. Not all the ratios in the original diagrams have been repeated—only those which provide the links between one diagram and another. The links and the missing ratios within the diagrams are represented by the dotted lines.

Diagram 12-9 should be used in conjunction with Diagram 12-1 which shows, as well as the major pattern of ratios, the nature of indirect outside influences as well.

Analysis can start at any point along the path and will finish when sufficient information has been obtained in order to indicate the nature of the action required. As Diagram 12-1 shows, no one individual has access to all the information in all the diagrams. Moreover, different individuals have different degrees of interest in the ratios shown. For brevity of description in what follows, these different individuals are referred to by the generic title 'the analyst'.

If an analyst is dissatisfied with the return on his investment (ratio Q1) he will look at the ratios in Diagram 8-5. If this does not give him his answer he will move either downwards to Diagram 8-6 (Stock Exchange ratios) or sideways to Diagram 5-8 (growth ratios).

If the analyst needs to proceed further he will move to Diagram 8-7 (overall company ratios). If it seems that the cause of what he is looking for is in the field of interest paid or capital gearing (ratios R11 and R12), he may need to examine the ratios in Diagrams 8-2, 8-4, or 8-3.

However, the analyst may be more concerned with the return on the total capital of the company (ratio R10), in which case he will proceed to Diagram 5-1 (investment in divisions). Having narrowed down which division is of interest, the analyst is faced with a choice between the methods of analysis suggested in Diagram 5-2 (based on products) or one of Diagrams 5-3, 5-4 or 5-5 (based on the Du Pont analysis or variations of that) or using the ratios based on the concept of capacity utilisation, shown in Diagram 5-6 or, finally, the concept of departmental contribution on which the bulk of this book has been based.

If it turns out that it is the buyer's contribution that is of most interest, the analyst proceeds to the ratios set out in Diagram 7-1. If it is the production department's contribution that is of concern to the analyst, he has a choice between the ratios in

Diagram 9-1 or in 9-2, depending on whether the company has a meaningful measure of capacity utilisation. From the ratios in these diagrams again there is a choice, depending on whether the company is labour or machine intensive. If it is the former the ratios in Diagram 9-3 require to be examined; if the latter, the ratios in Diagram 9-4 should be of interest.

If the analyst requires further information about marketing contribution he again has a choice of method. Diagram 6-1 is suitable for manufacturing industry; Diagram 6-5 approaches the problem of marketing contribution from a product analysis viewpoint. Diagram 6-6 is for firms who manufacture on long-term contracts.

In the general field of marketing, three areas have been provided with examples of more detailed analysis. Diagram 6-8 is of interest where distribution costs are a major item. Diagram 6-3 contains ratios of relevance to a firm with a substantial amount of export business. Diagram 6-7 concentrates on that aspect of marketing under the control of a sales manager—particularly one using representatives and agents.

12.3 Using Ratios for Planning

The integrated approach already described in the preceding section on analysis has another practical use in planning the future of the company because:

1   It can be used to demonstrate some of the major results of various courses of action under consideration.
2   It is a constant reminder that it is dangerous to consider any item in isolation.

To use the ratios for planning it is desirable to start with the activities measured by grass root ratios and to move up the analytical pathway to observe what the effect of proposed changes will be on the higher ratios which will be used to measure the success (or otherwise) of the implementation of the proposals.

It is quite likely that any proposal will affect more than one grass root ratio. The first thing to do in fact is to make a thorough check of how many ratios are indeed likely to be affected. The next step is to quantify the likely change in each of the ratios concerned. Then, using the formulae in the relevant diagrams, work out the consequential changes to the ratios higher up in the analytical path. One must continue to move upwards until one reaches the first ratio at which all the paths (along which the consequences have been flowing) converge. Only if that ratio improves is the proposed action likely to be worthwhile.

The integrated set of ratios shown in the analytical path diagram can also be used to help evaluate alternative proposals. The repercussions of each proposal are followed upwards until a ratio common to all proposals is reached. The proposal which improves that ratio by the greatest amount is, prima facie, the most attractive. Obviously for any major proposal one must also explore the likely repercussions if the proposal does not run according to plan (and how many projects do?!) It could well be that proposal A, which is prima facie the most attractive, is found to be much more sensitive to things going wrong than project B, and management could be justified in selecting the less hazardous project.

12.4 Using Ratios for Monitoring and Control

Once a plan has been agreed and action has commenced to implement it, it is highly desirable to monitor its progress. The integrated set of ratios may be used for this purpose as well as during the planning process.

Each ratio (or at least each major ratio) that is likely to be affected by the plan should be given a chart. Charts will be needed not only for ratios which it is intended should change but also for ratios which it is intended should not change as a result of the plan's implementation.

The numerical value of the ratios should be put on the vertical axis, and the horizontal axis used for the time scale extending over the estimated time required to complete the implementation of the plan. The planned change in the ratio over time can then be plotted on the chart using a dotted line. As the actual results are measured they can be marked in with a full line. Any deviation from plan can then be quickly seen and management is alerted to the need for action.

It is useful to arrange the charts for each ratio in a similar manner to Diagram 12-10. The key ratio at the top is the ratio described earlier in this chapter at the point of intersection of the analytical paths from all the grass root ratios affected by the particular plan. The key ratio may therefore be different for different plans. An intermediate ratio is one where a number of analytical paths from some grass root ratios converge but is not the point at which all converge.

With this arrangement of charts senior management would look first at the key ratio. If the actual for this was on plan, there would be no need to look further. If it was deviating from plan they would look to see which intermediate ratio was off course and then look only at the grass root ratios under that particular intermediate ratio. This arrangement of charts and the use of them just described is, of course, just another application of the principle of management by exception, in this case in a graphic or pictorial form.

At this stage management will initiate corrective action and/or modify the plan. If the latter course is taken the new plan should be added to the original chart by means of another dotted line distinguished from the original plan by a different pattern of dots.

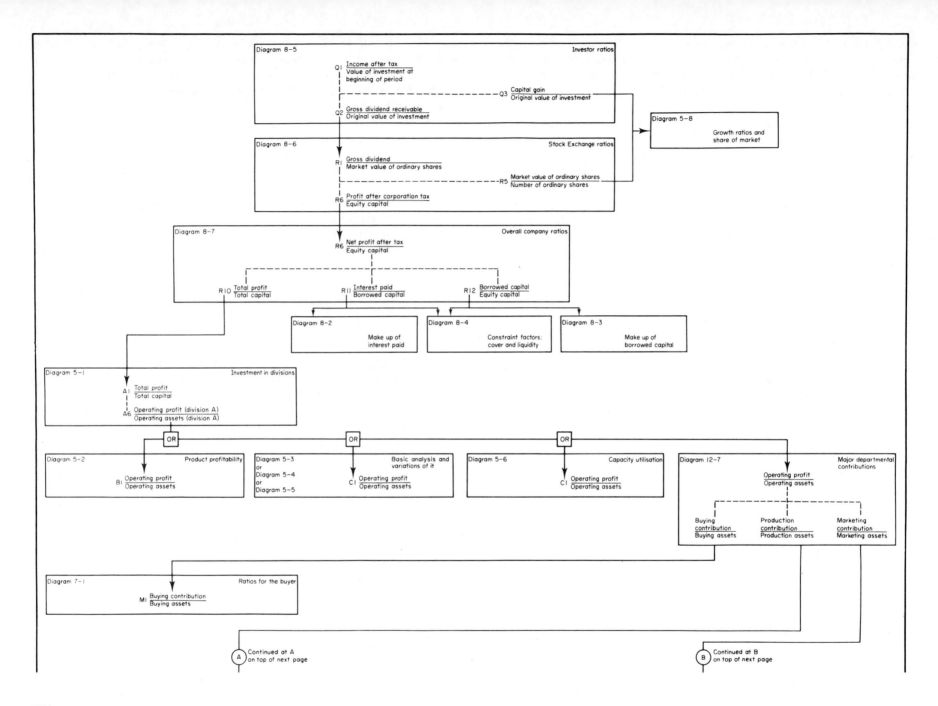

Diagram 8-5   Investor ratios

Q1 $\dfrac{\text{Income after tax}}{\text{Value of investment at beginning of period}}$

Q3 $\dfrac{\text{Capital gain}}{\text{Original value of investment}}$

Q2 $\dfrac{\text{Gross dividend receivable}}{\text{Original value of investment}}$

Diagram 5-8   Growth ratios and share of market

Diagram 8-6   Stock Exchange ratios

R1 $\dfrac{\text{Gross dividend}}{\text{Market value of ordinary shares}}$

R5 $\dfrac{\text{Market value of ordinary shares}}{\text{Number of ordinary shares}}$

R6 $\dfrac{\text{Profit after corporation tax}}{\text{Equity capital}}$

Diagram 8-7   Overall company ratios

R6 $\dfrac{\text{Net profit after tax}}{\text{Equity capital}}$

R10 $\dfrac{\text{Total profit}}{\text{Total capital}}$

R11 $\dfrac{\text{Interest paid}}{\text{Borrowed capital}}$

R12 $\dfrac{\text{Borrowed capital}}{\text{Equity capital}}$

Diagram 8-2   Make up of interest paid

Diagram 8-4   Constraint factors: cover and liquidity

Diagram 8-3   Make up of borrowed capital

Diagram 5-1   Investment in divisions

A1 $\dfrac{\text{Total profit}}{\text{Total capital}}$

A6 $\dfrac{\text{Operating profit (division A)}}{\text{Operating assets (division A)}}$

OR

Diagram 5-2   Product profitability

B1 $\dfrac{\text{Operating profit}}{\text{Operating assets}}$

OR

Diagram 5-3
or
Diagram 5-4
or
Diagram 5-5   Basic analysis and variations of it

C1 $\dfrac{\text{Operating profit}}{\text{Operating assets}}$

OR

Diagram 5-6   Capacity utilisation

C1 $\dfrac{\text{Operating profit}}{\text{Operating assets}}$

Diagram 12-7   Major departmental contributions

$\dfrac{\text{Operating profit}}{\text{Operating assets}}$

$\dfrac{\text{Buying contribution}}{\text{Buying assets}}$ $\dfrac{\text{Production contribution}}{\text{Production assets}}$ $\dfrac{\text{Marketing contribution}}{\text{Marketing assets}}$

Diagram 7-1   Ratios for the buyer

M1 $\dfrac{\text{Buying contribution}}{\text{Buying assets}}$

A   Continued at A on top of next page

B   Continued at B on top of next page

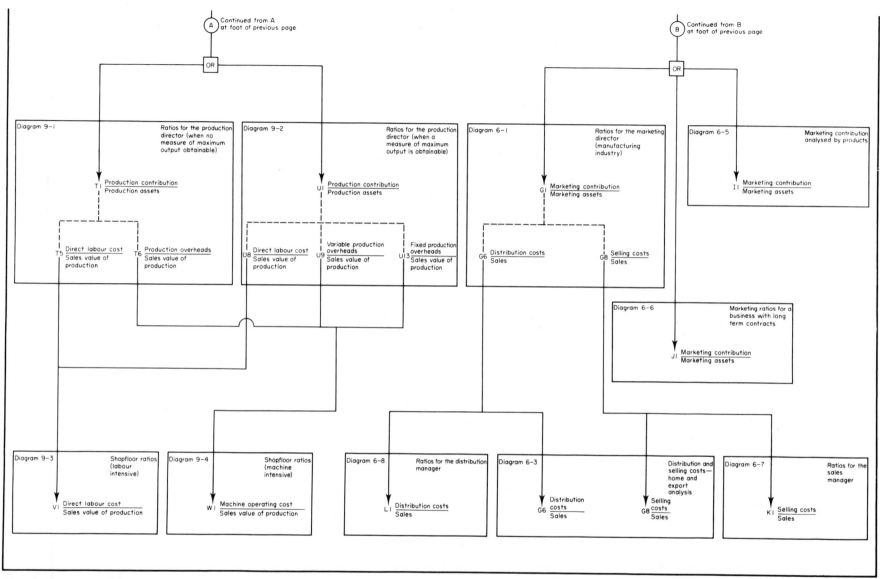

A — Continued from A at foot of previous page

B — Continued from B at foot of previous page

OR

OR

Diagram 9-1 — Ratios for the production director (when no measure of maximum output obtainable)

T I — $\dfrac{\text{Production contribution}}{\text{Production assets}}$

T5 — $\dfrac{\text{Direct labour cost}}{\text{Sales value of production}}$

T6 — $\dfrac{\text{Production overheads}}{\text{Sales value of production}}$

Diagram 9-2 — Ratios for the production director (when a measure of maximum output is obtainable)

U I — $\dfrac{\text{Production contribution}}{\text{Production assets}}$

U8 — $\dfrac{\text{Direct labour cost}}{\text{Sales value of production}}$

U9 — $\dfrac{\text{Variable production overheads}}{\text{Sales value of production}}$

UI3 — $\dfrac{\text{Fixed production overheads}}{\text{Sales value of production}}$

Diagram 6-1 — Ratios for the marketing director (manufacturing industry)

G I — $\dfrac{\text{Marketing contribution}}{\text{Marketing assets}}$

G6 — $\dfrac{\text{Distribution costs}}{\text{Sales}}$

G8 — $\dfrac{\text{Selling costs}}{\text{Sales}}$

Diagram 6-5 — Marketing contribution analysed by products

I I — $\dfrac{\text{Marketing contribution}}{\text{Marketing assets}}$

Diagram 6-6 — Marketing ratios for a business with long term contracts

J I — $\dfrac{\text{Marketing contribution}}{\text{Marketing assets}}$

Diagram 9-3 — Shopfloor ratios (labour intensive)

V I — $\dfrac{\text{Direct labour cost}}{\text{Sales value of production}}$

Diagram 9-4 — Shopfloor ratios (machine intensive)

W I — $\dfrac{\text{Machine operating cost}}{\text{Sales value of production}}$

Diagram 6-8 — Ratios for the distribution manager

L I — $\dfrac{\text{Distribution costs}}{\text{Sales}}$

Diagram 6-3 — Distribution and selling costs—home and export analysis

G6 — $\dfrac{\text{Distribution costs}}{\text{Sales}}$

G8 — $\dfrac{\text{Selling costs}}{\text{Sales}}$

Diagram 6-7 — Ratios for the sales manager

K I — $\dfrac{\text{Selling costs}}{\text{Sales}}$

Diagram 12-9   The analytical path

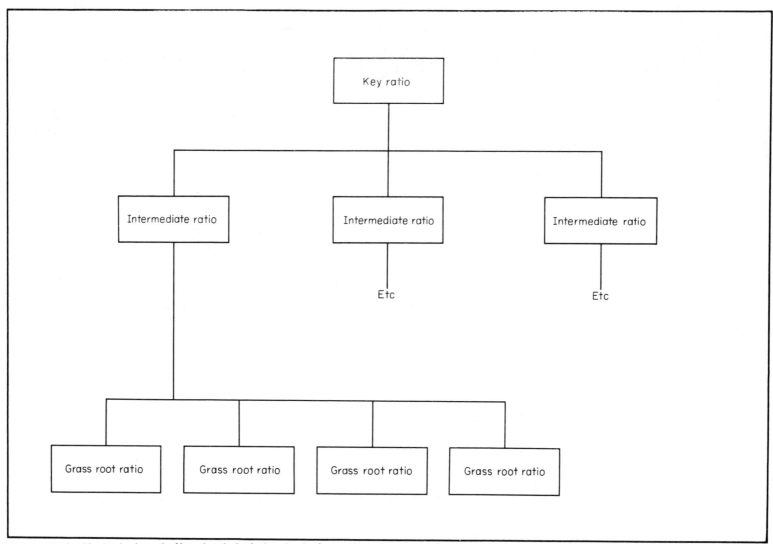

Diagram 12-10   Monitoring by ratio. Note that the basic three levels of control have been proven in use at the Centre for Interfirm Comparison.

Suggestions for further reading

For those who want to follow up any aspect of the subjects covered in this book the following selection of articles and books is recommended. Apart from the first section it is set out in the chapter order of this book. Within each section publications are in alphabetical order of their title.

General

Efficiency Comparison Within Large Organisations, Study Group of B.I.M. member firms, British Institute of Management and The Centre for Interfirm Comparison, 1962*

The Meaningful Interpretation of Financial Statements, D.E. Miller, American Management Association, 1966

'Ratio Analysis for small business'. R. Sanzo, *Small Business Administration*, 1957

'Ratios and performance', Chapter 17 in *Business Planning*, D.R.C. Halford, Pan, 1968

Successful Managerial Control by Ratio-analysis, S. Tucker, McGraw-Hill, 1961

The Use of Ratios in the Study of Business Fluctuations and Trends, K.W. Bevan, Institute of Chartered Accountants, 1966

Introduction

The du Pont Chart System for Appraising Operating Performance, C.A. Kline, Jr. and Howard L. Hessler, N.A.C.A. Bulletin, Conference Proceedings, August 1952, pp 1595-1619

'Pyramid structure—a pattern for comparative measurements', H. Ingham and L.T. Harrington, *The Manager*, September 1956, pp 657-660

Chapter 1—Principles of ratio selection

Facts From Figures, M.J. Moroney, Penguin, 1965

'The use of ratios in measuring asset utilisation', *The Accountant*, 23 December 1967

Chapter 2—Standards of comparison

Business Efficiency: An ABC of Advisory Services, NEDO, HMSO, 1968

'The Companies Act 1967 and its implications for interfirm comparison,' C.A. Westwick, *Business Ratios*, Spring 1968

Interfirm Comparison for Management, H. Ingham and L. Taylor Harrington, B.I.M., 1958*

Introduction to Work Study, International Labour Office, Geneva, 1969

Productivity Measurement—a Symposium for the 70's, R. Allard *et al.*, Institute of Personnel Management, 1971*

Productivity Measurement Review, Number 26, August 1961, published by the Productivity Measurement Advisory Service of the European Productivity Agency

A Study of Profitability in the Hosiery and Knitwear Industry, C.A. Westwick, NEDO, 1971

Survey of Published Accounts 1970-71, Institute of Chartered Accountants in England and Wales, 1972

Chapter 3—Principles of ratio definition and calculation

Accounting for Stewardship in a Period of Inflation, The Institute of Chartered Accountants in England and Wales, 1968

'How to read a balance sheet', Learning Systems, International Labour Office, Geneva, 1966

How to Read A Financial Report, Merrill Lynch, Pierce, Fenner & Smith

Inflation and Accounts: Discussion Paper and Fact Sheet The Institute of Chartered Accountants in England and Wales, 1971

The Meaning of Company Accounts W. Reid and D.R. Myddelton, Gower Press, 1971

Chapter 4—Priority ratios for the chief executive

Managing for Results, P.F. Drucker, Heinemann, 1964

Chapter 5—Ratios for overall control

Corporate Planning: A Practical Guide, J. Argenti, Allen & Unwin, 1968

Management of Research, Development and Design in Industry, T.S. McLeod, Gower Press, 1969

Problems of Using 'Return on Capital' as a Measure of Success, L. Taylor Harrington, Manchester Statistical Society, 1961

'Return on capital employed as a measure of efficiency', R.C. Skinner, *Accountancy*, June 1965

You Can Profit from Product Life Cycle J.S. Bridges, Rydges, April 1971

Chapter 6—Ratios for marketing management

'Creating a Market', *Learning Systems*, International Labour Office, Geneva, 1968

Creativity in Marketing, Remus A. Harris, American Marketing Foundation, Southampton, (N.Y.), 1960

'The evaluation of direct sales campaigns', W.N.S. Calvert, *Business Ratios*, Spring 1968

'The financial control of advertising', D. Britton, *Accountancy*, November 1971

Handbook of Advertising Management, R. Barton (editor), McGraw-Hill, New York, 1970

How British Industry Buys: An Enquiry, H. Buckner, Hutchinson, 1967

How to Win Customers, H.M. Goldmann, Staples Press, 1960

Management in Marketing: Text and Cases, H. Lazo and A. Corbin, McGraw-Hill, 1961

Marketing, C. McIver, Business Publications, 3rd edition revised and edited by G.C. Wilson, 1968

Marketing and Higher Management, E. Pearce, Allen & Unwin, 1970

Marketing for Profit, L. Hardy, Longmans Green, 1962

Marketing—the Sales Manager's Role, A. & G. Tack, World's Work, 1968

Physical Distribution Management, F.R.L. Wentworth (editor), Gower Press, 1970 *

Planning a Distribution System, P.R. Attwood, Gower Press, 1971

The Practical Approach to Marketing Management, S. Morse, McGraw-Hill, 1967 *

The Principles of Marketing, Learning Systems, Business Books, 1969

Product Management in Action, R.H. Offord (editor), Business Publication, 1967

Profitable Marketing for the Smaller Company, C.G. Roe, Gower Press, 1969

Sales Management, Cunliffe L. Bolling, Pitman Paperbacks, 5th edition, 1971

Chapter 7—Ratios for purchasing management

Cutting Costs by Analysing Values—A Practical Purchasing Programme, National Association of Purchasing Agents, New York, 1963

Design of Stock Control Systems and Records, P. Baily and G. Tavernier, Gower Press, 1970

A Guide to Stock Control, A. Battersby, Pitman, 1962 *

Improving the Purchasing Function Through Cost and Price Analysis, C.C. Chauvin, Materials Management Institute, Boston, USA 1961

Purchasing Principles and Techniques, P. Baily, and D. Farmer, Pitman 1968 *

Scientific Inventory Control, C.D. Lewis, Butterworths, 1970

Stock Control in Manufacturing Industries, A.B. Thomas, Gower Press, 1968

Chapter 8—Ratios for financial management,

'Analysing return on equity capital', C.A. Westwick, *The Manager,* January 1965

Business Finance and the Capital Market, K. Midgley and R.G. Burns, Macmillan, 1969

Capital Budgetin & Company Finance, A.J. Merrett and A. Sykes, Longmans, 1966

Computer Appreciation, T.F. Fry, Butterworths, 1970

Differential Costs and Management Decisions, D.R.C. Halford, Pitman, 1959

Discounted Cash Flow, A.M. Alfred, and J.B. Evans, Chapman & Hall, 3rd edition, 1971

Effective Use of Business Consultants, W. Seney, Financial Executives Institute, New York, 1963

Effective Use of Computers in Business, P.A. Losty, Cassell, 1969 *

Electronic Data Processing, G. Emery, Pitman, 1968 *

The Financing of Industry and Trade, D.J. Darby, Pitman, 1970 *

Gearing in British quoted companies', D. Prusmann, and G. Murphy, *Business Ratios,* Winter 1968

Investment Analysis, D. Weaver, Longmans and the Society of Investment Analysts, 1971

Investment Arithmetic, M.S. Rix, Pitman, 1964

Management Accounting, J. Batty, MacDonald & Evans, 3rd edition, 1970

Management Accounting: Text and Cases, R.N. Anthony, Irwin, 1956

Management of Trade Credit, T.G. Hutson, and J. Butterworth, Gower Press, 1968

Managerial Finance, J.F. Weston and E.F. Brigham, Holt Rinehart and Winston, 3rd edition, 1969

Managing for Profit. The Added Value Concept, R.R. Gilchrist, Allen & Unwin, 1971*

Managing Money and Finance, G.P.E. Clarkson and B.J. Elliott, Gower Press, 1969.

The Money Game, Adam Smith, Michael Joseph, 1968

Parkinson's Law, C.N. Parkinson, John Murray, 1958

Practical Financial Statement Analysis, R.A. Foulke, McGraw-Hill, 1968

Profit Management and Control, F.V. Gardner, Macdonald, 1971

Studies in Management Information, The Institute of Chartered Accountants in England and Wales, 1969

Take-overs and Mergers, M.A. Weinberg, Sweet & Maxwell, 3rd edition, 1971

'Towards a new measure and use of gearing', C.A. Westwick, *Accounting and Business Research,* Winter 1970

Up the Organisation, R. Townsend, Michael Joseph, 1970

Chapter 9—Ratios for production management

Analysis for Production and Operations Management, E.H. Bowman and R.B. Fetter, Irwin, Illinois, 3rd edition, 1967

Control Techniques for Production Management, R.H. Offord (editor), Business Publications, 1967

Design of Project Management Systems and Records, A.T. Peart, Gower Press, 1971 *

Modern Production Management, E.S. Buffa, Wiley, New York, 2nd edition, 1965

Principles of Production Control, J.L. Burbidge, MacDonald & Evans, 2nd edition, 1968

Production and Inventory control—Principles and Techniques, G.W. Plossl and O.W. Wight, Prentice-Hall, 1967 *

Production Control in Practice, K.G. Lockyer, Pitman, 1966

Production Planning, J.L. Burbidge, Heinemann, 1971 *

Production Planning and Inventory Control, J.F. Magee and D.M. Boodman, McGraw-Hill, 1958

Scientific Method in Production Management, G.R. Gedge, Oxford University Press, 1965 *

Chapter 10—Ratios for personnel management

Analysis and Costing of Company Training, J.R. Talbot and C.D. Ellis, Gower Press, 1969*

An Employers Guide to the Industrial Relations Act, P. Paterson, Kogan Page, 1971

Design of Personnel Systems and Records, Industrial Society, Gower Press, 1969

Guide to the Industrial Relations Act, 1971, N.M. Selwyn, Butterworths, 1971

Industrial Relations and Communications, W. Walsh, Gee, 1970 *

Industrial Training Management, J. Finnigan, Business Books, 1970

Labour Turnover? Towards a Solution, P.J. Samuel, Institute of Personnel Management, 1969

Manpower Planning, G. Stainer, Heinemann, 1971*

Personnel Administration and Industrial Relations, J.V. Grant and G.J. Smith, Longmans, 1969 *

Personnel and Industrial Relations: A Managerial Approach, J.B. Miner, Collier-Macmillan, 1969

The Personnel Management Handbook, J. Larkcom (editor), Business Publications, 4th edition, 1967 *

Personnel Management—Principles and Practice, C.H. Northcott, Pitman, 4th edition, 1960 *

The Personnel Management Process, W. French, Houghton Mifflin & Co. 2nd edition, 1970 *

Productivity Agreements and Wage Systems, D.T.B. North and G. Buckingham, Gower Press, 1969

Recruitment Handbook, B. Ungerson (editor), Gower Press, 1970

Chapter 11—Operating ratios for non-manufacturing organisations

'Assessing the efficiency of an accounting firm', M.H. Cabourn Smith, *Accountancy,* December 1970

Management and Financial Control in the Professional Office, P.J. Grant, Business Books, 1971

The Practice Administration Series of booklets published by The Institute of Chartered Accountants in England and Wales

A Standard System of Hotel Accounting, Hotels and Catering EDC, HMSO, 1969

Stock Exchange Journal, June 1968.

* These books contain a bibliography

Index to ratios

In this index all the ratios described in this book are listed in alphabetical order. The code letters and numbers have the following meaning:

(a)   the first reference (in **bold** type) is the ratio's code letter and number (eg **AD2**), or, in the case of the priority ratios for the chief executive, the ratio's code number (eg **5.4**)

(b)   the second reference (in roman type) indicates on which page or pages the ratio will be found.

Some ratios have colloquial names (eg stock turnover) as well as their more formal description (eg stock/cost of sales). Such ratios are indexed under both headings. Some ratios have more than one code letter and number because they are of use in more than one situation.

Subject index